Mountain Rescue Doctor

ALSO BY CHRISTOPHER VAN TILBURG, M.D.

Introducing Your Kids to the Outdoors

Watersports Safety and Emergency First Aid: A Handbook for Boaters, Anglers, Kayakers, River Runners, and Surfriders

Emergency Survival: A Pocket Guide

First Aid: A Pocket Guide (Editor)

Backcountry Ski! Oregon: Classic Descents for Skiers and Snowboarders, Including Southwest Washington

Canyoneering: Beginning to Advanced Techniques

Backcountry Snowboarding

MOUNTAIN RESCUE DOCTOR

Wilderness Medicine in the Extremes of Nature

CHRISTOPHER VAN TILBURG, M.D.

St. Martin's Press • New York

www.stmartins.com

Book design by Spring Hoteling

Library of Congress Cataloging-in-Publication Data

Van Tilburg, Christopher.
    Mountain rescue doctor : wilderness medicine in the extremes of nature / Christopher Van Tilburg.—1st ed.
             p.   cm.
    ISBN-13: 978-0-312-35888-7
    ISBN-10: 0-312-35887-3
    1. Van Tilburg, Christopher   2. Mountaineering injuries—United States.
3. Mountaineering accidents—United States.   4. Rescue work—United
States.   5. Emergency physicians—United States—Biography.   I. Title.
        [DNLM: 1. Mountaineering—injuries—Personal Narratives.
2. Rescue Work—Personal Narratives.   3. First Aid—Personal Narratives.
QT 260.5.M9 V216m 2007]

RC88.9.M6 V37 2007
616.02'52—dc22   2007028304

First Edition: November 2007

10   9   8   7   6   5   4   3   2   1

Contents

AUTHOR'S NOTE

This is a work of nonfiction, but identifying characteristics of certain people, places, and times have been changed. The names of all living patients have been changed. The dialogue and actual facts of rescues are based on my recollections and my notes taken afterward. Considering the tension involved in a mountain search and rescue mission, the descriptions are as accurate as possible. The rescues occurred during the many years that I have participated in mountain rescue and worked at the mountain clinic. Although I relied on many sources writing this book, the bulk content of these tales came from my brain, and thus is subject to the limitation of my human mind.

I thank colleagues and friends who commented critically on the manuscript: Craig Danner, Mark Nykanen, Andrew McElderry, and Crag Rats Jay Sherrerd, Dave Wagg, and Paul Crowley. Joelle Delbourgo has been a believer ever since my one-sentence e-mail about the project years ago. John Paine lent a keen eye to the words. Nichole Argyres at St. Martin's shaped this manuscript expertly and enthusiastically. Getting this book to press required the effort of a team, to which I owe thanks: Kylah McNeill and David Stanford Burr at St. Martin's, copyeditor Martha Schwartz, and Kevin Goering.

I thank my parents, Wayne and Eleanor Van Tilburg, for immeasurable support for my doctoring and writing endeavors, and my siblings, Jennifer Sato, Suzy Rylander, Peter Van Tilburg, and Joanne Guralnick, who provided incalculable and intangible support during the December 2006 Mount Hood search.

I recognize my daughters, Skylar and Avrie, for their help with rescue call outs and for their deep concern for those injured and for the families of those who did not return from the mountain.

I admire and am grateful for every member of the Crag Rats and the search and rescue community across the globe, who save lives and make the beautiful wilderness of our world a safer place.

—CHRISTOPHER VAN TILBURG,
    Cloud Cap Inn,
    Mount Hood

SPRING

CHAPTER I

Resuscitation

B elay on?" I shout.
"On belay," yells Jim.

"Send me down!" I holler back as Jim begins to lower me into the crack in the earth. I can't see much. Not the bottom of the canyon. Not the cliff. Not the nearly dead patient lying on a ledge halfway to the creek. The hillside is thickly tangled with vine maple, ferns, and poison oak. I drop backward in a blind descent on the rope and plow through the brush with my butt and back. A branch catches my helmet and twists my neck. I duck my head to release the branch, which snaps back and pops me again in the face. My boots squelch into the thick muck and leave deep footprints. When I hit soft forest duff, the thickly matted decaying leaves and branches of the forest floor, my feet slip. My knees slam the ground with a sickening thud. Pain shoots into my legs. I hope I didn't break my kneecaps. I start to slide on my knees. The rope holds fast.

As Jim lowers me into the abyss, I also have to haul down the stretcher and medical bag, as the brush is too thick and entangled to drop the gear down on a rope. So in addition to keeping myself upright, bushwhacking backward down the hillside, and trying to watch for the upcoming cliff edge, I am dragging the stretcher. Wiry vine maple branches reach out, grab the stretcher, and pull it back up the hill. As I tug, the vine maple fights back and tears my shirt. Finally I yank the stretcher with all my might. It pops free, slides another ten feet, and nearly bowls me over. The rope goes taut again: Jim's got me.

I am worried. I am dangling on a rope on the edge of a cliff, descending into a remote, rugged canyon in the mountain wilderness. I have the utmost trust in my partner, fellow mountain rescuer Jim Wells, climber and orchardist. When the rescue page goes out, Jim is always among the first to respond. He has me locked securely on the rope. I trust him with my life—no second thoughts. What I'm worried about is the patient, who looks from my vantage point, to be very near death. Earlier, from high on the trail, we spied him through a thin fissure in the rock. She was perilously balanced on a small rocky ledge near the bottom of the cliff but far from the floor of the canyon. Blood was spattered on the rocks. She was not moving.

If that isn't enough, Jim and I are acutely troubled by the four people—two volunteer firefighters and two hikers—who are with the woman on the ledge. The two hikers heard cries for help and the two firefighters from the closest town, Cascade Locks, hiked down an old deer trail to the scene. The mantra of mountain rescue is in the forefront of my mind: no one else gets hurt. Even before rescuing an injured person, protection of the rescuers always comes first. A rescuer does no good, and puts many at risk, if he or she becomes injured. Our own safety is most important: if we can't reach an injured person safely, we won't. Second, protect the team. Third, rescue the patient. The safety of the team is part of Jim's responsibility as incident commander and mine as a member of the rescue team. I am anxious to drop over the cliff and get to the ledge but need to do so safely.

Hood River County, Oregon, is sprawling, rural, and rugged. Forty miles from the town of Hood River at the south end of the county, lies Mount Hood—the 11,239-foot-high, perennially snowcapped, active volcano that dominates the landscape. The mountain lies in the Mount Hood Wilderness, a subsection of the Mount Hood National Forest. The land is populated by old- and second-growth mixed conifer forests. The patriarchal Douglas fir intermingles with noble fir, white pine, western red cedar, mountain hemlock, and western hemlock. The rich green understory is thick and lush with vine maple, sword ferns, thinleaf huckleberry, Oregon grape, salal, rhododendron, kinnikinnick, and vanilla leaf.

To the north, adjacent to the town of Hood River, lies the great Columbia River. The 1,243-mile-long stream originates in Canada and spews into the Pacific Ocean. The river slices through the Cascade Mountains and flows west past Hood River County. Near the town of Hood River, the river meanders through a deep gorge marked by 4,000-foot-high cliffs, waterfalls, rock pinnacles, deep gullies, narrow canyons, lava beds, and volcanic cinder cones. This area is so beautiful that Congress created the Columbia River Gorge National Scenic Area: a section of land in northern Oregon and southern Washington that begins in the outskirts of Portland and stretches 90 miles east.

When people are injured or lost in Hood River County—most often hikers, bikers, and climbers—they call 911. Our sheriff, like these in most states, is in charge of search and rescue, or SAR. Most rescues in Hood River County occur on Mount

Hood or, like today, in the Columbia River Gorge National Scenic Area. The sheriff responds with as many deputies as he can spare and as many volunteers as are available. That's us—Crag Rats, an independent, nonprofit club with a mission to provide search and rescue services. In a rescue, we are officially activated by the sheriff's office and work directly under that authority.

This rescue started an hour before. Crag Rats had been dispatched to the most popular hiking spot in Columbia Gorge National Scenic Area. Bubbling rapids, high waterfalls, large boulders, and lush vegetation create a picturesque and tranquil Narnia only a thirty-minute drive from Portland. Through thick groves of Douglas fir, western hemlock, and western red cedar, the trail gently rises above the creek. After two miles of meandering through the forest, the trail hugs a steep hillside 500 feet above the streambed. This is the most treacherous spot on the trail, the point at which we found the injured hiker and where Jim lowered me over the cliff.

After thirty feet of descending the steep embankment, I reach the cliff. I should be able to drop right onto the ledge where the patient lies, but I find myself thirty yards up the canyon. I hear water running but can't see a stream; and because he can't see me, Jim keeps lowering me through a trickling spring-fed waterfall, which appears lower on the rock face as if by magic. The seemingly gentle spring spills over jagged basalt, which is intermittently covered in bright green moss and thick patches of mud. I brace myself, but my boots slip on the wet moss and I slam into the incline, knees first again. I try to steer the stretcher down the cliff, but it bangs into me.

Thankfully, the cliff at last becomes a sheer wall and I dangle freely in midair. My harness cuts into my groin and the weight of my heavy rescue backpack pulls me backward, so I have to cling to the rope to avoid flipping upside down. Below me, I see the motionless patient.

Suddenly the heavy *thowck, thowck, thowck* of a helicopter swamps all other sounds, and the rotor wash pummels me with a blustery whirlwind of leaves, dirt, and water. The helicopter swoops up the canyon as if in a scene from a war movie. I can't see through the dirt and spray, and I can't let Jim know when I'm at the bottom of the cliff. He's still lowering me. In the next instant, my feet hit ground at the bottom of the cliff. With a thundering clang, the stretcher crashes on the rocks right beside me, barely missing my legs.

My footing is anything but secure. The damp mud- and moss-coated talus is as slippery as ice. Barely able to stand upright, I cautiously unhook myself from the rope, then yank it a couple of times, hoping Jim realizes that I am off belay. Maybe a spotter will tell him.

The patient is lying on a rocky ledge, across the dangerous talus slope from where I stand. I make a mental note: wide stance, keep a low center of gravity, make two trips if needed. I wave to the two firefighters, who come over to help pass the stretcher and medical bag across the slope. One heaves it up to the ledge effortlessly like a teenager tossing a hay bale onto a flatbed.

When I reach the patient, I see she is struggling to breathe, her head is matted with blood, and she's unconscious. She's dying. I take a few seconds to size up the situation, to ensure the safety of the rescuers.

"Be careful. Watch your eyes," I shout when the chopper sends another wave of debris flying. "Watch your head." The scene on the ledge is doubly dangerous now. The helicopter buzzes even closer to the canyon wall and blasts us again with its powerful rotor wash. Overhead, a medic twirls precariously on the cable, an umbilical cord stretching thinly from the giant aircraft. He spins seemingly out of control, dangerously close to the branches of the tall conifers. A gloved hand reaches out from the helicopter bay and tries to steady the cable, but with no luck.

The four volunteers on the ledge with me have no protective helmets, goggles, or gloves, no proper footwear, no personal survival gear. The ledge is a pile of melon-sized, sharply pointed rocks coated in moss, mud, and water: large enough for the five of us, but barely. A gentle slope leads down the canyon, so we are okay without a safety line, which would tether us to the cliff and prevent us from falling. At any moment, the medic whirling above could land right on top of us, and the downdraft from the chopper is still showering us with sticks, rocks, leaves, and dirt.

"Everyone, stay low! Don't look up!" I shout.

Then I turn to the patient and pull on my medical gloves. Emergency doctors speak about the golden hour, the first sixty minutes after a patient has suffered severe trauma, during which doctors have the best chance of saving a life—whether the patient has a collapsed lung, a brain injury, or is bleeding severely. This is the time to quickly put the patient on life support, staunch bleeding, and stabilize any fractures. After that first hour, it is more difficult to save a life.

The patient is on her back, unresponsive. Bright red blood oozes from her scalp and face, coagulating on the rocks. A loud stridor—a gurgling, snoring, grunting sound—means her airway is quickly clogging with saliva, mucus, vomit, and blood. Every ten seconds she takes a deep gulp of air: an ominous sign. I've seen this condition in the emergency room and recognize it immediately. It isn't likely a collapsed lung or broken ribs but the apnea caused by a severe brain injury that is interrupting the stimulus to breathe.

Her pulse is weakly palpable at eighty beats per minute. Her skin is cool, pale, and slightly purple, or cyanotic. This means that although her heart is beating and desperately trying to circulate blood, the patient is not breathing enough. You need both—lungs to draw in air and deliver oxygen to the bloodstream and the heart to pump the oxygenated blood to vital organs. This patient has lost a fair amount of blood; so there is less of it to circulate. Thankfully, we don't need to start chest compressions. If her heart stops beating, it will be extremely difficult—almost impossible—to keep her alive with CPR. The ground is unstable, we have only the basic life-support equipment, and we are far from help. If this patient were in a hospital, I would have access to highly trained staff and state-of-the-art lifesaving equipment. On the ledge, I have whatever gear that can be lowered down the cliff and run on batteries.

After many years working as an emergency and wilderness physician, I complete this primary survey in five seconds, much less time than it takes to read about it. Doctors use the mnemonic acronym ABCDE, or ABCs for short, when evaluating a trauma patient. Airway and breathing are the most vital. Circulation comes next and includes both a check to make sure the heart is beating and that there's no catastrophic bleeding. Next: D for disability. The neurologic exam yields one of four basic findings: alert, responsive to verbal stimuli, responsive to pain, and unresponsive. This patient's neurology exam shows she is unresponsive to all stimuli. In addition to her poor neurologic status, the patient has a head trauma and possibly a cervical spine injury—an injury at one of the seven neck bones, or cervical vertebrae—that can cause paralysis or even death. Emergency doctors have a mnemonic, "C three, four, and five, keep the diaphragm alive." In other words, any spine injury above the fifth cervical vertebrae disrupts the nerves that control breathing and thus the patient cannot live without life support. If the spine is injured below neck bone number five, the patient can breathe but can't move arms, legs, or torso. In trauma cases, we always immobilize the patient's neck and entire spine in case he or she has a back or neck fracture, using a hard plastic cervical collar and a backboard.

Finally, E for exposure: protect the patient from hypothermia. I'll deal with that later. Right now, we have to keep this patient from dying. She needs advanced life support immediately. One hiker reports that she was alert and whimpering a half hour ago. Now she is in a coma. This is a bad sign: she is getting worse quickly.

I pause to make sure everyone is still on the ledge and aware of the rotor wash from the chopper, which continues to hover overhead. It appears that the medic is being winched back to the belly of the two-hundred-ton machine. But he begins to swing back and forth, wildly spinning in big loops as wide as the rotor blades.

"I need help holding her head," I shout over the cacophony. One of the hikers stabilizes the patient's head. I quickly place a three-inch curved plastic oral airway in the patient's mouth to keep her tongue from blocking her throat. Then I gently but rapidly strap on a cervical collar. I have to get this patient's airway secured before she stops breathing altogether.

"Can you get the airway equipment for me, please!" I shout to one firefighter without looking up. I need a laryngoscope, a device that pushes the tongue to the floor of the mouth so I can visualize the vocal cords, and an endotracheal tube that I will pass into the patient's windpipe to breathe for her, a procedure called intubation.

"Can you monitor the pulse for me, please," I ask the other firefighter. "Let me know if it drops below sixty. I'm going to intubate."

In the muck and dripping spring water, I swiftly ready the airway equipment and check it over, and make sure everyone has a job: one Good Samaritan stabilizes the head, one firefighter keeps the pulse, and another helps me with the airway gear. I ask the fourth person to get the stretcher ready. *Thank God for the extra help,* I think.

An endotracheal intubation is by far the most difficult procedure I do as a doctor; in fact, it is one of the most difficult in all medicine. First, this lifesaving breathing tube always is inserted when patients are on the brink of death: bad asthma causing lungs to fail, a heart attack causing the heart to fail, or congestive heart failure causing both to stop. Or, as in this case, head trauma. Second, it is a difficult procedure; many ER docs do this procedure infrequently. You have to insert the laryngoscope in the patient's mouth, carefully push the tongue out of the way without breaking the teeth, and get a visual on the vocal cords. While holding the scope with one hand, you slide the narrow tube into the windpipe, or trachea. The problem is that the throat is usually full of vomit and sputum and the vocal cords are usually in spasm, blocking the trachea. Third, you only have a few minutes to complete the procedure before the patient begins to suffocate. It is an extremely difficult procedure in a clean, well-lit hospital room with familiar equipment, nurses, and special drugs to sedate, alleviate pain, and temporarily paralyze the patient. Here I am kneeling on the sharp rocks, with the medical bag splayed open, helicopter rotor wash blasting us with debris, and spring water spraying on my helmet. I focus intensely, blocking out distractions, hugely thankful that I have help from the firefighters and hikers.

There's another complication: I'm trying to keep myself clean. I'm not worried about mud on my search and rescue clothing but rather about following universal precautions, techniques that protect healthcare providers from the bodily fluids of patients. Universal precautions came into widespread use with the increasing prevalence of HIV, hepatitis B and C, and other deadly blood-borne pathogens. Medical professionals risk being splashed in the face or mouth during procedures and contracting life-threatening, chronic, irreversible illnesses in the line of duty. Universal precautions help minimize this risk.

This is my one big fear in the uncontrolled setting of a trauma in the mountains. I'm a doctor, but I'm also a father and a husband. For this procedure, I have gloves on, and I pull on my old pair of clear-lens ski goggles, which I keep strapped to my helmet. I'm ready to instantly duck if the patient vomits food, stomach acid, yellow bile, blood, or all four.

"Here we go," I shout as I pry open the patients swollen, blood-caked lips. I push down her tongue to uncover scant mucus and blood. The tongue is swollen and stiff. I see the throat: if I miss and pass the tube into the esophagus, the air meant to go into her lungs to keep her alive will flow into her stomach instead and she will suffocate. I search harder: I see only a mass of red tissue with gobs of mucus, blood, stomach contents, and dirt. I take aim and try a blind intubation: I cannot see the vocal cords. As precious minutes pass, I place the tube, hook up a large plastic breathing bag, and start squeezing it to force air into the patient's lungs to keep her alive. One of the firefighters puts an ear to the patient's chest until we locate a stethoscope.

The helicopter is now hovering directly above us and the medic is still unable to reach the ground. The turbulence is causing so much spray from the spring water, leaves, and dirt that the firefighters have to shield their eyes. I look up, and my goggles get splashed with muddy water. The chopper finally drifts away from the trees, dangling the medic at the end of the cable. The forest becomes quiet, save the gurgling, irregular snort of the patient trying to suck in air.

"Doesn't sound right," says one of the firefighters, pointing at the patient's breathing tube.

"You're right," I say. The patient's stridor worsens, and her skin turns a dusky purple. I check the tube and realize it is in the esophagus. Now I begin to doubly worry. I take another look with the laryngoscope and peer down the patient's throat. I pull out the first tube, and start over with a new tube. This time I stick it in the trachea.

"That's it," says the firefighter as the stridor abruptly ceases. The patient's chest rises and falls, and her skin turns from blue-purple to pale white to light pink in fifteen seconds.

"Thanks," I say. "Good call. Great call." I'm relieved. We now have her on advanced life support and we can breathe for her. The intubation, which usually takes five minutes in the ER, has taken fifteen.

"Can you bag her?" I ask the firefighter. In the hospital the patient would be hooked up to a ventilator that would fill her lungs with air at a scientifically optimized rate, volume, and pressure. Out here, we use a vinyl breathing bag and anyone with a spare hand. I ask the other firefighter to monitor the pulse. It beats a steady eighty times per minute, a good sign. Clearly the heart is beating okay and the patient has not bled to death. Her lungs are working properly, but the head injury has disrupted the stimulus to breathe. With her ABCs stable, I do a quick secondary survey, the rapid head-to-toe exam to check for other major injuries. Chest, abdomen, pelvis, and extremities appear uninjured.

I stand up, work a spasm out of my back and neck, size up the scene, and take a deep breath. The first part of the mission is complete: we have reached the patient in the golden hour and stabilized her at least temporarily. But, we now have the daunting task of extrication.

We have a critically ill patient stranded on a cliff ledge. In an hour the sun will dip behind the trees. A helicopter rescue appears to be out of the question. How are we going to get her out of here?

"Good work, guys," I say in a weak voice. Color disappears from the volunteers' faces. It seems as if all color drains out of the trees and sky and dirt, too. We are like actors in a black-and-white film; real life could not be this bad.

This day started out rather typically for an emergency doctor, adventure sport enthusiast, author, husband, and father. At 8 A.M., I got off night shift in the ER. Six hours of sleep interrupted by routine cases was a bonus: no major illnesses or accidents. At home I share a pancake breakfast with my wife, Jennifer, and our two school-age daughters, Skylar and Avrie. I cycle fifty miles at race pace with my regular biking buddies. After the ride, we take the kids swimming—eleven kids under age seven in the local pool, pure delight for them. Back home, we lunch on the deck in the warm sun: leftover salmon and rice balls. Afterward, my girls giggle in their fort with the neighbor kids, my wife gardens, I check my e-mail.

Suddenly my phone vibrates and beeps once, jolting me from my computer daze. From the tone I know it is a text message before I dig the cell phone out of my front pocket. Only one place ever sends me a text message: Hood River County sheriff's office. My muscles and mind instantly go from fully relaxed to taut. It's like when you awake suddenly from a nap and realize you overslept: you rev up to full speed in a flash. The glowing phone screen reads: *High-angle rescue. Call Penny.* This is not a dog rescue or transport for a stranded hiker. It is life and death.

"Honey," I say with a high-pitched and strained voice.

"Oh no," Jennifer says. She knows by my grimace and the way I have my phone jammed against my ear that I have received a mountain rescue call out.

I run upstairs to change clothes and call Penny Hunting, the call out coordinator for Crag Rats. My kids, having been through this countless times, jump up excitedly to explain to their friends what is going on. Skylar, my seven-year-old, runs in to fill water bottles for me.

"There's an injured woman about two miles up the creek. Bad head injury. High-angle rescue," says Penny in a clipped voice. "That's all I've got right now. Jim, Dennis, and Todd just called in. Dwayne has the truck," Penny says, referring to the other members of my unit and the heavy-duty 4×4 crew cab pickup that contains our search and rescue equipment. I get off the phone quickly, grab food and water, and toss my search and rescue pack in my truck. We still are within the golden hour: I need to hurry.

The sense of urgency is infectious: my kids get excited, too.

"Those are his poison oak pants," says Skylar. "Last time, someone died," she adds, referring to a body we retrieved from the mountain. Avrie's eyes sparkle, soaking up the excitement.

I am out the door ten minutes after the page. A mountain rescue call out is quite different from the adrenaline rush of outdoor adventure sports like surfing or mountaineering in which the peak moment of thrill can be planned, anticipated, calculated, and sometimes even controlled. Often you can turn back at any moment. In mountain rescue the call out comes unexpectedly and suddenly: at a dinner party, in the middle of the night, at work, or in the backyard on a Sunday afternoon. You gather your gear as fast as you can because someone may be dying. You don't necessarily know where you are going, what condition you will find the patient in, or who will show up to help.

I gun my truck out of the driveway. As I drive I guzzle water, knowing I may not have time later to drink. My phone rings.

"We'll be a few minutes behind you," says Dennis. "Todd had to run home for his pack." Dennis Klein is a former ski patroller turned mountain manager for our tiny one-chairlift Cooper Spur Resort in winter and a state forestry firefighter in summer. Todd Wells is a carpenter and expert skier and ice climber. These guys combined have more rope-rescue knowledge than almost anyone in our group. They are the guys you want on a rescue, hauling you out of a canyon.

Twenty minutes later, I reach the creek's trailhead parking lot, the staging area, the gathering place for launching the rescue. Forest Service trucks, an ambulance, and sheriff's department vehicles are parked haphazardly. A loosely organized crowd of officials and support staff huddles around our huge search and rescue pickup. I quickly spot Sheriff Joe Wampler and Chief Deputy Dwayne Troxell, who are discussing the situation.

"What's the story?" I ask anxiously.

"Someone fell about two miles up: head injury," explains Dwayne. "Hurt bad. Might be unconscious."

"You'd better head the trail, Doc," says Joe. "We need you up there."

Earlier that day, the hiker was leisurely bounding down the trail after a half-day hike. At a muddy bend, where a spring trickles across the trail, she slipped. At other sections of the trail, she might have landed in a bed of ferns, bounced over a log, or skidded on the trail. But at this spot she tumbled down a steep embankment, badly scratching her arms, legs, and face on the thick brush that hid a cliff just ten feet from the trail. She flew over the precipice headfirst and landed on a ledge of sharp rocks fifty feet below. Her partner on the trail above did the right thing. He tried to call 911 on his cell phone and when he didn't get reception, he ran for help.

"Oh, and I activated the National Guard out of Salem," says Dwayne, "Helicopter en route. ETA twenty minutes."

"Okay. Todd and Dennis are right behind me," I say.

Spiked with adrenaline, I nearly knock over the Forest Service ranger who is keeping hikers off the trail. "Search and rescue," I say as I career by with my forty-pound pack. The trail is eerily vacant for a sunny weekend afternoon, so I have room to run. But I force myself to slow down to a fast trot: the last thing I need is to sprain my ankle running up the trail.

When I reach the accident site twenty minutes later, I find a slew of hikers, Forest Service workers, volunteer firefighters, and a reserve deputy sheriff standing on the trail. They can see the patient through a small fissure in the cliff, but all are untrained and ill equipped to respond. Panting, I approach Jim Wells.

"Hey, Jim, where do you need me?" I ask. I'm willing to perform as a doctor when needed, but many times, when my medical skills are unneeded, I've pulled a rope or schlepped gear.

"I need you to go over the edge. Now."

Immediately I dig into my pack, strap on my helmet, pull a climbing harness over my pants, and put on heavy leather gloves. Meanwhile, Jim sets up an anchor for the rope by tying a length of sturdy one-inch nylon webbing around a stout tree. He clips a carabiner, an aluminum snap link used by climbers, around the webbing and threads a rope through a belay tube. This friction device allows the rope to slide through freely, and the rope can be easily slowed or stopped by pinning it against the aluminum tube. This controls the rate of descent of a person or gear being lowered down the cliff.

I instantly put aside emotions and all extraneous thoughts. I concentrate on avoiding critical mistakes like forgetting a vital piece of equipment or missing a safety line. I have a job to do and I have to be careful.

"The lady's in bad shape," explains Jim. "There are two Good Samaritan hikers and two volunteer firefighters with the patient, but they have no gear. I'm worried about their safety. I'm rigging a belay line and a rescue line. We will send a stretcher down with you," he says, pointing to a heavy steel-cage basket stretcher from the ambulance crew that was meant for car crashes, not wilderness rescue.

"Where's our gear?" I ask.

"You'll take down the ambulance gear," says Jim. "Our stuff is still at the trailhead." I frown, knowing it would be best to work with our lightweight litter that is rigged for technical extractions like rope rescue and helicopter hoists. And since I packed our medical bag, I know where everything is.

But the patient may be dying.

I hook into Jim's rope and double-check everything: harness on tight, anchor secure, carabiner locked. Then I go over the edge and disappear into the narrow, yawning abyss.

When the helicopter peels off without dropping the medic, how daunting the task of extrication and evacuation is becomes apparent. The tinkling of the dripping spring is juxtaposed with the whoosh of air being forced into the patient's lungs. As I try to figure out the next course of action, out of the corner of my eye I see a flicker in the brush. An animal? The wind? What could complicate this rescue more? Then I spy a camouflaged figure moving slowly up the slick talus slope: the medic is making his way up from the bottom of the canyon from where the helicopter had lowered him. I feel a wave of relief, as the much-needed medical assistance and equipment are arriving. In addition, I'm going to need highly skilled help to evacuate this patient.

"Okay. We need to get this patient on the backboard and in the litter," I say with renewed energy. "And we need to start thinking about how everyone is getting out of here." My mind clicks back into emergency-doctor mode: define problems, figure out solutions, multitask. Keep everyone safe.

"Can't we just get pulled up the rope after the patient goes up?" one firefighter asks.

"No, that's too difficult and dangerous. I think you might have to hike out the way you came in," I say.

I call Jim on the radio. "We're packaging the patient and she's now on life support. I'm not sure if we can use the helicopter from here."

"Okay. We're preparing for plan B: take her up the cliff," says Jim. Typical of a well-seasoned rescuer, Jim has already constructed a complicated rope-raising system on the trail above us in case the chopper can't snatch the patient from the ledge. Because of the thick trees and narrow canyon, the chopper can't get close enough to haul the patient up a cable into the helicopter. We'll have to carry her right off the ledge using a rope, which means the crew above has to find anchors, build a rope-raising system, and drop down two more ropes. A red rope will be the primary rescue line to lift the patient. A yellow rope will be the belay line, a backup in case the primary fails. To a recreational climber, using two ropes may seem redundant, since ropes are designed to be fifteen times stronger than needed; each is rated to hold more than nine thousand pounds. But this is mountain rescue. We don't like to take chances.

I coordinate the group on the ledge as we gently move the patient onto the backboard, then nestle her inside the litter. The two firefighters continue to monitor her pulse and pump air into her lungs. The medic finally arrives.

"What'd'ya got?" he says, chipper and upbeat as if his near-death cable ride was just another day's work. He unholsters his compact medical pack.

"Open head injury. GCS three. Just intubated. Pulse steady at eighty." The GCS, or Glasgow Coma Scale, describes brain function in head trauma by observing and rating the patients eye opening, verbal response, and motor response. Three is the lowest on a scale of one to fifteen. This patient is in a deep coma, unresponsive to all stimuli. The medic pulls out a capnometer, a device that measures the carbon dioxide content from the breathing tube, which confirms it is placed in the lungs. His pulse oximeter, a device that measures the percent of oxygen in the blood, glows 98 percent: the patient is getting enough air to stay alive. I am grateful to have both confirmed.

"We can't lift with the helicopter from here," the medic says. "Too tight with the big trees. They had to drop me in the creek." His pants are soaked to the knees.

"Can we head down to the water?" I ask, since hiking down through thick brush is much safer than going up a cliff on a rope.

"The brush is way too thick. It would take until dark. My pilot isn't certified for a night-vision hoist."

"Okay." Frowning, I call Jim on the radio. "We can't use the helicopter. We need to bring her up the cliff."

"Roger. We'll be ready soon," says Jim.

Unlike a paramedic doing a scoop and run with a car crash victim, we need a more extensive patient package to take her up the cliff. Because the patient is on life support, she can't go up alone. We will need two people by her side: I have to keep her alive using the breathing bag and someone else needs to steer the litter so it doesn't get wedged against the cliff. To add to the complicated extrication, we are not using our mountain rescue litter, which means we need to be extra careful strapping her in. I need someone more experienced in rope work to back me up. Todd rappels down to help. He always gives pointed, clear recommendations, not instructions. Even with all his years of experience at rope rescue, he listens to others and helps forge a cooperative decision, despite the fact that we always follow his advice. He's been a Crag Rat since he was eighteen; his dad, uncle, and cousin are Crag Rats, too.

We use lines of 8-millimeter climbing cord rated at 10 kilonewtons, or 2,250 pounds of force, and 1-inch-wide military-grade tubular nylon webbing, strong enough to hoist a Humvee. Todd and I tightly tie the patient to the backboard, then anchor the backboard to the stretcher. We tie a climbing harness around the patient's waist for backup, and we add webbing straps around the patient's pelvis and shoulders, which prevent her from sliding up or down in the stretcher. We don't have head stabilizers, foam blocks that keep the head tight, so we wad up some jackets and tape her head down to the backboard. Finally we tie the stretcher to the red rescue rope and the patient to the yellow belay line. When we finish, the patient is snug and stable. Even if the stretcher were to flip upside down, the patient will remain strapped in.

All the while I hear the artificial, uneven flow of the breathing bag every three seconds and the firefighter calling out "eighty and stable" every few minutes.

"I'll activate medevac," says the firefighter, referring to the hospital-based helicopter. If we can't lift her off the ledge with the military helicopter, we can carry her to the road and pass her off to medevac. That thought may very well save the patient's life, since it will prevent a long drive in the ambulance and eliminate the need for a risky military helicopter extrication.

"Great idea," I say to the medic. Then on the radio, "Jim, we're ready down here."

"Okay. Stand by to raise," says Jim. As the sun begins to touch the treetops, shadows lengthen. We grow chilled. The spring water has soaked through our clothes and still drips off the cliff. Mud cakes our pants. We gather our gear and prepare to evacuate. We wait nearly twenty minutes, getting colder and more forlorn.

The medic takes over squeezing the bag and monitoring the patient's pulse, so I ask the firefighters and hikers to start down the trail. The medic is the only person Todd and I need to help lift the patient off the ledge. The group sets off but decides to scramble up a muddy chute at the end of the cliff. Halfway up, the chute becomes steep and slimy: the foursome slip in the mud, slide twenty feet, and land in the brush. I am relieved to see them stand up, unhurt. They turn and head down the canyon in search of the deer trail.

Todd and I tie ourselves to both the red and yellow ropes. My job now is to keep the patient alive by using the breathing bag to force air into her lungs and to keep the tube in her trachea. Todd will steer the stretcher up the cliff and keep it from becoming wedged in a crack or flipped over. The medic lifts us off the ledge and keeps us from getting pulled under an overhang where we could get stuck. Finally airborne, the patient goes up completely vertical, head up.

The ascent is slow and painful. I'm dangling on the rope next to the litter. My face is about ten inches from the patient so my arms are bent close to my body. This makes it extremely difficult to maintain the airflow by squeezing the bag. I get a cramp in my right hand, but I can't switch hands. I can't even check the patient's pulse. I use my left hand to keep from being pinned against the rock by the litter. As my knuckles scrape against the rock, I can feel my skin tear despite the thick leather gloves and thin medical gloves I'm wearing. My harness digs into my groin so that my legs tingle. I'm drenched in water.

On the trail above, at least a dozen rescuers pull hand over hand on the rope. With every yank the litter jerks slightly. We are dragged and banged against the cliff. To make matters worse, the rope crew doesn't have enough room to haul us all the way up the one-hundred foot cliff in one pull. They have only twenty feet of trail to work with, so they pull twenty feet, lock off the rope, reset, then pull again.

Todd looks just as bad as I feel. Using all four limbs to stabilize the litter, he fights with all his strength to keep from being pinned against a large crack in the rocky cliff.

Eighty feet, fifteen minutes, and four big pulls later, the litter scrapes wickedly against rocks as we crest the lip of the cliff. The litter tilts slowly from vertical to a forty-five degree angle as it comes to rest on the steep embankment above the cliff. I am hugely thankful to see one of my colleagues at the edge.

"Stay on the rope," he says. "We still have a way to go." Another twenty feet of steep slope and thick brush remain before we reach the trail. I climb on top of the litter, kneel on the metal rails, and use both hands to hyperventilate the patient to drive in extra oxygen and remove excess carbon dioxide. I'm trying to make up for the last twenty minutes of difficult bagging. Todd bushwhacks alongside to keep the stretcher from tipping or becoming caught in the thick brush. As the rope crew drags us up the embankment, we flatten everything in our way, leaving a three-foot swath of dirt among the ferns and vine maple.

Finally we approach the trail. The crew up top looks exhausted. The raising system is complex because the trees being used as anchors are twenty feet from the trail. The master belay plate, a six-inch sheet of thick aluminum with ten holes, is suspended like a trapeze in midair. It has a half dozen ropes attached to it: rescue and belay lines, anchor ropes, safety cords.

Even after we reach the top of the cliff and the trail, we are far from the end of the mission. Instantly a flurry of rescuers unties the ropes. I don't stop squeezing the breathing bag. Pulse seventy. Glasgow six. The patient's neurologic status has technically improved slightly, but I fear it is actually a turn for the worse. The patient's skin looks waxy and pale. Her chest is barely rising with the ventilations. There is a trace of left eyelid flutter and some flexion of her right hand and wrist. The patient's brain stem functions are likely taking over, an automatic life-preserving function of the body that occurs when the brain function begins to dwindle. But I know we still have a chance. She has one thing going for her: we reached her in the golden hour.

"The helicopter guys can pluck her off the trail," yells Jim. "About a half mile down there's a clearing." Everyone on the trail is ready for the helicopter to snatch the patient and whisk her away to the hospital. The team dismantles the rope-raising system.

"I don't know about that," I say incredulously. A few volunteers at the trail look shocked.

"What do you think, Doc?" says Jim.

"This woman has been stable for two hours. I think that's too dangerous." I still have visions of the medic nearly being wrapped around a tree. "It wouldn't buy us much time. Do we have medevac?"

"Standing by." The nearest landing zone is five miles away.

"We can get her down the trail in twenty minutes," says Todd. "We've got the wheel and plenty of help."

"I don't think a helo evac is worth the risk," I say.

"Me neither," says Todd. With the patient back on the trail, everyone is ready to do anything it takes to save her life. It would be easy to take the most daring solution, which is also the most dangerous and not necessarily the quickest. Todd and I are clearly in favor of maximum safety at this point. Jim looks around and pauses for two seconds to let everyone know he has weighed the options. The forest is quiet; a dozen rescuers are staring at Jim when he shouts, "Down the trail!"

I have no time to breathe a sigh of relief because the team is already attaching a wheel to the bottom of the litter in order to steer the patient quickly down the path. As Todd and fresh rescuers wheel the cumbersome stretcher down the trail, I trot alongside continuing with the breathing bag and monitoring the pulse. Losing a pulse now would mean a full cardiac arrest, and we'd have to start chest compressions. I try to suppress the thought, but my mind automatically prepares for it.

A rescuer runs ahead to clear the media; a film crew has hiked up the trail with video cameras. Ten minutes later we hear a bone-chilling, ear-piercing shriek. A woman sobs loudly, runs up, and almost careens into the litter. Luckily, one of the volunteer firefighters has experience in crisis management. The rescuer immediately corrals the woman, who is the patient's family member, explains the situation, and offers some hope. We don't break stride.

At the trailhead, news crews and several dozen people stare

transfixed as we untie the patient and whisk her, backboard and all, into a waiting ambulance. I jump inside without taking off my helmet or backpack. With lights flashing and sirens blaring, the ambulance speeds to the landing zone. Tucked inside the cramped vehicle, I continue to squeeze the breathing bag while the Cascade Locks volunteer paramedic starts an IV and attaches heart and oxygen monitors. I fumble for the suction with one hand, then topple against the supply cabinet as we take the exit turn. My hands are cold and cramped and I am barely able to hook oxygen up to the mask. It is my job to keep this patient alive and it is taking all my concentration to do so.

At the landing strip, security waves us through to an empty parking lot where the helicopter waits.

"Oh good—she's intubated," says the flight nurse, surprised.

"An open head injury, found two hours ago. Intubated. Pulse stable at eighty. GCS was three on scene, now five. No other trauma. Sats ninety-five percent bagged," I report to the flight nurse. Then we quickly lift the patient into the helicopter and step back just as quickly. The flight nurse slams the door, the chopper powers up, and the pilot signals thumbs-up. This time the rotor wash is warm and free of debris and spray.

Exhausted, I sit down on the bumper of the ambulance and watch the chopper follow the Columbia River west. A full trauma team waits: neurosurgeon, trauma surgeon, full operating room staff, respiratory therapy, IV team, and a multitude of others ready to roll the minute the helicopter touches down. The sun sneaks behind the mountains in a warm yellow-orange glow. I dig some water out of my pack and tip the bottle to the sky.

Four hours have passed since the call-out page. In mountain rescue terms, that is very fast. In this case, reaching the patient immediately, in the golden hour, proved lifesaving. And no rescuers got hurt. Now I feel the adrenaline fade, and fatigue hits me like a tidal wave. I am hungry, dirty, exhausted. I had completely forgotten I'd worked the night shift and ridden my bike fifty miles. I ask the ambulance guys for a ride back to my truck at the trailhead. I quickly call home.

"We're finished," I say to my wife.

"Is the patient okay?" she asks.

"I'll tell you about it when I get home. I'll be an hour," I say. *Welcome to mountain rescue,* I think.

CHAPTER 2

Into the Slot

When I drop into the slot, I have no idea what I'll find at the bottom. The man is critically injured, but that's all I know. From a cliff high above a remote canyon in a neighboring county, I check and recheck my harness, carabiner, and figure-eight rappel device. I'm about to drop into a deep, dark crack in the mountain. Despite the warm spring sun and clear skies, the canyon bottom is obscured by the depth of the canyon, the thick foliage lining the cliff, and the giant trees embedded in the earth and towering a hundred feet. In addition, the vine maples at the staging area are barely thick enough to provide solid anchors, we don't have enough rescuers at the scene yet, and thick mud from spring rains makes our footing precarious. The worst part of this rescue—of any rescue—is the unknown. Unknown location, unknown situation, unknown injuries. The rescue may take a few hours or a couple of days. It all adds up to a difficult, dangerous situation.

Jim Wells has just dropped over the edge. A few minutes pass and then the rope goes from being tight as a guitar string to slack. Jim has reached the bottom, at the end of a fifty-meter rope. We wait for five minutes.

"He's alive but injured badly. We need medical down here now," he says over a static-clogged radio, his speech sparked with urgency. "I have to secure the scene." Although trained as an EMT, Jim also needs to assess the safety of the scene and begin extrication. I need to get down there to attend to the medical needs of the patient. Preparing for the worst possible situation, I take my big SAR backpack. "And you'll need a life jacket," Jim says over the radio. "No one can come down without one."

I can hear Jim on a radio from the ground team, but no one from the other agencies on scene can. That is another complication: our radios don't have the the correct frequency, so communication with the volunteer firefighters and sheriff is not optimal. Shouting becomes our modus operandi.

I drop in. I squat and hunch to duck under the wiry vine maples and dense undergrowth of ferns, manzanita, and huckleberry. I wince as branches scrape my helmet and arms. While plowing backward through a huge crop of poison oak, I feel the soft velvety leaves kiss my neck and I wince again. That loving touch will give me a miserable rash for two weeks.

My right hand—my break hand, my lifeline—tightens on the rope. I use my left to hold onto branches, logs, and rocks on the way down. In addition to my typical rescue gear, I wear a large foam life vest, the kind designed for boating. It is like an elaborate Halloween costume: the bulk obstructs my vision and constrains my shoulders and abdomen so I move stiffly, like a robot.

After fifty feet of gnarly bushwhacking, I reach a sheer cliff covered in moss, mud, and water. I spot the patient and Jim far below, thirty yards upriver. They are tiny colored specks against a dull background. The light gray basalt of the canyon walls is marked with clumps of bright green moss and trickles of water. River-smoothed logs are stuffed in the canyon at odd angles like pickup sticks. The black water is laced with silver ripples that spangle in the sole shaft of sunlight that reaches into the canyon.

My rappel gets even more difficult after my hands become cold and wet and the rope slippery. Finally, I thud to a halt at the bottom. The rope, which was fully stretched, recoils a few feet, yanking me with it. My harness digs into my groin and I dangle for a few seconds before slamming into the rock wall at the canyon bottom again. I am relieved to have made it, but I'm still tight on the rope. It is too dangerous to untie because I am standing on a six-inch-wide rock ledge on the river's edge. The sheer walls tower one hundred feet high on both sides. Giant old-growth conifers rise another hundred feet. Despite the warm day, it is chilly here. A quarter mile upstream water rushes over the spillway of a small dam. The stream is barely thirty feet wide, plugged with the unsteadily bobbing logjam. I suspect the water just below the logs is flowing swiftly, ice cold, and deadly.

I lean toward the cliff, grip the rock with both hands, and sidestep slowly upriver on the ledge. The canyon wall is slick, and the weight of my pack pulls me away from the rock. At one point I slip, and my foot dunks between logs, into the frigid waters. Finally, with one foot on the moss-covered canyon wall and one foot on a floating log, I stop before Jim and the patient.

Earlier on this bright, warm Sunday morning in April, Mark decided to walk his dogs. He started down the rural gravel road around 10:00 A.M., and when he came to the dam, he couldn't resist having a peek.

A small dam plugs the steepest, narrowest part of the this river. Only fifty feet high and fifty feet wide, it is rather puny as far as dams go. Because the canyon is too steep and deep for a powerhouse, behind the dam a twenty-foot-diameter wood pipe draws water out of the lake and shunts it a mile downstream to a tiny powerhouse. The pipe is fenced off in most places, but in one spot along the road, the fence is broken after a winter of storms.

Mark stepped onto the pipe by crossing a two-foot-wide log, probably put there by some kids. The only pathway on top of the giant tube was a six-inch-wide board slippery with moss and dew. Suddenly Mark's two dogs took off after a squirrel, leaping off the far of the pipe and darting into the brush. Mark clambered down a ladder after them and headed into the thick undergrowth. After only a few steps he tumbled, twisted, bounced, and flew headfirst off the cliff.

Had it not been for the logs, he would have hit the freezing torrent and been washed over the rapids downstream. But he landed in the middle of the tightly packed logs, hitting them very hard, and he probably passed out.

H igh-angle rescue. Major injury. Call Penny." The page came when I was playing with the kids, and my wife was just leaving to go to the grocery store.

"Honey, we have a call out, sounds bad."

"Oh no, not again," she said. "I'll take the kids to the store with me."

I hurried around the house, getting ready. *Damn,* I thought when I reached for my pack, *I should have converted it over.* My winter gear includes skis, poles, climbing skins, crampons, avalanche-rescue gear, ski helmet, winter clothing, ski boots, and other special equipment. In the summer, I carry rope-rescue equipment, a climbing helmet, my canvas poison-oak-proof clothing, and lightweight boots. I pile my gear in my car, taking more than I will probably need.

"Dad, food," Skylar said as she handed me a bag of Goldfish

crackers. I took them with a smile and a hug. I knew they'd end up as crumbs in my pack, so I'd probably leave them in my car. Avrie brought a water bottle and kid-sized juice box.

In fifteen minutes I pulled out of the driveway. Penny had given me what information she had. The volunteer firefighters had received a 911 call for a missing man from a neighboring county. After an hour of searching, they could hear but could not reach him. They contacted the sheriff, who contacted our county sheriff, who sent out our page and called Penny. In her typical calm and deliberate manner, Penny instructed, "Head to the dangerous road; you'll see the rescue rigs. Bring rope gear."

Jim dropped everything and headed over with our SAR truck. The usual crew—Cam Axford, Todd Wells, Paul Crowley, and Steve Castagnoli—were not far behind. When I arrived at the broken fence, I found six agencies on the scene: a slew of volunteer firefighters, deputies, a handful from a neighboring county's SAR group, personnel from the power company that operates the dam, and a hospital-based ambulance crew. The first Crag Rats, Cam and Jim, were on the other side of the conduit, assembling rope-rescue equipment, taking charge of a situation in which no one else knew what to do. The otherwise highly trained fire, sheriff, and ambulance crew members had neither the knowledge nor the equipment for high-angle rope extrication.

I cautiously walked a hundred yards north on top of the conduit's slick, narrow catwalk, scrambled thirty feet down a slippery metal ladder, and walked a hundred yards back to the cliff again. At the edge, Cam and Todd had tied webbing around a vine maple for an anchor. Jim had just gone over the edge. Then I heard his call for medical help and the need for a life jacket.

"You'd better head down," said Cam. "I'll be rope safety."

"I'll get to the edge on another rope," said Todd.

"I'll fetch the litter from the truck," said Steve.

Sometime after noon, Mark's brother realized that Mark's quick walk had lasted several hours. After a short search, Mark's brother returned to the house and called 911.

Now, our crew works fast, trying to save Mark's life.

"Chris, this is Mark," says Jim. He is busy untangling a rope and preparing to receive a litter.

"Okay," I say and go to work.

I approach Mark extremely slowly, for every time I shift my weight on the logjam, he winces. Also, I am afraid of falling under a log myself and getting sucked into the churning water.

I quickly interview the patient, conduct a primary survey, and make a cursory secondary survey.

"Mark, I'm Christopher, the search and rescue doctor. How do you feel?"

"Oh, thank God," he sighs, and almost passes out again from sheer relief. "I hurt all over, especially my leg and my elbow and my wrist and my head. And I'm very cold." He looks distraught, shivers almost to the point of convulsions, and slurs his words.

"Do you have any chest pain?"

"No."

"Abdominal pain?"

"Um, I don't think so."

"Oh, Chris," says Jim. "He can't move his left leg. Forgot to mention that." He coordinates the ropes with Todd, who has rappelled to the edge of the cliff. "And we have a helicopter on the way. MAST from Yakima." U.S. Army's Military Assistance to Safety and Traffic air evacuation helicopter team is designed to augment local fire and sheriff departments in precisely these types of situations.

First, we have to move the patient to a safer spot. Jim helps me carefully drag Mark the ten feet from the middle of the log-jam to the edge of the canyon so that he is still floating on a log, but now his back rests against the canyon wall. This is not only a safer position for all of us, but the canyon wall will stabilize his back.

I review the ABCDEs. I determine that his airway is intact and breathing is normal. His pulse is faint and thready, and his skin is pale and cold. I see no pools or spurts of blood, but I sur-mise that he has probably lost a significant amount, since the logs are splattered. He's fallen over a cliff and has a large laceration and bruise on his forehead, so we have to treat the head injury and prevent possible spinal cord and brain injuries. He is already suf-fering from mild to moderate hypothermia.

"We need a C-collar, blanket, and helmet!" I shout, referring to a cervical collar to immobilize his head.

I do my rapid head-to-toe secondary survey. His neck is not tender and he has no visible deformity or pain on his spine. He cradles his left elbow, so I cut away a part of his fleece jacket with heavy trauma shears.

A bone sticks out of a matted clump of blood, twigs, and dirt. I stuff the fleece back against the wound. The open fracture wor-ries me: a life-threatening infection can set deep in the bone. However, if I were to open the wound and clean it to prevent in-fection, it would certainly start bleeding again and he can't afford any more blood loss here.

Mark also can't move his right wrist. I palpate an obvious de-formity. But there is no bleeding; he can move his fingers; he can feel me touching them; and his skin is only slightly cool and pale.

From this I can tell the wrist fracture is not cutting off his circulation or nerve impulses, so I'll deal with this less serious injury later.

Thankfully, his abdomen and chest are not tender. I will assume his spleen and liver are uninjured, but I keep the possibility of blunt abdominal injury in the back of my mind to be rechecked for later. I test for obvious swelling and deformity of his legs the best I can through his soaked jeans. He can't move his left leg, but he wiggles his toes, moves his ankle slightly, has a faint pulse in his foot, and has minimal sensation when I touch his toes; these signs mean that his neurovascular function is intact all the way to his toes. If he does have a fracture, at least it is not cutting off the blood or nerve impulses to his foot. He has lost his left shoe and hadn't been wearing socks: I'll have to watch for frostbite, too.

Jim brings over the helmet, C-collar, and blanket. Jim and I gently place the C-collar on Mark's neck and the helmet on his head. Opening my medical pack, I tape a big wad of gauze over the exposed bone of his left elbow. Then I wrap the elbow tightly with a gauze roll and stabilize the entire arm with a malleable aluminum splint covered in soft foam. I use safety pins to attach his sweater sleeve to the front of his sweater and tape his arm to his chest using big wraps of two-inch cloth medical tape. Finally I cross his right arm over his left to stabilize both. All the while we exercise extreme caution not to move his neck or back. I'm thankful Jim is on scene with me because he's a seasoned firefighter and emergency medical technician. He automatically keeps Mark's neck and spine protected as do I. We cover him with the blanket.

"Thanks," Mark says faintly.

Mark's airway, breathing, and circulation are stable, his spine is immobilized, the hypothermia is treated as best I can for now, and the left elbow and right wrist fractures are splinted. I do another quick exam of his left leg because a femur or pelvis fracture could be serious; either can bleed so profusely than people can die in a matter of hours. Mark has no visible leg injury but feels more pain on his hip bone than his leg. He has excruciating pain every time Jim and I shift our weight on the logjam. But when Mark remains still, he doesn't have pain. This seems more like a pelvis fracture than a femur fracture to me.

"Jim, what's the plan?" I ask. "We have to get him out of here."

"They are sending down a litter," says Jim. "We can't take him up the line we came down. Todd's at the edge above us. They are rigging a raising system."

I feel a sinking feeling in my gut. The raising system will be one of the most difficult we've ever done: up the cliff, through the thick brush, and to the top. A single rope will probably not be long enough, we may have to do a more complicated raising system with multiple ropes. The extrication could take hours. If the patient passes out again, he may not be able to breathe properly if he has a serious head injury like a concussion.

What's more, once at the top of the canyon, we'll have to rig a secondary raising system to get him up and over the twenty-foot-high pipe.

Just then a helicopter roars up the canyon. The thundering rotors create a whirlwind, pelting us with rocks, sticks, and dirt. I cover Mark with a blanket and shield his eyes with my gloved hands. To do so, I have to bend awkwardly against the rock wall and move my feet to a more stable position. The logjam wobbles, Mark winces, and more debris showers down upon us. Someone from dispatch called the helicopter, arriving with a medic and hoist to evacuate the patient.

"Rock!" yells Todd from above. I hug the cliff tighter and

shield Mark's face with my chest. A bowling-ball-sized rock comes from the sky, hits Jim square in the back between his shoulder blades, and bounces off. I wait for him to collapse into the water and I'm just about to lunge toward him.

Instead, he looks over, smiles, and yells: "Was that a rock?"

"Big one." I smile. Luckily, he is wearing the heavy foam life jacket. This is dangerous: falling rocks, narrow canyon, unstable log jam, swift water. No to mention we have several agencies from two states, which don't usually work together.

The litter is finally lowered bringing with it a slew of pebbles and dirt. Jim grabs the lightweight fiberglass stretcher to keep it from sliding into the water. At the same time, a medic is lowered on a cable from the chopper. The medic and litter converge right on top of us. There's little room on the logjam, and they bang together, almost knocking Jim into the water. The medic finds a perch on the cliff above us, and he unhooks himself from the cable. Jim grabs the litter and slides it onto the logjam. All the while I'm shielding Mark from the rotor wash, trying to keep his head and neck stabilized, and making sure no one falls into the water or between two logs.

Finally, the chopper flies away and we regroup. I immediately wonder if we can extricate the patient with the helicopter hoist. As in the earlier rescue, the chopper might not be able to fly close enough.

With the added weight of the medic and the litter, the logjam starts quivering. Dazed and pale, Mark's face is a flat mask of pain, and his hypothermia has worsened. I worry about the logjam breaking up and sending us all into the river. We stand still and wait for the vibrations to dissipate. I later find out that the power company shut the dam spillways to lessen the stream flow and help keep us stable on the logjam.

I summarize the situation to the medic as tersely as possible: "Adult male, fell a hundred feet about eight hours ago. He's alert and talking. GCS fifteen initially. Head injury, open elbow fracture, wrist fracture, possible hip or femur fracture. No major chest or abdomen injury. In C-collar and arms splinted. He's pretty hypothermic. I'm worried about his head and neck and that left leg. He's lost some blood."

"You guys have done most of my job," he says. "Let's get him out of here." He radios the helicopter while Jim and I lift the patient onto the hard plywood backboard that's nestled inside the litter and strap him in. We remove the rope bridle that we use for rope extrication so that the medic can attach his cable bridle, one designed to minimize spinning when the litter is winched up into the chopper.

We wait ten minutes. Finally, the helicopter zooms back, hovers, and drops a cable. The medic nods. Jim and I hook in the cable, attach a tag line that also helps keep the litter from spinning, and recheck everything. The medic radios the pilot that all is a go.

I give Mark instructions: "Relax, you are strapped in tight. Keep your eyes closed—it will be windy. Don't move. You may spin a bit. Just don't move," I say. "There's a medic in the chopper. You'll be at the hospital in fifteen minutes."

"Okay, thanks," he mumbles.

The litter lifts off the logjam, and the medic hold a tag line to keep the litter from spinning. The litter, suspended in midair, wobbles a bit in the downdraft. It clears the branches of the giant Douglas fir and is drawn under the belly of the big chopper and up to the door. From below, all I see is a gloved hand reach out, grab the litter, and drag it inside.

The canyon is too narrow for the helicopter to hover for

much longer, as the downdraft creates unstable air that can suck it downward. The helicopter flies away, makes another pass, settles into the same position, and drops the cable again.

The medic hooks on.

"Thanks, guys. We'll leave your litter at the hospital," he says like it's all in a day's work. The chopper winches him up, then flies away. Jim and I are left on the logjam, with blood spattered on the logs and rock wall and debris floating in the now calm water.

As always with the end of a rescue, I breathe a huge sigh of relief and feel a wave of fatigue wash over me. Now all we need is for our buddies to haul us up the cliff and we can head home.

"We're not finished," Jim says as though he'd read my mind. He points to two shivering dogs about twenty feet upstream. "We can't leave them here."

The dogs are perched on two rock ledges. One is just on the edge of the water and the other is on the cliff twenty feet above us. Because of the sheer walls and the logjam, we can't reach them easily. To reach the lower dog, Jim and I traverse a thin ledge upriver while tied to a safety line.

Todd, still above us on the ledge, can reach the higher dog. Todd puts the young puppy in Cam's empty backpack, hoists it onto his back, and has the team haul him up. It takes twenty minutes. Jim and I wait near the second dog, and we cling to the rock wall, getting cold.

Finally, Todd bushwhacks back to the edge on the rope and drops an empty pack on a second line. I cradle the shivering, whimpering dog in my arms. It doesn't appear to have any broken legs or ribs. I gently put it into the empty backpack with its head sticking out. I hoist the pack and dog onto Jim's shoulders, trying to keep my footing on the ledge.

"Ready for Jim!" I yell to Todd. He then radios above. The

team begins to haul up Jim and the dog. After twenty vertical feet, an overhang in the cliff makes it impossible for Todd to see Jim. The rope stops when the team above resets the line. But it stops at the most inopportune moment, when Jim is not quite cresting the overhang. He swings violently into the wall and slams his knees. He can't let go of the rope to cushion the blow because he is carrying the dog. Later when I look at his knee, I tell him to go to the hospital for stitches. The small but deep cut is dripping blood.

Finally, two hours after rappelling into the canyon, the crew hauls up Jim and then me. I guzzle two bottles of water. It is close to 7:00 P.M. and I want to head home, but we are not quite finished. We quickly repack the truck. I drive to the hospital to check on the patient, see to Jim's stitches, and retrieve our backboard, litter, and other gear. When I walk in, the charge nurse frowns at my filthy pants and scratched face and arms. She doesn't recognize me.

"Can I help you?" She scowls. "Patient registration is around the corner."

"I'm Dr. Van Tilburg," I say softly. "We extricated the trauma patient from Washington."

"Oh, hi," she says, smiling broadly.

The patient is still in the CT scanner. The ER doctor on duty doesn't know much yet, other than Mark has warmed up and is getting IV fluids to counteract the blood loss. A preliminary scan showed no major brain bleed and no neck fracture. The trauma surgeon taking care of the patient is at the desk scribbling in the chart. His eyes sparkle when he sees me. I give him the full report, supplying more details than he needs to treat the patient. He asks about joining the Crag Rats.

"Send me an e-mail. We could use you," I say, too tired to write anything down. I know he'll be a good addition to our team.

Two days later when I see the surgeon in town, he recaps Mark's final diagnoses. Mark's open left elbow fracture required surgery and intravenous antibiotics. His right wrist fracture healed without surgery. His pelvis was fractured but was also stable: it needed no treatment to heal on its own. His femur was unbroken. His head injuries included abrasions, lacerations, contusions, and a mild concussion. He received a few stitches on his forehead and scalp. Amazingly, he had no major brain or spine injury. Dehydration and hypothermia were corrected with warm IV fluids.

I meet Jim outside the ER. After the few stitches, he would report the biggest hassle would be getting the bill paid. "You repack the medical, I'll take care of the ropes," says Jim. "I'll ask Devon to wash them at the fire department," he says, smiling, referring to his son, a firefighter and member of our team.

"See you, Jim. Good rescue."

"Yeah, good rescue."

CHAPTER 3

Crag Rats

It's your birthday, your choice," my wife says when I ask if I can
cancel our bike ride because I need to head out on another rescue. It is very difficult to be the significant other of a mountain
rescue volunteer. Sometimes Jennifer supports me and the greater
mission without too much complaint. She fills water bottles and
assembles a bag of food for me, even usually has dinner ready
when I return. She will watch the kids at unexpected times. She's
supporting her husband and, indirectly, the community. Like
many outdoor-adventure enthusiasts, she feels bad for the injured
or lost person. And she knows that someday, if she needs rescue,
she'll want people like the Crag Rats, and spouses of the Crag
Rats, to help. But it does create some friction in my marriage. I
miss dinner parties. I shirk household duties like mowing the
lawn.

I decided long ago to continue to volunteer for mountain
rescue, even after we had kids. I don't have boys nights out with
the guys or go on many personal trips. I'm focused on spending
as much time as possible with my daughters. My twenty-four-
hour shifts working as an emergency doctor allows me to work
ten days a month and give me more time with my kids than most

dads. I also decided to work less and create a world in which I need less money to live on. No one ever gets to the end of life wishing he'd worked more. But, as a result, leaving on another mountain rescue call out during a what will become a very busy year is not exactly greeted with smiles from my wife. Jennifer gave me a cold, raised-eyebrow stare when I mentioned earlier this year I might like to join the volunteer fire department.

"Are they okay?" she asks, worried about the climber.

"Don't know," I say, while I change clothes and call Penny.

"Who is it?" she asks, hoping it is not a friend.

"Don't know."

"Are they hurt?"

"I think so, but I'm not really sure"

"How bad?"

"I don't know."

So on my birthday, Todd Wells and I lumber up Cloud Cap Road, again. The gate, which blocks the road in winter, is locked so we drive around while Bernie Wells and Kirk Worrill, two Crag Rats, wait for the Forest Service to unlock the gate so they can drive through with our truck and snowcat. The road is dry, so the deep ruts explode with clouds of powdered dirt and clog my car's air filter. Sharp rocks threaten my tires. I seem to get one flat a year driving up and down this road. At mile four, a juvenile black bear sprints across our path and dives into the dense mixed conifer forest. At mile six, a downed Douglas fir as thick as a sewer main stymies our progress. It would take forever to cut it with the small folding saw I carry in my truck. We can't go much farther anyway, since the road still has patches of snow in the north-facing shadowed switchbacks.

Hood River County—including the valley, town, and river of the same name—is a rural mountain community. Five hundred feet above sea level, we are sandwiched between two great volcanoes of the South Cascade Range, Mount Hood and Mount Adams, in Washington, right where the Columbia River slices through. For years Hood River was primarily a fruit-growing community and a truck stop for loggers hauling old-growth timber out of the thick forest. In the early 1980s, windsurfers found the Columbia River Gorge. The cool marine air from the Pacific Ocean wafts inland to Portland. The scorched desert air of eastern Oregon and Washington rises and sucks the cool air up the natural hundred-mile-long, four-thousand-foot-high wind tunnel. Because the wind runs opposite the river flow, up to ten feet waves build on the water. The wind, which had been bothersome to orchardists and backyard picnicers for decades, was found to be ideal for windsurfing. Thus, Hood River became one of the premier windsurfing destinations in the world. And with the outdoor adventure sport craze of the 1990s, Hood River became jam-packed with more than windsurfers: it saw an influx of fly-fishers, mountaineers, mountain bikers, skiers, snowboarders, kayakers, and other adventure sport enthusiasts, the so-called adrenaline junkies.

Despite the worrisome trend of razing orchards for housing developments, Hood River still has a smattering of family-run orchards growing Bartlett and Anjou pears, peaches, Granny Smith and Fuji apples, and, in the east side of the county where it is slightly warmer and drier, Bing and Queen Anne cherries. The downtown strip, once filled with cheap diners and surf shops, has of late metamorphosed into a slew of Aspenesque boutiques: specialty shops for shoes, kids clothing, toys, jewelry, dog paraphernalia, gelato, coffee, and women's clothing. People drive an hour from Portland just to shop here on weekends and holidays.

Fortunately, though, our town retains its rural farming and

mountain cultures. Our community's true spirit is embodied by our mountain rescue history. The tale of sturdy volunteers donating their time to help those in dire predicaments is an inspiring one. Especially considering Crag Rats was the first official volunteer mountain rescue group in the nation.

For centuries, volunteers, just like those in Hood River, have been saving lives in the world's harshest environments: mountains, deserts, jungles, forests, and oceans. Some of the earliest rescue volunteers were the Augustine monks of the monastery founded 1050 by Bernard of Menthon, archdeacon of Aosta. The monastery still operates at 8,110 feet in the Alps of Italy and Switzerland, in the pass in the Pennine Pass in the Valais Alps. The monks became most famous for their highly regarded SAR dogs. Originally used for pulling dairy carts, the Roman Molossus breed was preferred for their thick coat, warm personality, sturdy legs, and keen smell. Also called Hospice Dogs and later renamed St. Bernard, they have saved over two thousand lives since 1707. The Augustine monks built aid posts and hospices across the Alps. So highly regarded were the Augustine monks that Bernard of Menthon was named the patron saint of mountain climbers in 1923 by Pope Pius XI.

In the late 1700s, mountaineering flourished in the Alps and organized mountain search and rescue, by necessity, soon followed. In the late 1700s the Duchy of Savoy released men from military duty to form a volunteer guide and rescue service. In 1821 the king of Sardinia founded a guide and rescue organization called the Syndicate des Guides de Chamonix to safeguard Mont Blanc. The Swiss Alpine Club formed in 1863 to perform mountain search and rescue in the Alps. Swiss Parsenndienst, a winter ski rescue group, organized to haul injured skiers off the mountains. In 1948, Europe's mountain rescue volunteers banded together to organize the International Commission for Alpine Rescue.

In the United States, search and rescue dates back to 1848, when the Life-Saving Service was created to provide rescue for sea mishaps on the eastern seaboard. By 1915 the country's first SAR agency, the United States Coast Guard, was formed. As the West became settled, Americans also began climbing mountains for sport. Enter the Pacific Northwest's Cascade Range, a string of perennially snowcapped volcanoes that extend from British Columbia to northern California. Until the 1920s, rescue on these peaks—especially on Mount Hood and Mount Rainer, in Washington State, was coordinated by the scant few national Forest Service rangers with help from groups of volunteer climbers, guides, and military personnel. But in 1926, in the tiny mountain community of Hood River, that changed.

August 10, 1926, was likely a warm summer day in the Pacific Northwest. The sky was probably sunny, temperatures warm, and perhaps a faint breeze drifted across the treetops. The tip of Mount Hood was probably encircled by a cloud cap, a ring of clouds that form as the warm marine air hits the year-round snowfields, condenses, then lingers atop the peak.

Eleven-year-old Jackie Strong set out on a fishing trip on Mount Hood's Lost Creek with his older brothers and became lost above timberline on Vista Ridge. For three nights he huddled in the open, sipped water from a creek, and devoured every huckleberry he could find. The sheriff gathered hundreds of volunteer rangers, police, deputies, hikers, neighbors, and soldiers from Portland's Seventh Infantry to search for the boy. During the search, it was Hood River mountain climbers who were the only ones with skills and equipment to hike high above timberline to the permanent snowfields and glaciers. Climber Mace Baldwin studied the maps and interviewed the brothers, then exclaimed "I know where the boy is!" On August 13, Baldwin, Percy Bucklin, and Jess Puddy found the boy perched on a rocky outcrop above the tree line. He was shivering uncontrollably. The mountaineers lit a fire and fired a single rifle shot to signal that the boy had been found. The men jubilantly walked off the mountain the next morning carrying the boy. The media asked who they were.

"We're Crag Rats," said Baldwin, grinning. Mace recalled a climber's wife saying that "the guys are just a bunch of rats climbing crags on weekends."

The name stuck.

Soon thereafter, volunteer mountain rescue groups began to form up and down the mountainous West. In 1936 on Mount Hood, Charles Minot Dole began organizing what would become National Ski Patrol to assist the burgeoning ski industry with first aid and rescues. Ski Patrol units quickly formed at emerging ski resorts and eventually became a 2,800-member organization with 600 patrols across the nation. In 1941, Dole was hired to train military troops in mountain search, rescue, and warfare. Thus the U.S. Army's famous 10th Mountain Division was established and began training first on Mount Rainier, then at Camp Hale in Colorado. The American Alpine Club—formed in 1902 to promote mountain skills, scientific exploration, conservation, and access—organized a safety committee in 1947. The committee published "Mountaineering Safety," which was distributed among climbing enthusiasts.

On June 6 to 7, 1959, at Mount Hood's Timberline Lodge, West Coast mountain rescue volunteers gathered to form Mountain Rescue Association. The two goals described in 1959 still are followed to this day: to provide mountain search and rescue and mountain-safety education.

Today, more than eighty-five units and 2,500 volunteers in the Mountain Rescue Association (the National Association for Search and Rescue, our sister organization that deals with non-mountainous SAR, has some 14,000 members) attend to thousands of rescues in the United States every year. Some teams are called out ten times a year; others have more than a hundred missions annually. Rescuers are primarily volunteer climbers, but some teams include paid personnel like the climbing rangers at Denali, Yosemite, and Grand Teton National Parks; Air Force Pararescue Jumpers; sheriff deputies; and select fire-rescue paramedic teams. With outdoor sports becoming more widespread and extreme sports becoming more popular, disciplines within mountain search and rescue have broadened. Nowadays, a team may be called upon to participate in a desert search, swift-water rescue on a river, or confined-space extrication from a cave. Most units are supported by grants, taxes, and donations. And as it was from the beginning, rescue has its core in the willingness of townsfolk to help those in distress in the wild country.

Like many mountain rescuers past and present, Crag Rats is a group of folks with families and outdoor lifestyles. We are orchardists, carpenters, and teachers. We have volunteer firefighters, paramedics, and an occupational therapist. We count lawyers, horticulturists, and the only two judges in the county as members. We rarely go more than a few days without running, mountain biking, cycling, skiing, snowboarding, climbing, kayaking, or hiking. We have a single underlying bond: a passion for the outdoors underscored by a deep love, respect, and awe for the high country, the wide-open snowfields and glaciers, tall peaks, thick forests, and wild rivers.

Everyone comes to the group skilled in mountain craft at some level. Some members are expert in technical mountaineering and ice climbing. Some are knowledgeable in basic glacier climbing (the only requirement for membership is to have summited both Mount Hood and Mount Adams and to live in Hood River County). We have assembled with a common, specific, highly specialized, highly focused goal: to head into the backcountry to search for the lost and rescue the injured.

We donate time, energy, and personal resources to the group and to the community. We don't get paid for the fifteen to twenty missions we perform every year. Typically, an active member donates twenty to forty hours on rescues and another twenty to forty on nonrescue duties. We have monthly meetings, six to eight trainings a year, social functions, and outdoor trips. We maintain and repair equipment, and our two buildings.

In a rescue, not everyone rappels into a slot canyon, but everyone has a job. One person is at home coordinating the rescue. One or two will function as the hasty team, to race up the trail and assess the situation. One person becomes incident commander in the field. Another is assigned to be the medical person. One member may shuttle rescuers in a vehicle, deliver food, or hump gear up the trail. Sometimes that gear saves a life; but other times it is not needed and we haul it back down the trail. Sometimes we wait for instructions, wait to be needed, or wait to be unneeded. Once in a while we drive home after doing nothing whatsoever.

Unlike most volunteer groups, except volunteer firefighters, we need to be available 24/7 for a mission. Often we know very little about the patient, the location, and the situation. It might be life or death or it might be to escort someone out of the woods. A "head injury up Eagle Creek" can turn out to be an ankle sprain up Ruckel Creek. A "heart attack at Elk Meadow" can be an uninjured but stranded hiker in Newton Creek Canyon. We leave work, household projects, dinner parties, a warm bed, and family with no advance notice and precious little time to prepare.

Individually, we desire to be mountain rescuers for many reasons. It is a community service, we build up good karma, we might need help one day. The camaraderie is different from the other aspects of our lives here; we are brought together for a common, specific task that few can complete, is often performed under tense circumstances, and usually has unpredictable obstacles. Highly specialized, dangerous, physically demanding, mentally exhausting life-or-death missions are intensely powerful stimuli. We gain a deep satisfaction when applying our skill and knowledge of the mountains, forests, and rivers to helping those in need. We thrive on the adventure—the adrenaline rush begins with the call-out page and doesn't dissipate until the mission is complete. The thrill is compelling, the danger alluring, and the personal gratification is hedonistic. It is a pure, unadulterated form of pleasure. Altruism has rewards, too; otherwise it would be tough to roll out of bed for the next call out.

Now, nearly eight decades after Crag Rats were formed, Todd and I drive up the road to Cloud Cap, a saddle at six thousand feet on the north side of Mount Hood. Sometimes we race up to rescues because it's an emergency or we don't know if it is an emergency. Today we take more time. This call out actually began last night. The sheriff's office got a 911 call about a missing climber on the north side of Mount Hood. Sheriff Joe went up in the Piper Cub. The subject, Pat, was climbing the difficult route with some friends over Cooper Spur, a ridge that juts out from the northeast corner of the mountain. Lower, the spur is broad, steep, and for much of the year, snow-covered. Higher up, the slope steepens. From Tie-in Rock, a huge boulder at more than 8,300 feet, the climb is an exposed, treacherous, 2,000-foot pitch to the summit of the mountain. Just above Tie-in Rock, Pat felt ill, likely from acute mountain sickness (AMS).

Also called altitude illness, AMS can be a minor illness or a life-threatening disaster caused by the lower concentration of oxygen and the lower air pressure. The lungs need both an adequate amount of oxygen as well as enough air pressure to drive it across the lung membranes into the blood. In the blood, oxygen attaches to the hemoglobin in red blood cells and is carried to the tissues of the body. At high altitudes—and less oxygen in the air—the body tries to compensate by taking more and deeper breaths. The heart pumps faster to force blood more quickly through the body; speeding up absorption of oxygen in the lungs and delivery of oxygen to tissues. The blood vessels dilate, which also allows more blood to flow to the organs and muscles.

All these changes can improve oxygenation of the body's tissues; but they also have side effects. Symptoms include a headache, which is probably caused by a combination of less oxygen delivered to the brain and increased blood flow, causing congestion beneath the skull; fatigue, dizziness, nausea, lethargy, difficulty breathing, chills, and irritability. It can be difficult to distinguish AMS from fatigue, sun exposure, hunger, and thirst, all of which can afflict mountain climbers.

AMS can occur at elevations as low as five thousand feet, but it is more common above eight thousand feet, the elevation of many American ski resorts as well as many hiking trails and climbs in the West. Altitude illness can become life threatening. Advanced stages can lead to difficulty concentrating, and walking, and even vomiting. High-altitude pulmonary edema occurs when the heart and lungs are working overtime and fluid leaks into the lungs. The same leaking can occur in the capillaries in the brain, called high-altitude cerebral edema, which causes disorientation, delirium, and eventually coma.

Prevention is paramount. In addition to staying in good shape, nourished, and hydrated, the key is proper acclimation. *Sleep low, climb high* is the common axiom of climbers. When ascending a mountain, a gradual ascent is recommended, especially if the mountain is taller than ten thousand feet. Recreational climbers and winter sports enthusiasts, who may only have a week off to ski or climb, are at higher risk for AMS. This is especially true of people who live at sea level and fly to Western ski resorts or mountain climbing locals. They ascend a mountain in one day and fall ill.

If you recognize that you have mild AMS, the best initial treatment is rest, food, and fluids. If symptoms don't resolve in a few minutes, treatment is simple but extremely difficult: go down. Immediate descent is not always possible. Mountain doctors can use medicines like steroids and diuretics to counteract the symptoms. With life-threatening AMS, climbers can be put in an altitude bag, a sealed chamber which, when pumped up with the patient inside, simulates the oxygen pressure of a lower altitude and drives more oxygen into the bloodstream.

Fortunately, Pat had the wits to abandon his climb of Mount Hood's Cooper Spur well before the summit. But Pat had another problem: he descended alone. His partners continued climbing. After ascending the north side, they would take the safer, gentler descent on the south side, where they had a second car parked at Timberline Ski Area. Pat's route down seemed straightforward: *hike down and in a few hours I'll be back at the car.* It was a warm, sunny afternoon and he could see the entire Hood River Valley and Mounts Adams, St. Helens, and Rainier to the north. But he did not have a map or compass. He had no spare clothes and not enough food or water. In addition, he wasn't paying attention on either the way up or down. He didn't realize that the route home (there is no distinct trail when the spur is covered in snow) is a subtle traverse. From Cooper Spur, Pat needed to catch the Timberline Trail, which would take him a mile northwest, back to the Cloud Cap. From there, he could follow Tilly Jane Trail two miles northeast back to his car. Instead, he followed Cooper Spur down the fall line, the natural course a rock would take when propelled by gravity. The snow was soft, so he was likely plunging ankle and knee deep into it, fatiguing him more. Eventually Pat entered dense woods and reached the terminus of the spur, which is flanked by the two impassible sheer cliffs of Pollalie Creek. He didn't realize he was off course, until the sun dipped low on the horizon. Pat recognized that he was lost. With dusk approaching, he stopped hiking, made himself a tiny shelter in the trees, put on his only extra layer, and rationed his food and water. He didn't have a cell phone, so he hunkered in for the evening.

Meanwhile, his partners had reached the summit, hiked down to Timberline, picked up their second car, and drove around to the north side. But instead of searching or waiting, they switched cars, reported their friend missing by cell phone, left the keys hidden in Pat's vehicle, and drove home to Portland.

Near dusk, Sheriff Joe Wampler in his airplane located Pat in thick trees. Joe has a foot-long foam-padded capsule with a three-foot-diameter parachute. He stuffed in a water bottle, cell phone, and map. After dropping the capsule, Joe talked with Pat, realized he'd be okay to spend the night, and notified the Crag Rats to head up the mountain first thing in the morning.

In the early morning hours on my birthday Todd and I hike through dirty, compacted snowbanks nestled in the switchbacks. We reach Cloud Cap saddle and continue up through the woods to the timberline. The forest is empty and peaceful. The sun has warmed the day. Todd and I stop to shed a layer of clothing and guzzle water. At the tree line, we start yelling. After an hour a guy emerges through the woods, stumbling beneath the weight of a big pack, almost running right toward us.

"You Pat?" asks Todd.

"Yeah," he said in a weak voice.

"We're search and rescue. How you doing?"

"I'm okay. I'm really glad to see you," he says, talking faster. "Boy, the sheriff dropped me this map last night. I had no idea I was so far off the route. I could have gone off the cliff." He shows me where Joe had written in big red marker "cliff" just below Pat's bivouac site. The adrenaline that had been keeping him juiced all night was waning. As so often when we find an injured or lost person, the sudden relief can almost put them in shock. They are famished, thirsty, and tired. Todd and I watch Pat closely.

"Your friends are gone," Todd says.

"Where's my car?" Pat asks.

"Red Honda?" asks Todd.

"Yep."

"Tilly Jane," says Todd, referring to the parking area that is two hours by foot below us. Pat seems dismayed that his partners abandoned him.

Pat was smart enough to turn back. Many climbers get caught up in the goal of reaching the top and keep going despite multiple warning signs that should urge them to turn around. People are embarrassed by the fact that no one else wants to turn back. Or they think; *I've been planning this weekend for months*, or *I'm in too good shape to turn around.* For Todd and I, this is a simple walk out, not really a medical evacuation, not really much of a search. I might be able to still catch my wife and her friends riding up Dog River Trail; I've got my mountain bike and gear in the back of my truck.

Todd, Pat, and I stop at one of my favorite places: Cloud Cap Inn, the Crag Rat cabin perched on a rocky outcrop at 6,000 feet on Mount Hood's north side. We sit on the deck, gawk at the mountain, and relax. We are waiting for our backup crew in the snowcat, now plowing up a trail called Old Wagon Road, named when the inn was a bed-and-breakfast after it was built in 1889. Todd opens up the cabin and gets water from the spring-fed faucet. We feed Pat and give him water, which rejuvenates him like a magical elixir. I soak up the high mountain sun and suck in lungfuls of the cool, clean air on my birthday, as I reflect on the mountain and this thorny business of mountain rescue.

Mount Hood, one of the most accessible and popular mountains in the world to climb, has seen its share of mishaps. First known as Wy'East, or Son of the Great Spirit, by Native Americans it received its present name in 1792, when Lieutenant William Broughton sailed up the Columbia River and named it after Rear Admiral Samuel Hood of the British Navy. In 1857, Portland mountaineers William Buckley, W. Chittenden, James Deardorf, Henry Pittock, and L. Powell first reached the summit of the 11,239-foot volcano. It is close to Portland and relatively easy to climb, and is one of the most popular mountain climbs in the world, with some ten thousand attempting to climb to the top every year. On July 18, 1889, the first mountaineering club in the United States was formed on the summit of Mount Hood and christened the Mazamas, after the mountain goat. Their motto is "*Nesika klalawa sahale,*" Chinook for "We Climb High."

Every year we have a rescue or two high on Mount Hood, often a fatality. Some reports put the death total at twenty-one on the north side. In fact, the Cooper Spur climbing route has been dubbed "the most popular route to die on." From the last pitch above Tie-in Rock, named after the spot where climbers band together with a rope, is two thousand feet up a steep slope that is off angle, meaning it is between side-hill traverse and a fall line. This route is an awkward, dangerous pitch, so when climbers fall, they slide off over the Eliot Glacier headwall, a two-thousand-foot rock cliff that lies between the summit and the Eliot Glacier.

Mount Hood is full of textbook examples of what not to do when climbing a mountain. Recently, for example, a thirty-four-year-old solo climber fell two thousand feet off Cooper Spur into the Newton Clark Glacier, a treacherous and remote spot on the mountain. Two climbers who witnessed the accident called 911. From the Piper Cub Sheriff Joe spotted the bloody body high on the glacier. He called in the Crag Rats and a helicopter from the National Guard. When the National Guard paramedics were lowered, they pronounced the climber dead. How did he fall? Maybe a falling rock hit him? Maybe his crampons (the metal spikes attached to his boots) balled up, and became compacted with snow and ineffective at providing purchase on ice. Maybe his attention drifted from climbing for the moment and he tripped on his ice ax or crampons.

Climbers carry an ice ax, a three-foot aluminum shaft with a sharp spike at one end and a pick and adze at the other. This tool is designed to anchor a climber or allow him or her to stop a sliding fall, a technique called self-arrest. But maybe the climber was not planting the ice ax properly to anchor his steps. Maybe once he fell, he began sliding too fast or the snow was too slushy for him to dig in with the ax. Maybe he dropped the ax.

It's not a good idea to climb without anchoring each step with an ice ax. And it is not a good idea to climb without a partner. Yet, even so, climbers fall because they neglect other basic precautions. A few years back a Hood River man also fell and died on Cooper Spur. He was climbing with an ice ax and a partner. In a letter to the Crag Rats, his climbing partner commented that although the dead man was an expert skier, he might not have had the climbing skills to anchor each step by driving the shaft of his ice ax deep into the snow. The fall might have been caused by his self-made gear. He was testing new climbing leg warmers like those used by dancers and cyclists. He had them pulled down off his legs and they were bunched up on the top of his boot. He might have caught his crampon on one, causing the fall. The two were not roped.

In another accident, a young couple in their thirties were roped together. The pair left Cloud Cap parking lot at 4:30 A.M. and reached the mountain summit at 8 A.M. Because of the combination of solar radiation and the high freezing level, the elevation where the air is 32° F, the firm morning snowpack turned to soft, slippery slush. This is dangerous because crampons don't provide much traction in slush, and a climber expends a lot of energy post-holing, that is, sinking ankle- or knee-deep in the snow. Recognizing the rapidly increasing danger, the couple started down from the summit immediately, but they did not descend the south side, a much safer route. A few steps off the summit, they fell. They were roped together, but that precaution alone is usually not sufficient for climbing steep, exposed slopes like Cooper Spur. In fact, tying into a rope with other climbers can be more dangerous than climbing without a rope, unless you use anchors, fixed-protection devices that when buried in the snow and clipped to the rope, will help stop a climber's fall. Such anchors include pickets (aluminum stakes), flukes (shovel-blade-shaped plates), and ice screws (six- or eight-inch long aluminum tubes).

The force of a climber sliding down the mountain is tremendous and will pull a rope with such huge force that it is almost impossible for a partner to withstand. Thus, if a falling climber is roped but unanchored, he or she often pulls the partner into the fall. The couple, who were training for Alaska's McKinley, fell twenty-five-hundred feet to the Eliot Glacier.

Some people have literally fallen right off the top of Mount Hood. One twenty-nine-year-old climber reached Mount Hood's summit via the south side route. She was posing for a picture with her climbing group when she fell. No one saw the fall, but they presumed she lost her balance near the edge. She too landed on the Eliot.

Similarly, a twenty-year-old snowboarder climbed from the south side and summited at 6:30 A.M. He planned to snowboard down Cooper Spur, climb back up, and descend the south side. He made only one turn on Cooper Spur and fell to the Eliot Glacier, to the same spot everyone else landed.

I first climbed Mount Hood via the south side with my brother Peter nearly two decades ago, the month before I married Jennifer. We hiked the dog route, the easiest way up, and chose March: a safe time to climb. The icy cliffs were still frozen, the crevasses were not yet open, the snow was firm for easy hiking, and the weather was clear. We left Timberline Lodge at dawn and reached the final ridge, Hogsback, by midmorning. We climbed the final chute, a narrow and steep gulley near the summit dubbed Pearly Gates because the summit rocks are coated with rime and glisten in the morning sun. I remember being frightened but not by the steep snow slope or the rock cliffs or the crevasse, which was only eight inches wide. I was worried about all the climbers—twenty packed into Pearly Gates chute.

"Keep moving," I yelled to Pete. "We need to get past everyone; someone's going to knock us off."

"Okay, I'm going," he yelled back, as he plowed onward to the top. Once on the summit, we shared a tiny airplane bottle of champagne, sliced salami, cheese, and French bread. But descending on a crowded section of the climb, Pete and I both realized this was a dangerous spot: many climbers, varying levels of experience, steep chute.

On May 30, 2002, Mount Hood had its worst accident in years. Many predicted it would come and it was exactly what I feared all those years ago. On the most popular climbing route in the world, three separate groups were ascending the final summit pitch, up Hogsback Ridge and through the Pearly Gates. The path was steep, narrow, crowded. It was a sunny warm day, with temperatures above freezing, and the many people on the route created an artificial sense of safety.

It started when a climber slipped, fell, and started sliding. The climber rapidly accelerated and was unable to self-arrest. His partners dropped instantly to self-arrest positions, gouging their axes into the ice slope to attempt to stop the fall. Then, one by one like dominos the other members of the team were jerked out of their self-arrest position on the rope that connected them to the sliding climber. Now four sliding climbers slammed into two additional groups, knocking more climbers over like bowling pins and tripping others up like a clothesline. Now nine climbers were sliding in three groups with no anchors to arrest their fall. Weak attempts at self-arrest failed: they were going too fast. They slammed into the Hogsback bergschrund, a large crevasse at the top of a glacier, and dropped in. Three died upon impact and six were stuck deep in the icy tomb. Jim Pennington, a local doctor, said the accident happened in about three seconds. He and his son and daughter were shocked, especially as they still had to descend the same slope.

A rescue was immediately initiated. Portland Mountain Rescue, Timberline Ski Patrol, and the local ambulance backcountry rescue team came up to help via snowcat. Helicopters were requested. Portland's Air Force Reserve 304th brought a combat-ready HH-60G Pave Hawk, and Salem's Army National Guard 1034th responded with two Black Hawks.

As quickly as rescuers could extricate the injured climbers using rope-raising systems, the helicopters began lifting them off the mountain. During the winching operation above the crevasse, the heavy Air Force Pave Hawk started settling, which is when the helicopter's downdraft creates suction that draws the helicopter closer to the ground. The huge chopper began a slow, out-of-control, downward spin. Thinking quickly, the crew chief fired the explosive to cut the cable; the patient on the other end of the cable had not yet been lifted off the mountain and did not get dragged down with the chopper. Then the Pave Hawk dropped out of the sky, smacked into the glacier, rolled down the slope, and tossed the five members of the crew out the open doors. Miraculously, not one of the helicopter crew members died, and no one on the ground was hit by the chopper or flying debris.

But now there were two rescues: the climbers and the downed helicopter—eleven injured, three dead. The injured climbers and crew members were evacuated by the lighter-weight Black Hawks and the Timberline Ski Area snowcat. The bodies were recovered the following day by ground. The mountain was closed for climbing for a week. The hulk of the chopper was evacuated by a giant twin rotor Chinook helicopter.

The Mount Hood South Side Rescue was not the worst climbing disaster on Mount Hood nor in the United States (however, it was perhaps the most costly ever with the loss of the $7.5 million Pave Hawk).

Back in 1986, the Oregon Episcopal School required that students participate in a climb of Mount Hood. Yet at Timberline Lodge on May 12, 1986, freezing temperatures thick clouds, and brisk winds made for a lousy day to be climbing. The weather was worse higher on the volcano, and it was predicted that a blustery spring storm would arrive. It was not, as the Portland *Oregonian* would later state in their front page headline, "an unexpected storm." Staff at Timberline Lodge warned the climbers against ascending the mountain. A climb planned by Rainier Mountaineering, one of the oldest and most respected mountain-guide services in the country, was canceled. Timberline Mountain Guides canceled a climb as well. Everyone hunkered down inside the lodge or headed home.

But Rev. Thomas Gorman, the OES trip leader and school faculty member, wanted to "give the summit a good shot." The group of seven adults and eleven teens left Timberline at 3 A.M., a bit late for such a climb in the spring, when warm afternoon temperatures heat the mountain, turn the snow to slush, and make climbing dangerous. Their progress was slow. In a short time three students and two adults turned back. But Gorman pressed on, despite the warnings of Ralph Summers, the paid "technical expert" and a local guide. The team was so slow that they didn't make it to Crater Rock, the final 1,500 feet leading up to the summit, until 3 P.M. Most parties climb to Crater Rock in six hours, which should have put the school kids here at well before noon.

With blowing snow and plummeting temperatures, climbing became dangerous. Gorman finally abandoned the climb at 10,000 feet. However it was late in the day and the group was trapped in the heart of the storm. The climbers couldn't even distinguish snow from sky. They hiked way off course, and stumbled downhill to 8,500 feet. Finally, after dark, with many of the kids hypothermic, they built a snow cave. The kids were shivering and crying. They had essentially no extra food, water, or clothing.

At 9 P.M., the adults and students back at Timberline called for help. One of the largest searches in Oregon began. By the next morning, May 13, rescuers scoured the mountain in search of the lost climbers, but the storm was still raging. Sometime that morning, the guide Summers and student Molly Schula left the snow cave and the freezing, crying students. Sixty mile per hour winds and two-foot visibility made travel treacherous. The two dropped into the mammoth White River Glacier, miraculously missed falling into a crevasse, and ended up at the Mount Hood Meadows Ski Resort, a dozen miles down the road from Timberline Lodge.

"Oh God, we're saved," exclaimed Molly when she saw the chairlifts of the resort.

"No," said Summers, "we have to wait until everybody is with us to celebrate." Summers would go on to search for two more days with hundreds of other rescuers.

On May 14, three more climbers were found in the snow at 7,500 feet: they were hypothermic and nearly dead. They had apparently left the snow cave and started down the mountain. Barely alive, they were airlifted to Portland trauma centers and later died, despite doctors working eight hours on one patient.

On May 15, after the weather finally cleared, the snow cave was located at the top of White River Glacier. The scene was grisly. Inside the cave were stacks of dead teens. Miraculously, two kids survived. One would later have bilateral leg amputations due to frostbite. In all, nine died.

The only North American mountaineering accident worse than the OES kids was when eleven climbers were killed on Mount Rainer when an icefall broke loose and avalanched into several rope teams on June 21, 1981.

I grew up skiing Mount Hood, climbed to the top, and still spend many days on the mountain. But accidents serve as vivid reminders as to what can go wrong on a mountain. One little mistake can turn to disaster. And even when everything is done correctly bad things happen to good people when climbing mountains.

Today, we find Pat and he is okay, despite having been abandoned by his partners and spending an unexpected night out above the tree line. Climbing, like all sports, contains varying levels of risk. Take surfing for example: if you head out on a clear day in southern California in small surf, you take much less risk than if you surf the huge waves of Hawaii's North Shore or on a hurricane surge on the East Coast. Same sport, much different risk. Climbing is the same: there are plenty of ways to minimize risks. The easiest, but also perhaps the most difficult, is to turn around and go home when conditions look unsafe. I am averse to putting myself at risk, especially when I think of my family back home. I love the outdoors: and I gain great pleasure from introducing my kids to the outdoors: camping, swimming, biking, hiking. But these days, I lean toward activities with much less risk.

Now, sitting on the front porch of Cloud Cap, I have a chance to reflect on what has been a busy year so far, my argument this morning with my wife about this rescue, and my devotion to Skylar and Avrie. This place, Cloud Cap Inn, is one of the most revered places in the world for me and a beautiful escape from the bustle of life. Now, it's peaceful and quiet, but in two more weeks, the road will open for the summer and there will be throngs of hikers and climbers up here.

Now, in the late spring sun, from my perch on the deck of Cloud Cap Inn, I'm content eating a peanut butter and honey sandwich, chatting with Todd about getting repairs done on the Crag Rat snowcat, affectionately named Pack Rat. We wait for Bernie and Kirk driving up in the Pack Rat to bring Todd, Pat, and me down the mountain.

I make a mental note to restock my personal box of gear up here and to call Jim Pennington. Maybe he's interested in joining the Crag Rats.

CHAPTER 4

The High Cost of High-Octane Sports

With the kids in school, Jennifer and I go on a long run to Post Canyon. Wiry vine maples and Douglas fir spread a canopy over an understory of greenery. After the run, with muscles tired and flamed, I coast into my driveway, dig my phone from my jersey, and see the text message and voice mail icons. I quickly scroll, see Jay's number, and hit speed dial.

"I'm just picking up the truck and I'm meeting Jeff Prichar at the Bridge Mart in fifteen minutes. Can you go?" asks Jay.

"What's up?"

"Mountain biker. Rode off the cliff. That's all I know." The news is an electric shock to my system. My muscles are already chockfull of lactic acid from the run—there's no room for the adrenaline infusion. But this is a double hit; this is an area I go mountain biking in all the time.

"I'm on my way," I say. Then in the same breath I look at Jen. It's not very often that color drains out of my face when I get a call out. I'm usually calm and collected, but this time, I get a chill deep inside, because I often ride there and because the victim may be one of my friends.

"A mountain biker just rode off the cliff. Can I go? Can you get the kids from school?" I ask even though I know it will cause some friction in my marriage. We just had a call out a few days ago. It's my afternoon with the kids and Jennifer already thinks I spend too much time with our two young daughters. So when a mountain rescue takes priority over time with my wife, things get a bit sticky between us. Call outs are never planned; they never come at a good time.

"Oh my God!" blurts Jen. "It is someone we know?"

"Don't know," I say as I quickly pull my canvas poison oak pants on right over my running shorts, change into a dry polyester shirt, and put on heavy socks. Back in the garage, I lace up my canvas hiking boots, grab two water bottles, and throw my ready pack into my truck.

As I race out of the driveway, I feel my legs starting to cramp from running without cooling down or stretching. Jen goes in the house and calls four of her riding buddies to make sure all are accounted for. The local bike store, where Jennifer works, quickly gets dozens of calls. Word spreads like wildfire through our small town. Jennifer and I planned to ride the same trail that very day with a group of friends but opted for a run instead.

Every time I ride it, I always think about riding off the cliff— everyone does. Now someone did. Locally well-known, the broad slope near Hood River is a plateau formed by a basalt flow fourteen million years ago. It's located at the sweet spot where the forested Cascade foothills meet the high desert. The ponderosa pine and scrub oak forest of the west section of the trail yields to the rabbitbrush and blue bunch wheatgrass of the sage steppe to the east. The Forest Service–owned area is home to a network of a dozen mountain bike trails that make it the favorite riding spot among locals. One of the most fun and popular rides is a trail that skirts the edge of a three-hundred-foot-high sheer basalt cliff.

We don't know much. It could be a major trauma and helicopter evacuation or could be a minor injury like a sprained ankle if the biker did not actually ride off the cliff. Penny has given Jay directions. The staging area is the backyard of someone's house. As Jay pushes the big truck up the road, my phone rings. It's a paramedic, who was first on scene with another EMT and a volunteer firefighter.

"The patient is dead, very dead," the medic says.

"Dead?" I ask.

"I've been up here an hour. He's dead. I'm sure."

"Body recovery," I say to Jay and Jeff, my ear still to the phone. The update immediately releases the sense of urgency. All of a sudden it's not an emergency. Not life or death. There will be no helicopter. As we take some deep breaths, the surge of electricity coursing through our blood vessels abates.

"Do you have any gear?" I ask.

"Our resuscitation kit," the medic chuckles "and it's not doing us any good up here." The laugh is a coping mechanism, not disrespect for the dead man.

"Okay. We've got a truck full. What do we need?" I ask, knowing he has enough climbing experience to at least give me the basic requirements.

"Bring a litter and a three-hundred-foot rope. We'll need to belay the body down this scree slope at the base of the cliff. We'll need just a basic lowering system. There's a big ponderosa we can use as an anchor."

"Okay, we're on our way," I say as Jay pulls into the staging area. "How do we get to the cliff?"

"Head up through the woods behind the yard that you're using as the staging area. You'll see us at the top of the scree slope."

"Okay, I'll call you by radio when we get closer." I click off my phone.

After Jay parks, we meet a deputy sheriff, and the county coroner. Both have just arrived and want to hike up with us. We gather gear from the truck. We pull out the new stretcher that breaks into two pieces, a long rope, enough webbing and hardware to lower the body on foot through waist-high poison oak.

Twenty minutes later we arrive at the base of a three-hundred-foot slope, where table- and car-size boulders of sharp-edged basalt have fallen off the cliff over the last million years. On the scree, every few steps a boulder shifts and I risk getting my foot wedged in a crack. In addition to my pack, I am hauling up the rope. But instead of grabbing the three-hundred-footer, I mistakenly grabbed the six-hundred-foot behemoth. Unfortunately I don't realize this until I get to the top.

"I think you got the long rope," Jay says, teasing me. "Nice going." He has more experience with rope rescue than I.

"No wonder it is so heavy."

When we finally reach the medic at the top of the slope at the base of the cliff, we are sweating. My legs are still nearly cramping from my run, followed by the sedentary drive in the truck, followed by the hike up the scree. At it turns out, the victim went out for a solo ride. It was a blustery spring day. Even though the trail in question can be ridden all winter, spring rains had made a few sections extra muddy. His bike tires were later found to be caked with mud. And because his chain was in the big ring in front and small ring in back, it was decided he was probably headed down the slope at high speed.

At one of the few spots the trail comes within three feet of the cliff and takes a sharp left turn, his front tire likely dropped into a rut and tweaked sideways. He went over the handlebars. At almost any other section of the trail, he would have tumbled and rolled to a stop. We've all done it. But the victim crashed in exactly the wrong spot and flew over the cliff. His bike was left teetering on the edge. He was airborne for one, two, three seconds. Then he smacked the rocks full force, and, from the looks of the crater about twenty feet above the body, bounced hard. He almost certainly died on impact.

That was yesterday. Today, two bikers riding down saw his bike on the cliff at 11:30 A.M. *That's odd*, they must have thought, *a bike in the middle of nowhere*. They crawled to the edge, saw the body below, and called 911 on a cell phone.

Bill, a local rider, appeared next. He, too, called 911 but stayed on the ridge, silhouetted on the cliff against the blue sky. This gave the first responders a visual reference, so they could drive as close as possible to the accident scene. If the victim had been injured but alive, Bill's quick thinking would have saved critical time. When I arrive at the scene, I see right away the victim had died instantly from injuries.

Rapidly we go to work. The coroner takes a few pictures. The deputy investigates the scene. A colleague and I package the body, wrapping it in two plastic tarps. We gently slide the stretcher next to the body and balance it on the rocks. It takes four of us: one to hold the litter and three of us to lift the body into the stretcher. We strap in the body. I cover the face and chest with another tarp and tape it closed.

Meanwhile, Jay and Jeff set up the belay on a thick ponderosa pine about twenty feet away. Jay ties a length of webbing around the tree, then clips a break rack to the webbing with a carabiner. The break rack is a U-shaped steel bar with several crossbars connecting the sides of the U. The rope is threaded through the break rack so Jay will be able to control the rate of descent of the litter. He tosses me an end of the rope, and I tie it around the rail of the litter.

However, Jay can't lower yet because we are standing across the slope at the same elevation. We need to haul the litter thirty yards across the scree and below the tree for Jay to start lowering. I don't feel comfortable doing this without a belay. Jeff pulls out a twenty-foot length of cord and clips one end to the litter. He wraps the other end around his torso in a body belay to stabilize the litter until we can traverse and descend to below Jay and the tree. Thankfully, two other Crag Rats, Bernie Wells and Roger Nelson, show up to help. We need six on the litter, one on the belay, and two more to carry down the paramedic gear.

About the time we begin to head down, a half dozen rescuers from local SAR group show up right below us, directly in the fall line. If a boulder were to rip loose, it could kill someone. We shout for them to get out of the way, but they can't hear. I pull out my radio and switch it from one frequency to the another.

"SAR from Crag Rats."

"Go ahead, Crag Rats," says the rescue leader.

"We'll need you guys at the base of the scree slope. Once we get down, we'll hand off to you." I smile at the idea, knowing I won't have to haul the body back through the poison oak thicket. "It'll probably take us thirty minutes to lower the body. Be careful of falling rocks." They get the message, find a safe spot, and wait for us to get down.

Close to an hour passes as we carry the heavy body up and over the large, sharp boulders. Every few steps one of the rescuers shifts his grip or steps awkwardly on a rock and throws all six people off balance. Jay stays up top to slowly pay out the rope. Eventually we reach the base of the slope and the edge of the poison oak thicket. We untie the rope and pass off the litter. They set off with the body while we pack up the rope and wait for Jay to hike down.

Back at the truck, we find the funeral home vehicle has arrived. Jay and I pull on another pair of gloves and lift the body into the funeral home van. Jeff swabs our litter with antibacterial wipes.

All of us, at some point, review the risks of outdoor adventure sports. And we all recognize the risk of riding off a cliff every time we skirt a cliff edge. The cliff is right there, three feet from the trail.

Why do we put ourselves at risk for these extreme sports?

The physical benefits of exercise are well known: you sleep better, feel better, look better. You are healthier and stave off all sorts of acute and chronic illnesses. You have a better self-image when slimmer, fitter, and stronger. Exercise is a great diversion from work and family duties: away from computers, faxes, and phones. (Although I run, bike, and ski with my phone because it doubles as my SAR pager, I love going on vacation and turning it off.) The clean air and scenery are rejuvenating and revitalizing.

But there is something much deeper—a chemical reaction to the movement, flow, and action of outdoor sports that creates an overwhelming sense of well-being. The appeal of outdoor adventure for some may be purely mental or purely physical, but it is likely a complex function of both. Some call it a "runners high," the euphoria and awe-inspiring good feeling that can make your toes and fingers tingle for hours. Sometimes the euphoria is so powerful that it blocks out the external world, blurs time and space, and transforms the familiar world into fantasy.

The sensation begins in the brain and in the muscles with serotonin, the pleasure hormone, and endorphin (a word formed from *endogenous morphine*, because they bind to the same pain receptors as opiates). These hormones mediate pain, hunger, sexual gratification, mood, memory, learning, and the sought-after euphoria that comes from physical activity.

In addition to this endorphin-mediated runner's high, another more powerful reaction is also present when one participates in outdoor adventure sports: the fight-or-flight reaction. Everyone has experienced this mechanism, often called an adrenaline rush, triggered when the body and mind are threatened. When someone is faced with excitement and/or fear, the adrenaline rush is launched by the body, mediated by a separate set of hormones: epinephrine (also known as adrenaline). The instant rev of an adrenaline rush is like stomping on the gas at a drag race, zero to sixty—taking one from calm and collected to frantic. The adrenaline rush is a tantalizing feeling that some athletes become addicted to, thus the moniker *adrenaline junky*.

Whereas a drag racer may experience the adrenaline rush, only outdoor adventurers can feel both the adrenaline rush and the runner's high. The two feelings become intertwined, touch us deep in our soul, in our mind, in our muscles. This hormone-mediated mental and physical sensation is animalistic, like sex, and the urge to reexperience the feeling becomes all encompassing and overpowering. Achieving this euphoria is the goal adventure athletes design their lives around. It becomes the sole focus of a sports or mountain community. Our lives are not built on work or social functions, nor structured around paying bills or working around the house. They are focused on what surfers call *tapping the source:* finding pure enjoyment in the actions and motions of sports in the outdoors via the search for adrenaline rush and runner's high.

All outdoor adventurers are vulnerable to injury and illness. We risk acute mountain sickness, hypothermia, or frostbite in the mountains. We risk heat exhaustion or heat stroke in the desert.

We risk injury from a fall off a bike, cliff, or glacier. We risk falling from a boulder or serac, which is an ice tower or pinnacle on a glacier, getting caught in an avalanche, or wiping out in surf. Some of us are aware and cautious: we have plenty of fun in the outdoors without taking extreme risks. But some push to the limits of their physical and mental abilities to get to the edge. This might be okay when you are young and free. But once you have kids, like me, you dial things back—way back. You take safer routes up mountains and climb in good conditions and clear weather. I don't go ripping down a mountain bike trail in tight trees and mud. I ski cautiously in avalanche country. But the thrill of adrenaline and endorphin can be overpowering. To consciously make a decision to be cautious in the heat of a blazing-fast mountain bike ride or a wide-open powder bowl can be difficult: the promptings of the brain have to overcome the deep physical and mental desire for the high and rush. It is like taking a few drinks and then having unprotected sex. No matter how smart you are, in the thick of passion, deep physical desire can overcome reason.

And sometimes, perhaps like the guy who rode off the cliff, you do everything right. You are safe and cautious, but all the little circumstances add up to catastrophe: new bike, blustery day, wind, muddy trail, deep ruts where there usually are none, slight turn in the trail, distraction caused by recent stress at work or home. The slightest trigger—we've all had it happen—and the tire sinks into a rut and jolts sideways, stops the bike, and you go over the handlebars.

I worry about getting injured when I'm on a mountain rescue mission, much more so now that I have kids. I don't mind putting myself in a little danger. But the difference between acceptable risk and danger is sometimes a thin line. This is one reason why the Crag Rats make it a bit of a chore for prospective members to sign up. The specific requirements are that you need to have climbed to the top of Mounts Hood and Adams, and you must live in Hood River County. You write a letter explaining why you want to join and what you can offer the group. The Crag Rats then need to approve you for membership in three meetings. But no one gets voted in until he or she participates and we, the Crag Rats, learn who you are. Your personality is perhaps more important than any specific outdoor skills. You have to fit in with the group: teamwork and levelheadedness are paramount. You have to trust your partners and instill trust in them. You have to have it in your blood, the desire to be outside—at night, in the mountains, or during a storm. You have to love the runner's high and adrenaline rush. But part of the thrill and passion of mountain rescue, the thing that separates a good rescuer from a dangerous one, is the ability to keep the rush and high in check. That is everyone on our team.

A few days after the mountain biker body recovery, his friends call me, wanting directions to the cliff. I try to discourage them from going there; the last thing we need is for someone looking at the scene to fall off the cliff. Despite my request to the contrary, a group wants to put a small memento on the cliff edge. A volunteer crew from the mountain bike association would reroute the trail to prevent a recurrence. The Forest Service contemplates closing the trail entirely to mountain biking, and I speak to the *Hood River News,* which runs a story in its next issue, discussing the accident and warning others. I speak with the man's family, and the Crag Rats receive a nice letter and a donation.

In the end, this death and body recovery would become indelibly associated with the other events of the years. Little did we know that this would be one of our busiest stretches of rescues in decades. The number of dead bodies we would pull out of the mountains over the past two years would come close to matching live ones.

CHAPTER 5

Flight for Life

"Doc to the clinic," I hear on the radio. "Backboard coming in."

"Okay, I'll be right in," I say.

I get the call while riding the chairlift at a Mount Hood ski resort. I'm riding the uppermost chairlift on the mountain because it is warm and sunny. Down in the base area and around the lower lifts, a thick, dank fog has blocked out the sun. As I snowboard down to the bottom, I descend into a gray soup. The same wet gray fog has settled in over the valley the past few weeks. Everyone flocks to the mountain for solar therapy.

In addition to my day job as an emergency doctor, I work as a doctor at the mountain clinic. Being a mountain doctor at a ski resort is not high paying, but it's a dream job, an opportunity to blend my passion and profession, play in the mountains I love, and use my skills as a doctor to help those in need. When conditions are stormy and powder snow abounds, the clinic is not busy. Many of the beginners stay in the lodge, and the skiers that do fall land in soft snow. By contrast, when the weather is sunny and warm and the snowpack is hard, the clinic's first injury of the day often arrives from the parking lot: a novice steps out of a car wearing ski boots, slips on a patch of ice or snow, and smacks his or her knee, hip, shoulder, wrist, or head. Most often I treat orthopedic injuries: sprained ankles and knees; fractured wrists, arms, shoulders, and ribs. Once in a while I stitch a laceration when someone is sliced by a tree branch or the edge of a ski or snowboard. Once a patient came in, quite literally, with a stick up his bottom. He fell while snowboarding, landed on a tree branch, and sliced his rectum. He tore his anal sphincter so badly that I transferred him to the trauma center to have it repaired by a specialist.

Today, Jonathan, our seasoned emergency nurse, is on duty. Sarah is our clerk and Mary is the X-ray technician. Sarah and Jonathan staff the clinic full-time, but Mary and I can head out to ski or snowboard when we don't have patients. This season has been an unusually light snow year. It has brought bad crashes because rocks, usually buried under several feet of snow, are hidden dangerously close to the surface. I'm riding up the chairlift when I get the radio call. Across a wide-open bowl I see three patrollers huddled over the patient. Another patroller stands in the sun at the top of the lift. When I exit the lift, I slide over next to him.

"What's up with that girl?" I point down the slope.

"She's all right, even though they're bringing her down on a backboard. Fell trying to get up to the ridge, face planted. Awake and alert, minor head injury." The skier is sitting up in the snow, about three hundred yards down the hill. The patrol brings everyone who has the slightest possibility of a head, neck, or back injury down on backboards to protect their spines and necks. Instead of snowboarding down to the patient, I head to the clinic so I can be ready when the patient arrives. At the clinic, I stash my gear and duck into the bathroom. When I step out of the bathroom, I hear a panicky flurry of activity outside.

"Doc, code red, stat," someone yells.

I run outside. Two patrollers and Jonathan lift the patient from the patrol sled to a clinic gurney. The skier from the hill is now unconscious with blood oozing from her head. She's breathing, but barely. I feel a faint pulse.

"She had a seizure," says a patroller. "She was just fine, alert and talking about three minutes ago, until we got halfway down the hill. She just passed out and had a seizure."

My heart and mind rev; instantly I kick the clinic into overdrive. "Sarah, activate medevac; get the ambulance team," I say, referring to the aeromedical chopper from Portland and the ambulance crew in a nearby town, respectively.

"Doing it," she says with her ear to the phone. Unlike the dramas shown on television, here no one shouts. Everyone does his or her job. Because we are high on the mountain, a good hour from the nearest hospital, I have to think and act quickly as well as plan ahead for transport.

"Jonathan, get the rapid sequence intubation kit from the lock box. Two large-bore IVs." He's already starting an IV, a Teflon catheter the diameter of a pencil lead and about an inch long. It will be inserted in an arm vein and allow us to deliver lifesaving medicines directly into the bloodstream.

I follow the ABCDE mnemonic acronym of the primary survey, starting with airway. The blood oozing from a depressed skull fracture is distracting, but the first order of business is always airway. Jonathan is busy with the IV, so I hurry over to the electronic lockbox that looks like a vending machine. I can't remember my login ID or password, the banes of modern technology. Jonathan comes over after he has placed the IV, and I return to the patient, grabbing the intubation kit on my way back to the gurney.

"Can you cut off her clothing?" I ask a patroller. Jonathan

hands me the needed drugs from the lockbox and places a second IV in the other arm. I bag the patient, forcing air into her lungs with a breathing bag and tight-fitting mask clamped over her face. Then I ask the second patroller to take over ventilation with the bag so I can ready the intubation kit. Bagging is a difficult job for one person, especially when cramped in the tiny one-room medical clinic and for the ski patroller, who does not do this procedure regularly. So Mary comes over to help the patroller: she holds the mask tight on the patient's face while the patroller squeezes the bag.

Normally, in a hospital, I'd have so much help I wouldn't have to do much but coordinate the code, shorthand for cardiopulmonary arrest, which is what is now happening. But in this case I need to draw up the medicine in three syringes, something nurses usually do. I choose three drugs from nine used for a code in the box. I use the universal adult weight of one hundred kilograms. Midazolam is a drug in the benzodiazepine class like Valium; it sedates the patient so she will not be conscious during the procedure, which will save her life. Fentanyl is a fast-acting pain medicine like morphine. Vecuronium, the most important to save her life, will paralyze all her skeletal muscles that move her arms and legs, help her breathe, and control her a gag reflex. The paralytic will allow me to pass the intubation tube past the vocal cords without the neck and throat muscles going into spasm or the gag reflex rejecting the tube. The drug does not affect the smooth muscle tissue of the heart or other internal organs. Once I've drawn up the meds, and organized the intubation equipment, I give everyone the heads-up, especially Jonathan.

"Meds going in, everyone ready?" To Mary and the patroller: "Keep bagging until I'm ready." To Sarah: "Transport coming?"

"On the way," says Sarah.

"Can you call the trauma center?" I ask.

"Doing it," says Sarah.

"Ready," says Jonathan. Timing here is critical as with the intubation I performed in an earlier chapter on the creek. I have about three minutes to complete the procedure after the medicines take effect, which occurs about thirty seconds after they are injected.

"Meds in," I say as I plunge the medicine into the patient's veins.

"Keep bagging," I say to the patroller and Mary when they start to remove the mask. I can tell by the patrollers' excited voices that they are a bit anxious. The one rookie patroller is finally cutting off clothes with heavy trauma shears.

"I need you to help me intubate," I say to the first patroller. "Do you know how to give cricoid pressure?"

"I think so."

"I want you to push down gently on her Adam's apple when I tell you to. Like this." I show him the procedure that will occlude the esophagus and open the windpipe.

"Jonathan, you ready?"

"Yup. Here's some suction." He hands me a flimsy hose hooked up to a low-power portable suction unit.

As the patient goes flaccid, I tell the patroller and Mary to stop bagging so I can get to the patient's throat and windpipe. I pry open the mouth with my right hand, using my thumb and index finger against the patient's teeth. With my left hand, I pass a laryngoscope between her teeth and over the tongue. With the scope I lift the tongue and open the throat. Thankfully, there's no blood or vomit. I've done this before when the airway is full of bodily fluids. I look at the vocal cords, put the tube into the windpipe with my right hand, remove the laryngoscope, and hold the tube tightly. I won't let go of the tube for five minutes until I can secure it with tape: it is the patient's lifeline. Many times, patients' medicines wear off, and their gag reflex causes them to expel the tube. Someone hands me the breathing bag and I connect it to the tube. I start forcing air into the patient's lungs, squeezing the bag with one hand.

With a stethoscope Mary places in my ears, I make sure the tube is in the right place. I hear air moving into the patient's lungs. Her pulse is steady at 95 beats per minute and her oxygen saturation is 99 percent: both normal. I hook up a monitor that shows carbon dioxide coming out of the tube. I also see moisture condensing on the walls of the tube. All these signs reveal I have placed the tube in the lungs; it is easy for even an experienced doctor to put the tube accidentally into the esophagus. Last, still holding the tube with one hand, I secure the tube to the patient's mouth and face with a special plastic device that slips over the patient's mouth.

Airway and breathing have been secured and stabilized. The process has taken about ten minutes. On to circulation.

I remove the pile of bloody gauze from the head wound. I see an open, depressed skull fracture: no brain tissue is leaking out, but bone fragments are jammed inward. The wound is partially obscured by clotted blood and matted hair. I decide it is best not to disturb the wound. I place a huge wad of clean gauze on the wound and, with a roll of stretchy gauze, wrap her head like a mummy's without lifting it off the table.

For disability, she is already in a cervical collar and on a backboard to protect her spine. If the patient comes out of her drug-induced coma, she will start to move her head, either consciously or as a reflex. For that reason, I reinforce the hard plastic collar with big loops of two-inch-wide medical tape, anchoring the patient's forehead to the backboard. The blood on the backboard prevents the tape sticking well, so I wrap a few extra loops.

For exposure, the ski patroller has removed all wet clothes and covered her with dry blankets.

"Sarah, ETA on transport?" I ask.

"Medevac en route, fifteen minutes. Ambulance in route, fifteen minutes." I charge one patroller with bagging the patient.

"Let me know if you get tired," I say. I ask the other to keep monitoring the pulse. If the heart stops, we'll need to start chest compressions.

On the radio, one of the senior patrollers instructs a crew to use cones and orange paint to mark a landing zone. Maintenance has turned off the lift and evacuated the slope above it. Another employee pulls up outside the clinic with a snowmobile with a toboggan on the back: we'll use it to pull the patient to the helicopter—if it can land in the fog that seems to have thickened over the base area.

I complete the secondary survey, the head-to-toe exam to check for other injuries. This is extremely important. I don't want to miss a ruptured spleen or hip fracture, either of which can cause the patient to bleed to death. A wrist or ankle fracture could cause the patient to lose circulation to her extremities and cause irreversible damage to the tissues.

I find no blood in her ears, and her pupils are equally round and reactive. Both suggest there is no severe brain injury. Face without injury. Chest without trauma. Abdomen soft, no trauma. Pelvis stable, no fractures. Arms and legs without obvious bruises, fractures, or abrasions. The patient face-planted, and hit her head on a rock beneath the snow. Because the patient had a hat on, the patrollers didn't see the open bleeding head wound. She was fine as long as she was lying down. Once she sat up, her blood pressure began dropping. Then she passed out, then had the seizure.

"Let's get a chest X-ray," I say. Before we fly her, it is useful to check for a punctured or collapsed lung. The change in altitude can cause a partially collapsed lung to completely deflate. If that were to happen, it wouldn't matter how much air was being pumped into the lungs: the patient would die. I lean over to the phone that Sarah holds up to my ear so I don't have to touch it with my bloody, gloved hands. I give report to the physician who will accept the patient at the trauma center.

Then, to add to the chaos in the jam-packed clinic, a slew of patrollers bring in *two* additional patients.

Another seasoned patroller, whose judgment I trust, barks out his assessment. "These patients are both green. Both green." Green is stable. Yellow is unstable. Red is critical. Although I trust him, out of instinct I rapidly conduct a triage, a rapid field assessment to confirm their status. A man with the hip injury is alert and talking. I quickly palpate his hip and pelvis: no catastrophic femur or hip fracture. The second patient holds his arm. I can see from across the room he's fine to wait, too—alert, talking, no visible blood or deformity, fingers pink and moving. I don't take any injury at the mountain clinic lightly. Even a simple arm or leg fracture can be life or limb threatening. I agree with Mark: both can wait. Later, I will diagnose one with an unusual pelvis fracture—he took a chunk out of the large hip bone—and ship him by ground ambulance to the trauma center in Portland. The other I will diagnose with a shattered elbow—six or seven pieces—and ship him to the trauma center by private car.

The head-injury patient starts squirming and moaning as the medicine wears off. I quickly give her another dose of sedative. Her natural reflex, to remove the foreign body that has been placed deep into her lungs, will kill her. Then Mary holds the chest X-ray in front of my face. I hold it up to the fluorescent ceiling lights, just like the trauma docs in the movies. I can see it: no collapsed lung, no broken ribs. That's all I really need to know at this point.

"Helicopter ETA five minutes," I hear a patroller yell.

"Okay, let's get ready for transport," I say. We pile on extra blankets. Wrap one around the patient's head. Tie down arms and legs. Secure IV lines, both going full bore with fluids to counteract blood loss. A patroller is still bagging her.

"Sarah, can you put on my helmet?" I want my helmet for the snowmobile ride and anytime I'm near a helicopter. But I don't want to touch it with my bloody gloves. She leans over, slides the snowboard helmet on my head, clips the strap.

"Everyone going near the helicopter needs a helmet," I say. "Are we ready with the sled?"

"Yup," says Jonathan.

"Okay, we're not moving until we're sure the helicopter can land," I tell them. The fog is still thick in the base area of the ski resort. "But let's get ready." The patient has had two full bags of IV fluids so I ask for a third. Recheck: pulse eighty, blood pressure 122/72, pulse oxygen saturation, 95 percent. Stable, at least for now.

We're listening to ski patrollers at the landing zone communicate with the helicopter pilot. They're trying to find a hole in the fog. The pilot cannot see the ground and cannot land. Then abruptly, the gray mist parts and a hole miraculously opens right over our landing zone. The chopper drops in and we get word it has touched down.

We carry the patient, still on the backboard, from the gurney to the toboggan. The patroller sits at the head squeezing the breathing bag. I straddle the woman's legs, notice blood has siphoned backward into the bag, and squeeze it hard to get the fluids pouring into the patient again.

It's a surreal vision of the mountain I started skiing on when I was seven years old. We speed across the snow in front of a thousand skiers and snowboarders, parents with kids, ski-school groups. The helicopter is perched on the snow, rotors still turning, powered up. Fluorescent orange dye and huge construction-zone cones mark the landing zone at the bottom of the vacant lift. We stop twenty feet in front of the helicopter and meet the aeromedical nurse. My report is brief, as I have to yell over the still-moving rotor and through the flight nurse's helmet.

"Open head injury. Intubated. Sedated fifteen minutes ago: ten of Midazolam, ten of Fentanyl, ten of vec. No other injury. No pneumo on X-ray."

The flight nurse nods. "Well, you've done everything. Let's get out of here." We lift the patient into the chopper, slam the doors, run back to the snowmobile, and watch the bird lift off. It disappears into the fog, and within seconds the thumping rotor noise dissolves into murkiness, too.

"Good work, everyone," I say.

We all relax, smile, high-five.

It is an uncommon privilege to be able to save a life, even for an emergency room doctor who does it more than the average physician. I have a strange mix of fleeting emotions, but I never have time to process them. On one hand, I'm hugely relieved we saved her and I passed her off to another team, which can complete the lifesaving measures. It's a combination of exhilaration, joy, accomplishment, and thankfulness. But I'm also saddened by the plight of the woman—a bad sports-related trauma in the mountains touches me more personally, as I could get hurt someday, too. That's in the back of my mind when I see a young woman injured doing a sport she loved: no recklessness, no irresponsible behavior, just fell at the wrong place, like the mountain biker on the cliff.

But, like many emergency doctors, the complex feelings quickly dissolve and I will remember it as another case, not the emotions that go with it. I don't have much time to process personal feelings, as the clinic has two more patients needing attention, not to mention the mound of paperwork I need to complete. It may seem odd to those not associated with health care, but we have to move on to the next patient and block out emotions from the previous one.

It would be nearly a year later that Jonathan would casually bring up the topic of the open depressed-skull-fracture patient.

"Remember the woman we intubated and medevaced last year?"

"Oh yes, quite well."

"She came in here with her boyfriend last week after he sprained his knee. Full recovery. No memory of the event but no neurologic deficits. She's back snowboarding."

Looking back, my life, and even the foundations that would lead me to being a doctor, began in these mountains, with skiing and snow. One of my earliest memories is of a January morning at our home in rural southwestern Washington, waking to a white blanket covering the fields and rooftops. Voluminous clouds, in every shade of gray imaginable, are Pacific Northwest constants. Every so often the omnipresent rain turns to a flurry of white flakes. Snowfall came only once or twice a year, so it was a pure delight, especially to a four-year-old.

I remember Dad had long red skis and I stood on top of

them. My red rubber boots nested in front of his worn leather lace-up ski boots, which were straight from Europe in the sixties, where he and Mom learned to ski in Switzerland. He grew up as the son of a farmer. My grandfather died when Dad was seventeen. With his brother at war and his sister too young, my dad ran the family farm with his mom. At the same time, he put himself through college in Ashland, Ohio, the first in his family to continue his education beyond high school. Dad went on to dental and orthodontic schools. He was always a focused man, at work and at play. After he graduated, he married Mom, joined the Army, and requested to be stationed in Europe to see the world. While he was in Germany, he got the ski bug.

That gray January morning we careened straight down a gentle hill through the cow pasture to the barn. Six inches of gooey snow over grass made skiing slow and spongy. With a cold wind in my smiling face, my stomach felt like I was on a roller coaster. Dad hiked back up the slope carrying me and his skis. We made another run, maybe two or three more. Later I ran inside, stripped off my soaked clothes, and huddled in a blanket by the fire with a cup of hot chocolate Mom had brewed up for me.

The next year we hit the ski resorts on Mount Hood. I remember the wind blowing in my face, the sun peeking through parting clouds, and thrills branding my thoughts. I had that wild feeling again in my stomach—in fact, in my whole body. The memory of skiing as a kid settled not in the thinking part of my brain but deeper in my brain stem, in the area responsible for more primal emotions. This feeling was euphoria.

My family went on annual ski trips in the West, Canada, and Europe. I learned to snowboard in college on a plywood Burton Backhill when snowboarding was just barely a sport. Almost three decades into life, in lieu of a bachelor party, my brother Pete took me up Mount Hood. We did not climb back down, Pete had skis and I my snowboard.

On the wall of my home office, I have no medical diplomas or certificates. Instead I have hung prints from my travels around the world, self-portraits by da Vinci and Michelangelo, art by my kids, and the framed picture of Pete and me at the summit of the mountain I now see every day. Little did I know back then how intimate I would become with this mountain in both my sporting life and my medical one.

With such intense interests in outdoor sports, traveling, and writing, I am often asked, "Why did you go to medical school?" Medical school, internship, and residency—seven years in all— involved a commitment of time, stress, sleepless nights, and money. The largest stress was not the money or sleeplessness, but the time: time away from all the other things I have on my life's to-do list. I didn't foresee this conflict when I applied to med school. Initially I wanted to help people and have a rewarding, satisfying career. I wanted to apply my skills in math, science, and analytical thought to a goal-orientated career. I grew up thinking that being a doctor was the apex of the career ladder: career stability, community respect, and a good way to earn a living. Little did I know then that medicine is a difficult and challenging way to earn a living, especially if you want to have a quality family life, time to play outside, and a job without stress.

Dad was the most powerful influence on both my decision to pursue medicine and my later deviation from the traditional path. When I was little, he told me that it didn't matter what I did with my life as long as I liked my job. Dad was an orthodontist who practiced four days a week, took three months of vacation annually, and participated in adventures like skiing, hunting, clam digging, and fishing. He worked hard, but he played hard, too; and usually took the whole family along. When I was in college, Dad sold his orthodontic practice and retired at age fifty-five. At that point, he gave me quite different advice. You want a career that provides you with a decent income so that you can do what you want in life, he told me, whether that is traveling, skiing, sending your kids to college, or buying a house. Work hard, invest your money, and retire early.

I was accepted to medical school at the University of Washington in Seattle in the summer of 1988. I was not ready to be locked into further schooling just a few months after finishing four years of college, so I went through the arduous task of requesting a year off. After some deliberation, the dean agreed to an rather obscure "deferral of enrollment," which allowed me to spend the year traveling the world. I didn't know it then, but that was the initial step—and one I look back on fondly—in establishing an atypical pattern in life and career.

I spent four months traveling around the world, then landed for the summer in Hood River, which at the time was the windsurfing capital of the world and a bourgeoning adventure sports town. I had to ask myself: Should I go to medical school or not? It would mean leaving the dirtbag outdoor-bum lifestyle forever, a way of living that was starting to appeal to me. I would miss the opportunity to go to Maui, live in a rundown bungalow, and surf all day or spend a winter snowboarding at Jackson Hole or spend three months windsurfing in Baja. On the other hand, I had a deep desire to learn about science, and, in particular, the human body. My college major was science communication, a field that distills science into terms laypeople can understand through words, photographs, drawings, and now computer graphics. Also, deeper down, I loved the idea of rescuing people, ever since watching John Gage and Roy DeSoto save lives on television's *Emergency* as young boy. I knew I had something to contribute.

Once I started medical school I was disheartened that I was tied up in classrooms all day long and had my nose in my book all night. I loved learning, but I wanted to be outside in the sun, wind, rain, and snow, too. I tried to strike a balance. I would always squeeze in a sport or exercise sometime in my day, even for an hour. I rode my bike to and from class. On weekends, I'd go on long road bike rides with my friends or I'd paddle a sea kayak around Seattle's Lake Washington. I learned to rock climb at the local crags and at Seattle's University of Washington outdoor climbing rock, and would often head to the ski resort with my classmates. I studied hard but not more than three hours a day, test or not. I'd sometimes steal a run at noon, after morning rounds, and before afternoon clinic.

Every summer off, while my colleagues were doing research or clinical rotations, I worked at a brew pub in Hood River. I would pour beer by night and windsurf the Columbia River during the day. I ascended and skied the trifecta of Mounts Hood, St. Helens, and Adams, rock-climbed the local crags, hiked any of the three dozen trails nearby to a waterfall, lake, or spectacular panorama vista, or rode my bikes. By the time medical school rolled around in the fall, I was relaxed, refreshed, and ready to get back to academic life.

I was not halfheartedly committed to medicine. Rather, I was wholly committed to life, all the many aspects of it. I wanted to be a doctor whose heart and mind were in the right place, one who could take life's experiences and apply them to healing and patient care, one who was a whole person that people liked and trusted. But I also wanted to be outside. The two concepts, in a traditional sense, conflicted. Doctoring is done in a hospital or clinic, with specialized equipment and tests. The outdoors are places that firefighters or ski patrollers worked, not doctors.

But outdoor adventure was a life-sustaining activity for me, both for physical conditioning and mental health. Being outside was pure and simply fun. I reap great enjoyment from interacting with the natural world in sport. And I felt that in some way doctoring and outdoors did not have to be mutually exclusive. I felt that it was not far-fetched to think I could retain both aspects of my life at a high level. I did not want to be a weekend warrior, someone who has time to pursue sports only on days off from work. Likewise, I did not want a nine-to-five doctor job: I needed something thrilling, exciting, stimulating. Eventually, I realized, I needed this connection to stay in medicine and to be fulfilled. Over the years, many of my colleagues and professors have regarded my double life of sports and medicine with bewilderment. I frequently had to justify this deep-set motivation to professors, parents, fellow students, advisers, and, eventually, even myself. How I chose to live was crucial for my development as a doctor. It kept my enthusiasm for medicine alive, it maintained my physical and mental health, and it allowed me to experience the varied aspects of life, which eventually made me better at many things, most important, at doctoring.

A fellow student once told me I should not be a doctor—I had too many interests in the outdoors, adventure, and travel. I should be a park ranger or a mountain guide, the colleague suggested. I quickly found out I wasn't cut out for clinic work, performing surgeries, delivering babies, doing research in a lab, or caring for chronic problems. These aspects of medicine were not enjoyable to me and thus I was not good at them. I struggled to find a career or niche in medicine, something I enjoyed. Nothing clicked and I was fast approaching decision time in choosing a specialty. I was worried I wouldn't find a rewarding, enjoyable career and I was worried I'd choose wrong. Once a doctor invests three to five years in residency training, it is very difficult to switch career paths.

One day, while researching a project on international health in the great stacks of the medical school library, I stumbled upon kindred spirits in an obscure, tiny medical field. I found the *Journal of Wilderness Medicine* buried in the stacks, and I was instantly captivated, overwhelmed. I delved into copies of the journal and read every book I could find on wilderness medicine. I learned that nearly every main exploration expedition of the nineteenth and twentieth centuries had physicians as members. Ernest Shackleton had two physicians on his legendary, ill-fated expedition to Antarctica in 1914. Edmund Hillary and Tenzing Norgay had a team doctor on their first ascent of Mount Everest in 1953. I learned that over the past thirty years, a burgeoning medical specialty has started: wilderness medicine.

Initially, noteworthy wilderness-medicine experts focused on high-altitude medicine research and the treatment of acute mountain sickness, but wilderness medicine today reaches far beyond mountain medicine. It includes desert and heat illness, natural disasters, drowning, diving and deep-sea injury, hazardous plants and animals, ethical and legal issues of wilderness treatment, aeromedical evacuation, survival skills, medicine in remote environments such as polar climes, expedition medicine, herbal and plant remedies, and international travel.

I thought: *wilderness medicine is my career, merging medicine and outdoors.* I wanted more information, so I started making phone calls, searching journals, and networking with friends and professors, a means of information gathering at a time before I could simply google "wilderness medicine" or network through e-mail. I finally talked my way into an elective at the family practice residency program in Boise, Idaho, which ran the Northern Rocky Mountain Center for Wilderness Medicine, a tiny research project on rattlesnakes. My month in Boise coincided with a wilderness-medicine conference a hundred miles up the road in Sun Valley. I bartered the conference admission fees for working at the front desk. I learned about mountain, dive, travel, and desert medicine.

As a young medical student, I didn't bother to think, *Can I make a living at wilderness medicine?* All I could focus on was that I was to begin the journey to specializing in wilderness medicine. I would forge a career that would take me far beyond medicine, and perhaps one day, merge my two lives.

Because there was no formal training for this specialty, the way was fraught with roadblocks. The biggest roadblock was that many colleagues and professors thought my career path was not a worthy pursuit. I had to educate myself. I attended more wilderness-medicine conferences during medical school. During my internship in internal medicine, I took my only two days off in July to fly to Squaw Valley, California, to present a research paper on medical-relief projects to developing countries (I was so poor, I slept in my car and showered in the media room). During family-medicine residency, I really pushed the limit, camouflaging wilderness-medicine electives to get them approved by my advisers. I organized a public-health and sports-medicine elective that allowed me to teach two classes on mountain survival and avalanche safety with my colleagues at Portland Mountain Rescue.

I designed a ski-patrol elective, which was approved under the radar by my adviser before my program director could squash it. I wanted to fulfill a lifelong dream to work as a ski patroller as well as learn how to be a ski-patrol physician. Medical director Rob Bates at Big Mountain in Whitefish, Montana, advised me, "You'd better do ten shifts with me in the emergency room. That's the only way you'll get this approved. We'll just call it emergency-and-mountain medicine." When on the mountain with ski patrollers and Rob, I sponged up knowledge about mountain medicine. I learned to strap patients on a backboard, conduct a field exam without undressing the patient, put a dislocated shoulder back in its socket on the ski slope without an X-ray, evaluate head trauma, and evacuate a chairlift when it breaks down.

In my spare time over the course of five years, I wrote articles for *Journal of Wilderness Medicine* and *Wilderness Medicine Letter* on snowboarding medicine and canyoneering medicine as well as book reviews and case reports. I'd write almost anything to establish my name as frequently as possible in the wilderness-medicine literature. I volunteered to speak at many conferences before a conference chair finally took me up on my offer to lecture on board sports (windsurfing, surfing, skateboarding, and snowboarding). Later, I became a regular conference lecturer on ski and snowboard medicine. After penning two unpublished novels, I finally sold my first book, *Backcountry Snowboarding*, and went on to write seven books on outdoor sports, survival, first aid, and introducing kids to adventure sports. When the editor of *Wilderness Medicine* magazine stepped down, I volunteered to succeed him. I eventually volunteered for a spot on the board of directors of the Wilderness Medical Society.

I did not squeeze this all into my life. I expanded the usual four years of medicine to five years. I completed an internship, then spent two years working three days a week at a state health department, before completing two more years of residency. What most doctors do in seven years—four of medical school and

three of residency—I completed in over ten. When I finally finished my formal training in family medicine, I realized I couldn't
make a living on wilderness medicine alone. So I gravitated toward the closest field, emergency medicine. It provides a similar
type of excitement to outdoor adventure sports. It also allowed
me a flexible schedule.

I discovered many things about myself and medicine in that
decade. I learned I liked certain aspects of medicine—science,
writing—and hated others, such as clinical rounds. I learned that
if I could work hard, I could find, develop, and nurture almost any
career, no matter how obscure. And I learned, after many years of
earning wilderness-medicine credentials the hard way, that the
question wasn't whether I should become a doctor, but what kind
of doctor I should become.

SUMMER

CHAPTER 6

The Moment of Fear

M y phone vibrates and beeps once. Again.

Sunrise Falls, call Roger for detail, reads the text message on my cell. Then my home phone rings. *Here we go again*, I think. I was just about to head on a mountain bike ride up Post Canyon.

"Jumper off the Sunrise Falls, back injury," says Roger Nelson. "That's about all I have right now." Roger, a retired high school science teacher, raises blueberries and volunteers for the American Red Cross. He has a head and beard of white hair and wire-rim glasses, and he skis every Christmas Day in a Santa suit. And he acts like Santa: kind, soft-spoken, wise, calm. His years of climbing experience and enthusiasm for volunteering make him the quintessential member of the Crag Rats. Roger can manage a soothing smile and quiet chuckle in almost any situation.

"Sunrise Falls?" I ask incredulously, "Again?" It is mid-afternoon, on a ninety-degree Fourth of July. This is our third of what will be six calls to the Falls this summer. "Who's going?" I ask.

"You're the first Crag Rat I've gotten a hold of," he says. "It may be tough getting a crew on a holiday weekend." Roger is co-ordinating call out because Penny is out of town.

"Okay, I can leave in five minutes," I say. I throw my pack in my truck and change into a pair of lightweight hiking boots.

A few seconds later the phone rings again.

"And can you get the truck?" asks Roger.

I call my wife, who is running errands with Skylar and Avrie; Jen is slightly irritated by another call out. I have a part-time job in the hospital and work at home, so I'm with the kids the majority of the week, volunteering in school, coaching soccer, or driving the kids to activities. I take very few personal trips that are not business related and never go out with "the guys." So I easily justify leaving at a moment's notice to head to a call out. Jen doesn't quite see things this way; it disrupts the entire day and causes tension. I zip two miles to the public-works yard, a five-acre fenced compound that houses the sheriff's office snowcat, snowmobiles, and our main rescue vehicle, a gargantuan four-door four-wheel-drive Chevy pickup. I jump in the truck, pop the keys from the visor, and fire it up. The one-ton stick shift is fun but difficult to drive. I speed out on the interstate, crank the truck up to seventy, and blast the air-conditioning for the short trip to Sunrise Falls. I flick on the sheriff radio as Steve Castagnoli, a viticulturist for the university extension in Hood River, calls on my cell phone. He's twenty minutes behind me; he had to run home for gear. John Ingles, a climber, backcountry skier, and carpenter, and Judge Paul Crowley are getting their packs, too, says Steve. Good crew for a rescue: skilled, levelheaded, and immediately available.

"One from five," the radio crackles. That is Sheriff Joe Wampler, number five, calling dispatch, number one. "I'm on the way to Sunrise Falls." I glance in my mirror. *Oh no.* I suddenly have a sinking feeling in my gut. Joe is right behind me in a white unmarked Ford Explorer. I slow to sixty-five and let him pass me.

It's bad form to drive faster than the sheriff, even on the way to a rescue.

I am the first Crag Rat to arrive at the staging area, but loads of other people are incoming. After careening down the off ramp, I roll the heavy truck to a stop. I quickly spot Joe, a seasoned four-term lawman transplanted from his native Hawaii. He possesses a magical calm voice: no matter the situation, he speaks softly, clearly, and succinctly. No matter how grim the situation, he manages a smile. He now stands in the parking lot wearing khaki shorts, walking boots, and a polo shirt with HRCSO AVIATION UNIT embroidered on the chest. He carries a radio, cell phone, and gun on his belt. He speaks with a deputy who is dressed head to toe in tactical gear. Seeing me, Joe pauses in his conversation.

"Head up the trail, Doc," he says. "There are a couple people ahead of you. Sunrise Falls."

I grab my SAR pack from the truck and start jogging. After two steep miles up the trail, I have to slow for rocks that are slippery and wet from springs seeping out of the canyon wall. The trail has been chipped out of a cliff here. I grab the old, rusty cable bolted to the rock wall to provide safety to hikers. I'm dripping with sweat on this ninety-degree day; my lone water bottle is stuffed deep in my pack. Higher up, the trail is dry and dusty, the loose soil slick. In ten minutes, I reach the intersection with Sunrise Falls, where a volunteer directs me to a large gravel bar on a creek. As if they have minds of their own, my boots slip and slide down the steep, muddy trail, which is wet from a spring trickling through a crack in the earth. But I stay on my feet.

At the gravel bar, I run into Charlie, a sheriff deputy. He answered the "all available units" call for a rescue.

"What's going on?" I ask.

"We just got here," says Charlie. "The jumper has a back injury. She's lying on a ledge around the corner, just out of the water. She has some friends with her. Apparently she's pretty cold and not moving." His eyes light up and he smiles; the expression shows confidence.

Up the creek, a fifty-foot waterfall thunders through a slot in the rocky box canyon and gushes into a plunge pool the size of an Olympic swimming pool. The hundred-foot cliffs are loose, columnar basalt stacked like child's blocks, ready to topple. The top of the cliff is lined with thick vegetation, patches of dirt, and piles of stones and sticks. Shadowy and dim, the box canyon looks like an icy, dark, foreboding Harry Potter cauldron.

"What do you think?" asks Charlie as he sees me open my pack and start digging around.

"Well, I'm swimming. You coming?" I ask.

"You bet!" He grins and his eyes light up again. Tired of busting drug traffickers and a summer of no rescues, Charlie is ready to swim. I'm always a bit nervous doing a complicated rescue with someone I don't know. Charlie strips off his shirt and leaves his gun belt with the volunteer. I unscrew the antenna from my radio and stuff both into a resealable plastic freezer bag. I cram in my wallet and keys, and seal it tight. I find a second freezer bag for my headlamp.

"You bringing your pack?" says Charlie.

"Well, you never know."

Charlie doesn't have any rescue gear, so it is up to me to bring medical and safety equipment. I don't know what I will need, so I bring my entire pack.

We Crag Rats have lots of gear. Most of us have a backpack devoted solely to rescues called a ready pack. I keep mine as light as possible and only half full so I can stuff in extra gear from the truck at the trailhead, like ropes, rescue hardware, and such, depending on the situation. I always carry a hooded rain jacket, a hat, and thin polyester gloves. No matter how hot and sunny the weather, midsummer mountain temperatures can be frigid, especially if we are out all night. I have a helmet, goggles, heavy leather gloves, a climbing harness, twenty meters of 7.5-mm escape rope for self-rescue or emergency access to a patient, three locking carabiners, a rappel device that allows me to either slide down a rope or pay out a rope tied to another rescuer, and three cords, that when tied in a special one-way Prusik slip knot, can wrap around a thicker diameter rope, slide up one direction and grip the rope tightly in the other. This allows one to slide the cord up a rope, then lock it off tightly. In *For Your Eyes Only,* James Bond used his shoe laces to tie Prusik knots and climb a rope after being knocked off the monastery in Meteora, Greece. I rode up the same elevator as a college student living in Europe and perhaps that one pop culture idol helped solidify my thirst for adventure and equipment.

I carry a water bottle, a couple of energy bars, a small survival kit, and a bulky medical kit. I have a ridiculous assemblage of electronics usually strapped to my chest or stashed in the top compartment of my pack: headlamp, SAR radio, Global Positioning System receiver, camera, cell phone, and sometimes a Family Radio Service walkie-talkie to contact a patient who may have one. I have everything marked with my name and orange tape so I can find it after a rescue, since gear can intermix among rescuers and units.

So while holding my pack overhead, I wade into the icy black water with Charlie. Ankle deep, knee deep, waist deep: the water is frigid, and I am immediately chilled as my socks and shoes sponge up the water. Charlie's eyes get big and round. He grins as if to say *it's cold, very cold* when the water hits his groin. I wince, too, when I wade up to my waist. Finally the water is deeper than I am tall so I start to swim by floating on my pack. The pack soaks up water and becomes heavier by the second. My head goes under and I get an ice-cream headache. Charlie swims to a boulder nearby and signals me to toss my pack. I heave the heavy, sopping-wet pack, and he catches it. Then I swim to a ledge on the canyon wall where I can stand waist deep in the freezing water. Charlie tosses the pack back to me and it almost knocks me over. We leapfrog across the pool and around a bend in the creek. We see a bystander perched on a small rock ledge. Charlie throws my pack up to the ledge and we climb out. My hands and feet are numb, my boots are heavy with water, and I am shivering. I can see Charlie is, too.

"Be careful," I say to the bystander. Instinctively I worry about the friend of the patient, dressed in nothing but swim trunks, who has climbed over to direct us to the injured woman. I don't want additional injuries. We scramble on all fours over rocks and dirt, squeeze through a crack in the basalt cliff, then climb down to a tiny gravel bar littered with river rock and driftwood, where we find the patient.

"What's your name?" asks Charlie.

"Bobbie," she says.

"Where do you hurt?" I ask.

"My back."

"Does your head hurt?"

"No."

"Does your chest or stomach hurt?"

"No."

"Legs? Arms?"

"No."

"Do you have any numbness or tingling?"

"No."

In ten seconds, I complete a primary survey, quickly examine the patient while Charlie talks to her. The patient is breathing, talking, and alert. She has no obvious major bleeding. Pulse is normal. Her spine needs to be protected and she is mildly hypothermic. After I dig the hard plastic cervical collar out of my pack, Charlie and I gently place it on her neck. I show a bystander how to hold her head. Then I rapidly complete the secondary survey. I peel back three layers of wet beach towels and scan Bobbie head to toe. Charlie gets some basic info: name, age, family members. Bobbie had been part of a group that came hiking today. She had been jumping from the seventy-five-foot cliff into the plunge pool when she jackknifed in the air, hit the water flat on her back, and felt a sharp stabbing pain. She struggled to shore but couldn't get out of the water. Her friends, who jumped after her, dragged her out to a thin rocky gravel bar at the base of the cliff. They laid her on a flat twelve-inch piece of driftwood to support her back and covered her with the wet towels. One friend went for help, while the others stayed with her. That was sometime after noon and it is now four o'clock.

No head trauma. Chest not tender. Breath sounds clear when I listen with a stethoscope. Abdomen soft. Spleen and liver not enlarged or tender. No leg or arm cuts, scrapes, bruises, or deformities. Her neurologic exam is normal. Last, I slip my hand between her back and the driftwood. On the middle of the spine I feel a large swelling. She winces. I suspect fractures of the thoracic spine bones and ribs. Not good. This means we will have to evacuate this patient in full-spine immobilization with hard plastic cervical collar and backboard. In this location, this instantly becomes a technically difficult and dangerous rescue.

"I'm going to call this in," I say to Charlie, as we both shiver uncontrollably. I dig my radio out of my pack and reassemble the antenna.

"SAR Base, from twenty-eight," I say into my radio, holding it up as high as possible to improve reception in this deep canyon. I identify myself by the Crag Rats universal SAR call number.

"Go, Doc," replies Joe.

"We're at the patient. Back and rib fractures. Hypothermic."

"Thanks, Chris," says Joe. "I need a transport recommendation."

"Stand by," I say.

Charlie and I look at the cliff and then at each other. Now that we have finished the medical assessment, we need to don the other hat of mountain rescue: technical extrication and evacuation.

"This is not going to be easy," I say. "She has to be on a backboard with full spine protection." I am thinking: *This will be extremely dangerous.*

"No kidding." Charlie smiles, relishing the challenge, eyes wide and sparkling again. I suspect immediately that Charlie is the type of person who is always in a good mood—a great guy to have on a rescue.

"We have to get her up the cliff or down the creek," he says.

Fear settles in my soul at these two perilous options. I instinctively dig to the bottom of my pack, pull out my helmet, and strap it on. Still shivering, I pull out my jacket, consider giving it to the patient, then pull it on over my wet clothes because I know I can't help the patient unless I warm up first. The jacket is soggy and cold; it offers little comfort. I eye the cliff again, feel another shuddering chill; this time fear runs like ice through my body. I am cold, wet, and tired. I'm hungry because I forgot to eat before leaving the house and I'm thirsty from the heat and physical effort of trying to reach the patient. But at this moment the specter of fear overshadows all.

Fear is one of the most poignant, powerful emotions in mountain rescue. On a gravel bar in a box canyon with a waterfall spilling into a plunge pool behind me, I am scared for my own safety: the worst fear of all. For the first time ever I question doing mountain rescue: not my skills or time commitment, but how it could affect my two daughters, Skylar and Avrie. Should I, as a father, be risking my life to save others?

Friend and fellow Crag Rat Jay Sherrerd once said, "Fear keeps us in check. If we see something that scares us, we pause, back up, and change the situation to make it safer." What about this scene is causing me to be scared? Can it be remedied? I know the patient needs to stay in full-spine immobilization, and she needs to be warmed up. But we cannot, with the equipment we have, transport her safely across the plunge pool. That means a rope rescue: haul her up the hundred-foot cliff to the trail above. That realization sends shivers down my spine.

"It's pretty rotten rock," says Charlie, still smiling. I would later learn he has a young son at home.

"Yeah—rocks, moss, brush, dirt. Not only do we have no good place to extricate her, we're going to get pummeled with debris." What's more, the usual rope-rescue crew is out of commission due to personal injuries or vacation. I would later find out from Jim Wells that when he was in the same spot on a rescue years ago, he had the same fear and deemed the cliff nearly impossible to rig a safe rope extrication.

"Joe from Chris," I say on the radio.

"Go, Doc."

"If we can get a helicopter in here, that would be best. Patient has a back fracture and we need a litter evacuation with full spine precautions. If we don't have a helicopter, we need to set up a rope-raising system. We're going to need to haul her up the cliff."

"I doubt a helicopter can get in here," says Charlie, pointing to the towering Douglas firs that line the hillsides above the box canyon.

"Two-hundred-fifty-foot cable, forty-eight-foot wingspan," I say, knowing the specs of a rescue chopper.

"But I'd love to see them try," says Charlie with a huge grin.

"Well, we have two choices, because we need her on a backboard. Up the cliff or across the pool." I think out loud. "We can't carry her across—it's too deep."

"What about a raft?" says Charlie. Never a negative thought—I like this guy.

"SAR Base. Do we have a raft?" I ask on the radio.

"Stand by," says a voice I don't recognize.

The wait would take forty-five minutes. Meanwhile, Paul Crowley, Steve Castignoli, and John Ingles have made it up the trail and are trying to locate the cliff from above, amid the thick brush. I blow my whistle loudly a few times so Steve can find the rim. Once there, he can't see over the edge because of the thick brush, loose rock and dirt, and gentle slope to the cliff edge. So the guys anchor a safety rope on a big fir so they can walk to the edge of the cliff and scout the situation from above. When a blue safety rope finally drops down, a shower of rocks and dirt falls over the edge about twenty yards from where we are standing.

"Is that where you need it?" asks Steve on the radio.

I look at Charlie and we shake our heads. We need the rope directly above the patient. But before the crew above drops another rope, we will need to find a place to move the patient and ourselves away from falling rock. Before we can move the patient, we need a backboard and litter. Even then, going up a cliff composed of loose basalt will be risky.

I'm about to get on the radio when it crackles to life.

"We have a floating stretcher en route," says SAR base. I heave a gargantuan sigh of relief. ETA: twenty minutes.

"Who's bringing it up?" I ask.

"Jeff Prichar." Jeff is a Crag Rat and Cascade Locks fire chief. He's hoofing it up the trail with the floats. This is good: another experienced member of our crew is on the way.

The sheriff has also called Oregon Emergency Management and ordered a helicopter. With the Afghanistan and Iraq wars and military base downsizing, we have only one helicopter service readily available for extrications: the National Guard's 1042nd Medical Company Air Ambulance. Unfortunately, on the Fourth of July, both primary and backup crews are on rescues elsewhere in the state. They are calling on a third crew from home. ETA: forty minutes at best.

I ask Steve and his team to meet Jeff at the gravel bar. I call SAR base and ask for warm blankets to be waiting as well. I also hear SAR base acquiring GPS coordinates for the landing zone at the gravel bar. Amid a constant stream of radio chatter, Charlie and I do what so often is part of a complex rescue: wait.

I think about my kids a lot these days: trying to get them into outdoor sports, guiding them on the path of learning good and bad, and becoming schooled in academics. Parenting is much like mountain rescue. You spend time with your kids, love them, guide them, and teach them things like math and following rules and kindness. But I also recognize they need some time to be kids, to run and play and live carefree. Those times as a child are precious: no responsibility, someone to watch over you, unconditional love. This, perhaps, is another deep-seated underlying attraction of mountain rescue for me: it harks back to simpler times. On a rescue, we're not worried about bills or phone calls or finances or e-mail. We're not contemplating divorce, buying a new car, or planning a trip. We're focused wholly on a specific task, with clear and direct goals and unbreakable rules of safety. This may be a complicated rescue, but the thought process in a rescuer's mind is crystal clear: stay safe, get the patient off the ledge, and keep her in spinal immobilization.

After a long wait, it's nearing six o'clock. Charlie and I have finally stopped shivering. Every twenty minutes I check on Bobbie's pain level, pulse, and neurologic status. I try to vary the questions, but eventually I ask her over and over if she knows the day, date, home phone number, and who is president of the United States. Charlie and I send all but one of her friends to swim back to the main gravel bar. The friend who remains tells us he came up last year and was hauled down the trail after hitting his face on the water.

"You should have seen my injuries last year." The friend laughs as he tells the story. "I had two black eyes." Bobbie smiles, too, a good sign.

"And you brought everyone back this year?" asks Charlie incredulously.

"Yup," he replies.

"You're the people," says Charlie, with a lighthearted laugh. "You know the saying, 'If he jumps off a cliff, would you follow him?' You're the people that do follow. You jump off the cliff after someone has already jumped off and hurt himself." The remark lightens the mood, and everyone laughs, even Bobbie. I couldn't have said it with the jocular tone that Charlie tactfully did; my comment would have come out stern and fatherly.

Deep down, Charlie and I are neither surprised nor judgmental; accidents occur time and again. We never criticize patients in the field, but during debriefings at the Crag Rats monthly meetings, routine questions alway comes up: *Why was this patient jumping off a cliff in the first place? Why did these people hike into a storm without proper clothing, food, and water? Why did they not have a map or flashlight?* Many of these questions are aimed to prevent accidents: the mission of the Mountain Rescue Association, our national umbrella organization, is mountain safety and education. We hope to prevent more accidents.

Sunrise Falls cliff jumpers will get injured again and again.

Finally we get word the floats have arrived at the gravel bar. Charlie swims back, and returns in ten minutes with Jeff and Steve. They are swimming and struggling, fully clothed and dragging the stretcher. Luckily Jeff has used the floats before. The guys climb out, shivering. I send the friend back to the gravel bar as we strap Bobbie in the litter.

"Team Two from Team One," I say on the radio

"Go, Team One." I hear a reply.

"We'll be entering the water in a few minutes. We'll be to you in five. I'll be out of radio contact for a few minutes. We'll need those blankets."

"Helicopter ETA thirty minutes," says SAR base. When the thirty-minute call comes in, I know the chopper must be in air, headed here. I unscrew my antenna and repack my radio in the freezer bag. We carry and slide the patient over the rocks to the pool. The metal rails of the litter scrape loudly on the rocks, but as it slides into the water, it becomes suddenly silent and weightless. The patient sinks up to her ears but floats.

"Hold still, don't move," I tell her. "We've got you."

"If this thing flips, we're in trouble," Jeff whispers to me, out of earshot of the patient. "You're the only one dry, you stay on shore. No reason for all of us to be shivering." I've been standing with the patient so long my clothes are dry.

"Thanks." I smile, knowing I still have to swim back to the gravel bar and haul my pack with me.

Jeff, Steve, and Charlie climb in with the litter. Steve and Charlie each take a side. Jeff, thankfully having done this once before, knows that he needs to be at the patient's feet pushing them down into the water, to keep her head out of water. I belay, or tether, the stretcher from shore and slowly pay out the waterproof rope, ready to yank it back should the litter flip. The guys ferry the litter across the pool. The cold water numbs their arms and legs, forcing them to keep moving despite the chance to pause at a shallow, submerged gravel bar halfway across the pool. They swim with the litter down the stream, around the corner, out of sight. When the rope runs out, I toss the end in the water. "Off belay," I yell. My voice echoes in the canyon. I'm alone. I pause for a few seconds, then plunge again into the icy pool. I'm too exhausted to hold my pack overhead, so I let it float upright. All but the very top compartment, which holds my electronics stashed in freezer bags, sponges up water.

I stumble out of the water with my sodden pack at the gravel bar, where help is waiting. Paul thoughtfully insists that I put on his dry fleece vest. At first I decline, then he makes me take it. I'm grateful for the vest and hugely relieved to be back on dry ground and that I didn't have to ascend the cliff.

Jeff has a full medical kit from the Cascade Locks fire department; he inserts an IV catheter in Bobbie and gives her a pain shot. We strip off Bobbie's clothing and wet towels and cover her with blankets. A young volunteer pulls out a thin Mylar space blanket, the kind that hikers carry for emergencies, then stuffs it back in his pack, probably thinking it won't do much good because it is so wimpy compared to the heavy wool blankets.

"Hey, bring that here," I say. I show the young volunteer how to wrap the space blanket around the patient's head like a hood to cover her wet hair, ears, and neck.

"Good job. Thanks," I say, and the young rescuer smiles. While the others sort gear and send bystanders down the trail, Jeff and I stay with the patient. I tell her she's going up in the helicopter and to the hospital. I recheck her vitals, ask about her pain level, and check another neuro exam: *"Wiggle toes. Who's the president?"*

We feel the downdraft seconds before we hear the heavy blades of the Black Hawk. Then it appears abruptly above the treetops. The feeling is like being momentarily lost in the woods, disoriented and confused, then suddenly recognizing a landmark and being profoundly relieved. Unlike the last critical patient, here the chopper has enough space to fly low, wench down a medic, and drop a litter. Over the blustery rotor wash I shout a brief history to the Army medic. "Jumped off the falls. Thoracic spine and rib fracture. No other injuries. Pulse eighty. Neuro normal. Eighteen gauge IV in left antecubital. Five of morphine. Needs some fluids when you get her up. And she's pretty cold." The hovering helicopter blasts us with warm summer wind that dries our wet hair and clothes.

As quickly as the chopper appeared, the patient goes up. The medic on the ground holds a tag line, a rope attached to the litter to keep it from spinning. When the litter disappears into the chopper, the tag line is released. On the end is a heavy steel carabiner that falls a hundred feet to the ground. It spirals down right above a dozen of us standing on the gravel bar. The steel carabiner smacks a rock and bounces three feet in the air very close to the young volunteer. The carabiner could have killed someone. Helicopter safety: we should have sent everyone out of the way. It's not necessarily my job, but it is a precaution I failed to consider. That was a close call.

I check my watch, 9 P.M., dusk. I have an hour until the fireworks start. *Just barely enough time,* I think. I jump in the truck and steer it toward Hood River, toward my daughters. I'm unsettled by the risky rescue. I feel the need to be close to loved ones.

An hour later, I pull alongside the vacant lot in Hood River, park the SAR truck haphazardly on the road, and scramble through a dark field. My clothes are soaked and I'm starving. My girls and Jen are sitting in the middle of the field of grass on a blanket. I huddle close to my daughters.

Just after I arrive, fireworks explode overhead. My girls giggle and *oooh* and *ahhh.*

CHAPTER 7

Timberline Trail

I gun my Chevy Suburban up primitive, rugged Cloud Cap Road on another midsummer day. Even with four-wheel drive and beefy tires, the driving is treacherous. The ten-mile unpaved road has many switchbacks. Large chunks of logging-grade gravel rattle my car so severely that the CDs drop one by one out of the sun-visor holder. I careen through thick bogs of mud, barely missing the mammoth Douglas firs that stretch their gawky limbs down toward the road. Higher up, I plow through a patch of snow in the north-facing shadows. I am only twenty miles from the town of Hood River, but I'm on one of the most remote roads in the county.

The frantic "Oh my God, I'm hurt, I broke my ankle, I can't move, I'm going to die, please help me!" cell phone call came less than an hour ago. A woman had injured her ankle and is stranded high on Mount Hood. Out for a day hike, the woman and her partner have no equipment for spending the night and are not sure of their location.

On my way up, I hear the SAR radio crackle to life and get a page on my cell phone for a second call out. "All Crag Rats. Need assistance for injured hiker, Eagle Creek." It will be hard enough to round up enough rescuers for one mission; two will be difficult during a weekday in midsummer: many of our crew are either working or vacationing. Dwayne Troxell, chief deputy of Hood River County, is a few miles behind me in the SAR pickup. I hear him on the radio coordinating both the Cloud Cap and Eagle Creek rescues with clear, soft-spoken directives. Dwayne is a former military helicopter pilot and former member of the Air Force Reserve 304th Air Rescue Wing.

"We'll need a minimum of four at Cloud Cap. See who you can get," says Dwayne when I finally reach him by cell. "We might be a bit shorthanded."

"I'm heading out with the fire department to a possible triple fatality on Whisky Creek Road," says Jim Wells when I reach him by cell phone. As chief of the Pine Grove Rural Fire Protection District, his first duty is the fire department and he can't respond to the mountain. Other Crag Rats—Tom Scully, Todd Wells, and Paul Crowley—I later learn, have received word of the rescue and are en route. Paul is at the courthouse and able to leave work. Tom is at the ski resort, where he is manager of maintenance; he, too, is able to leave work. Todd left his construction business the instant he was paged and is somewhere either just behind or in front of me. When I reach Inspiration Point, I am greeted by a glorious view of the mountain. I turn deeper into the mountains, lose cell reception, and focus on my driving.

Fifteen minutes later, I skid into Cloud Cap Saddle Campground and park among two dozen cars belonging to hikers, skiers, and climbers. The camping here is primitive: there is one small spring-fed spigot for water, a pit toilet, and dirt tent sites among the tall Douglas fir and Western hemlock. The summer day is just about perfect: not a cloud in the sky, sun shining brightly, and a faint wind.

I jump out, clamber up on a boulder twice the size of my truck, and make a few more calls on my cell. A camper scowls at me because I'm clearly disturbing the wilderness experience by shouting into my cell. Yet time is critical. The patient's status is unknown. Her location is vague. And I don't know how much help is on the way. Unable to stand idle, an idea pops into my head. I call dispatch for the cell number of the injured woman, whom we used to call *victim*, but now we call *subject* or *patient* so as not to imply blame.

"Hi, this is Search and Rescue," I say when a woman named Jeannie answers. "How are you doing?"

"It's my friend—she hurt her ankle. It's bad. We need help."

"Is she able to walk?" I ask.

"Yes, she's slowly limping down the trail."

"Which trail are you on?"

"I don't know."

"Are you west of the campground? Toward Timberline?"

"Yes."

"So you crossed the bridge over the creek, right?" I say to confirm.

"Yes."

"So you can see the valley?"

"Yes."

"Which direction are you walking?"

"Um, back to the parking area."

"Where? Cloud Cap?"

"Yes, we're parked at the campground."

"How far are you from the parking area?"

"Um, I'm not sure."

"How far are you from the bridge over the creek? Do you know that?"

"Um, I think it is right around the corner," says Jeannie.

This might be a simple walk out. "Okay, keep heading this way slowly!" I emphasize. "We'll meet you on the trail. Be careful. Don't leave the trail. If you get tired, stop right in the middle of the trail."

When Dwayne pulls up in the truck emblazed with SAR and sheriff logos, the camper's scowl is replaced by astonishment. I jog up to the SAR truck. Dwayne is still working his cell and his radio, so I wait for him to pause.

"Dwayne, I just talked to our injured woman's partner," I tell him. "She's one drainage west of the creek and walking this way. What do you say I head down the trail and confirm?" Usually our hasty team is a pair or trio of rescuers who hike up the mountain to assess the situation, render initial medical care, and determine the evacuation mode and equipment needed. Most of the time, we don't head out alone. But daylight is waning, and two other rescues have just started. The risk for me to head out alone in good weather on the well-known Timberline Trail is reasonable, considering the three rescues ongoing.

"Sounds great. I have other things I could be doing right now," says Dwayne. "Call me as soon as you know anything. If we can wrap this up quickly, that would be great."

I grab a radio out of the truck, a twenty-year-old Motorola as large and nearly as heavy as a brick. It's too big for my pocket, so I jam it in the top of my pack. I set off jogging westward on the Timberline Trail, crossing the same terrain where Jackie Strong was found eight decades ago. I hike to the tree line, then make my way down the treeless east lateral moraine of the glacier into the creek canyon. Filled with sand and boulders, the canyon looks like the moon except it has a few patches of lingering snow. I descend all the way to the stream before I realize the bridge had washed out earlier this year. The stream, usually a trickle, is a raging torrent from the summer afternoon sun: it is too dangerous to jump or wade across. I later find out I missed a small Forest Service sign that read: DETOUR, ¼ MILE UPSTREAM. So I climb back out of the canyon, hike farther up the mountain, then descend into the canyon again. This trail, being new, is pulverized sand, talus, and rocks. Pumice boulders the size of volleyballs and basketballs have been smoothed from years of being tumbled by the glacier. With every step I surf three feet down the steep slope, filling my shoes with sand. At one point, I bang my shins against a rock. I precariously scramble over the larger boulders and try not to get my feet wedged between them. I finally find the new bridge, cross, ascend the sand and pumice of the west lateral moraine, locate the trail, and set off westward at a trot.

At the first ridge past the drainage, I don't find the injured woman where she said she'd be. I reach the second drainage, but still no woman. At the third drainage, twenty minutes later, I pass some hikers.

"Did you see an injured woman down the trail?" I ask.

"Yes, she's a few miles down the trail," says one hiker. "We left someone to help her."

"Okay, great," I say. The news is a bit worrisome: she is actually quite far from Cloud Cap Saddle.

"She wasn't moving very fast. She didn't look too good," said the hiker. *Oh great,* I think. This is a major medical evacuation.

I call Dwayne on my cell phone because the radio is too busy with the Whisky Creek accident and an apparent drug bust going on in downtown Hood River. "I'm at the third drainage. Passed some hikers that said the woman's a few miles farther."

"Okay, keep going," says Dwayne. "Todd's on the way."

Finally, another thirty minutes later, I reach the woman. She is hobbling while her friend follows.

"Hi, I'm Search and Rescue."

"Oh, that was quick," she says. Obviously she has calmed down after the frantic 911 call. But I can see from her grimace that she is in pain. I take a look at the ankle. It was bandaged and splinted by another hiker who happened by. The hiker had also given the woman some pain pills, so she is a bit woozy.

"We have help on the way. Can you keep moving or do you want to stop?" I ask. I watch her face and that of her partner flush with relief.

"I'll try to keep going," she says.

I call Dwayne again, this time on the radio.

"We need a litter to carry her out. Anyone else show up to help?"

"Paul and John are just heading out. Todd's about halfway to you," says Dwayne. I can barely hear him as the radio is still clogged with chatter. "Do you need a backboard and straps? Do you need the wheel?"

"I just need the litter. No backboard and no ropes. Probably can't use the wheel."

Then I remember the bridge is washed out. Although this woman can hobble down the trail, we will never make it out by dusk unless we carry her. Plus if she continues to walk, she may risk another injury. She has a deep tendon laceration and the sedating pain pills given to her by the other hiker are really taking effect. After fifteen minutes of intermittent hobbling and resting, we've covered only a few hundred feet. Todd appears suddenly from the woods carrying the entire eight-foot lightweight fiberglass litter over his head.

"Hey, glad you're here," I say.

"What do you have?"

"Ankle torn up pretty bad. Can't walk much. Had some pain pills so she's getting tired. We need to carry her out."

"Okay," says Todd, ready to go to work.

"Nice radio, by the way," I say when I see that Todd has Dwayne's compact high-tech radio. "I've got a brick," I say.

We place the woman in the litter, pad it with a foam camping pad, strap her in, and lift. Todd and I have a difficult time carrying the heavy litter over rough terrain. We wobble and weave down the trail. Every time Todd or I stumble, it causes the other person to tweak his back and shoulders to keep from dropping the litter. We are not making much progress as the sun ducks behind the treetops to the west. Instantly, it becomes cold on the mountain.

Thankfully, Paul Crowley and another Crag Rat show up. Paul brings his clear, focused judgelike demeanor to rescues. I like having Paul around: never a confusing sentence. With four bearing the litter, we cruise more swiftly and safely down the trail. We slow to a crawl up inclines and speed up going downhill. Every few hundred feet, Paul, who is in the front, yells out "Roots on right!" or "Rocks on left!" to signal an obstacle in the trail that Todd and I can't see because we're in back.

When we come to the creek crossing, we carefully walk down on the loose sand and rocks of the west moraine, then pass the litter over the bridge, which is a mere eighteen inches wide and has a rickety handrail on one side only. It is bolted to two car-sized boulders just ten feet above the raging meltwater of the glacier. Hiking across by myself I didn't give it a second look. Transporting the patient over it is much more difficult.

Once across, we haul the stretcher up the sand and scree of the east moraine, which proves to be extremely difficult. For every three steps up, we slip and slide one step back. Paul stumbles on a rock he can't see and scrapes his shin. But he doesn't drop the litter. The moraine is the equivalent of ten flights of stairs; we have to pause four times to rest, reset our grips, or pass the litter over a boulder.

At the top of the moraine, Tom appears from the forest carrying the heavy, bulky wheel—an ATV tire mounted to a steel frame that fits under the litter. This allows us to wheel the patient on the litter down the trail instead of carrying it. Two people can steer a wheeled litter down the trail because they are not holding the weight of the patient.

We return to Cloud Cap just before dusk.

"Good turnout," says Paul.

"Yeah, five Rats. We can probably use more, don't you think?"

"Maybe we should recruit some young, strong bucks?" says Kirk Worrill later at a meeting.

"Maybe we should think about it—maybe get some guys from Washington," says Bernie Wells, a veteran Crag Rat who acts as our treasurer.

"It's a fine balance," explains Dwayne. "You need enough rescuers to complete the task, and enough rescues to keep everyone excited about showing up. But, if you have too many people standing around or too few rescues, people become uninterested." He's been doing this for a long time.

"And what about new radios?" I ask when I remove the heavy brick from my pack and wiggle it back in the truck's charger.

"Bring it up at a meeting," says Paul with a smile. In addition to working as a judge and playing bluegrass music, Paul is taking a turn as Crag Rat Pip Squeak which, in most organizations would be called secretary. It's a running joke that bringing up a topic at a meeting will likely stir heated discussion, many laughs, teasing (as in my being too wimpy to carry the brick), and a tabled decision. Our group is cautious and thoughtful about everything, from who we let join to how we spend our money. It is partly the culture of our eighty-year-old group and partly the necessity of a volunteer mountain rescue unit. We need members who are skilled, clear thinking, cautious, and team players.

The Crag Rats don't always have nail-biting excitement and nonstop action. We have as many social outings as trainings. Our social calendar begins in January with our annual banquet. In February, we Crag Rats ski up or ride the snowcat to the Winter Outing at Cloud Cap Inn. The cabin is full of Crag Rats and their families almost every weekend during the summer when the road is open and we can drive to the cabin.

With Jay, his family, and a troop of friends, we drive up to Cloud Cap Inn every Fourth of July. Skylar, Avrie, and I hike on the beautiful trails of the Tilly Jane Historic District. I love family time in the outdoors, but the kids sometimes grumble unless we can harangue another family to join us. In an old amphitheater built from downed logs, my daughters perform a song-and-dance number for us. We explore a dilapidated Forest Service building and an A-frame shelter that now serves as a backcountry ski hut. Skylar and Avrie adore playing in the cabin with their friends: it's a big clubhouse. Jay, Penny, Jen, and I sit on the deck, gawk at the spectacular view of Mount Hood, and sip ale. The kid pack is in constant motion, flowing in and out of the old cabin, following my rule to keep the cabin in sight at all times. Dee, another friend, comes up with her two kids. When Doug and Laurie show up, a couple I'd like to sign up as Crag Rats because their alpine skills and calm personalities would fit with our group, we head out for another hike. It's the same thing Crag Rats did in the fifties.

When the snow is good, the adults set off at dawn to climb for three hours up the west moraine of the glacier to the permanent snowfield called Snowdome. At first I was nervous leaving Skylar and Avrie asleep in a tent on the deck of the cabin high in the mountains. But my girls are strong, fit, smart, and independent. Skylar wakes, finds the chocolate milk in the cooler where I told her it was, then snuggles with Avrie until she wakes. They dress themselves, locate the babysitters Penny had brought along and the other kids, and eat the breakfast I left for them.

At 7:30 A.M. I call Skylar, who answers on the cabin's SAR radio.

"Papa, where are you?" she asks.

"I'm climbing the mountain. Everyone okay?" I check in, with doctorly and parental concern.

"Yeah, we're fine, Papa. We're trying to find you with the telescope."

"Okay. I'll wave."

"Got to go, Papa. We're having breakfast again. See you later." Skylar signs off, but I leave my radio on, knowing she might call me again to check in. More likely, I'll call her. At the top of Snowdome, nine thousand feet, we have a snack, admire the view, then ski—or, in my case, snowboard—three thousand feet in the smooth summer snow to the Timberline Trail. We're back to the cabin by noon, just in time for lunch.

In September Crag Rats host the Ice Follies, our Crag Rat annual crevasse rescue-training weekend on the glacier. Most years, all five Oregon mountain rescue units arrive to have a joint training exercise as well as the pararescue jumpers from the 304th Unit in Portland. It's a big group at Cloud Cap and a chance to get together with our colleagues.

Back in Hood River, Crag Rats have two meetings a month. The first is for business and the second for training. We meet upstairs in our Pine Grove hut in front of a big fireplace, hand-laid with basalt blocks. The twenty members who usually show up at the twice-monthly meeting relax in big couches at one end of an otherwise empty hall that seats a hundred people when the tables are set up. Everyone takes a turn on house committee, which means it is your turn to bring beer, snacks, and dessert.

Our meetings are packed with spirited discussion, controversy, and laugher about mundane but necessary aspects of any nonprofit club. We discuss correspondence, recent trips by members, rescues, equipment needs, upcoming social functions, and our liaisons with the sheriff and the Forest Service. We discuss how to raise, invest, and spend money. In our training meeting we sometimes rig ropes on the beams above the fireplace and ascend with Prusiks, a self-rescue extrication exercise. We recertify with CPR or drill on navigation, avalanche searches, litter packaging, splinting, helicopter operations, and radio use.

A week after the Timberline Trail rescue, at a meeting, I read an e-mail and show digital images that I received from the woman's friend we rescued. The e-mail reads: " 'We were amazed at not only your quick response but the depth of the crew that was deployed. Everyone was extremely efficient and skilled at getting my friend off the trail and on the way to the hospital.

'The hospital crew was so friendly. The X-rays showed no broken bones but a puncture to the tendon. This did cause leakage from the ankle joint, so they brought in an orthopedic surgeon. Meanwhile, they put her on IV antibiotics and morphine and decided she needed to go into surgery to investigate and clean up the wound. The ankle was stitched up, braced, and she was put in a room for an overnight stay around midnight.' "

The e-mail is a nice bonus. But we don't do it for the thanks and don't really ever expect any. We'll come to this mountain to rescue people time and again, the living and the dead, simple accidents and complex ones.

CHAPTER 8

Dial 911 for Mountain Rescue

Nowadays, rescues nearly always start with a cell phone call. Another summertime afternoon page zings invisibly to my phone. *Hiker needs assistance, Newton Creek.* I am faintly tempted to stay at the neighborhood barbeque that is just starting so I can spend time with my family. Yet someone may be hurt and I'm available to respond. So I really need to answer the call.

"It's a fifty-eight-year-old hiker having a heart attack."

"Okay—is anyone else going?"

Penny, an outdoor enthusiast, occupational therapist, mom, and wife of my friend Jay, has one of the most difficult and potentially frustrating jobs of our unit: call-out coordinator. "When I start making calls," she once said, "I end up talking to a lot of answering machines."

"I have Roger Nelson and Paul Crowley," she says. "And I left a lot of messages. It is Saturday afternoon too," she reminds me, "*and* the fair." Many of our members, as well as every spare deputy, are at the Hood River County Fair.

"I'll call you back." I change into my poison oak pants, toss my pack in the truck, and eek out of the driveway past the green space where the neighborhood gathers for the barbeque. My wife instantly knows. "Rescue?" She's a bit disappointed, perhaps since she's loosing me to another rescue. It's been a busy summer with rescues. Our marriage has been a bit rocky since we had kids: mostly because I spend so much time with Skylar and Avrie. And mountain rescue work is completely unpredictable.

"Heart attack, up by the ski resort. I need to go. The man or woman could be dying. They really need me." I say this knowing that no matter the situation, I will go on the rescue. I drive a mile to the county yard, pick up the SAR truck, and swing by Paul's house.

"I just opened a beer. My wife and I just got back from a wonderful bike ride," he says. "Man, I was looking forward to that beer." He tosses his pack in back and climbs in the cab. He's always excited and available for a rescue. "Sorry, I didn't get around to changing," indicating his bright Hawaiian shirt.

"Looks like a good outfit for a rescue if I ever saw one. I'm underdressed."

I creep through town amid heavy summer traffic. When I hit Highway 35, I stomp on the gas. In fifteen minutes, I pull into the shoulder at the Mount Hood Store, where Roger is standing on the side of the road wearing his trail-worn pack and blueberry-picking clothes. He looks like a beatnik hitchhiker.

"I'm getting out of a wedding," says Roger, smiling. "I really didn't want to go to that wedding. Thanks for the rescue." Roger's two grown girls are athletic and outdoorsy: one's a smoke jumper and ski patroller in Sun Valley, Idaho, and the other was a ski patroller on Mount Hood. He told me once, when I talked to him about dragging my two young daughters into the outdoors, "Get them outside, do the things you want to do, and they will do everything boys do. Usually better." I keep that advice in the forefront of my mind. Someday I hope they will want to be Crag Rats.

With our evening plans disrupted, Paul, Roger, and I head up the mountain. The subject, Kyle, had planned for several weeks to hike to Lamberson Butte on the rugged and remote northeast side of Mount Hood. His friends bailed at the last minute, so he went solo. He set off from the Teacup Lake parking lot and crossed Newton Creek in the early hours of a clear morning. The stream was a bubbling trickle. He'd been prepared with a backpack full of water, food, a whistle, an emergency Mylar space blanket, and a jacket. He reached Lamberson Butte via the Elk Meadows Trail at midday, ate some food, and took some pictures. But when he hiked down in the afternoon, Newton Creek had swelled into a raging torrent. The sun had baked the Newton and Clark glaciers, and, as so often happens in the afternoon, the creek quadrupled in volume. On the way down, Kyle walked up and down the creek, looking for a place to cross. Exasperated and desperate, he jumped to an island, then realized that from the island he could not complete the crossing. He turned to jump back to shore, but the water was too high and he was too frightened.

The call out was first billed as a heart attack. On the way up, I call dispatch and learn Kyle had actually called his wife in Portland, who then called 911. It is thirdhand info, which is typical for rescues. No, he's not having a heart attack, says dispatch. Rather he has a "heart condition." I call Kyle's cell phone.

"Hi. This is Search and Rescue."

"I need help. I'm trapped," I can hear the nervousness and tension in his voice. "When can you get here? I need help," he repeats, anxious and panicky.

"We're on our way. We will be coming in a half hour," I assure him, even though I suspect it may take us longer. "Stay where you are."

"Hurry—how long will it take you?" he asks again. "I need help. I'm trapped."

"Are you injured?"

"No."

"Are you having a heart attack?"

"No."

"Chest pain?"

"No, I'm fine. Just trapped. The water is raging all around me. It's very dangerous."

"Okay—we are on our way. We'll get to you as soon as we can. Stay where you are. Save your cell phone battery. Don't move." Since he doesn't have an injury and he is not having a heart attack, we're not racing, but this rescue is still urgent. With only two hours of daylight left, we'll eat up at least one driving and hiking. That will leave us little time to set up a technical extrication and hike out.

I condense the man's complicated directions into a single sentence to my partners. "He's up the Elk Meadows Trail, about two hundred yards downstream of where the trail crosses Newton Creek." I'm a bit unfamiliar with the area, but luckily Paul's along.

"Oh, great," he says. Paul's a veteran of multiple trips on the Timberline Trail, which circles the volcano. "I know a shortcut. It'll save us a half hour hike."

"We'll need some ropes and long anchor lines," Roger puts in. "There may not be too many trees for anchors, only boulders," he explains. "And they may be quite a distance from the creek."

Direct communication with a subject is a recent phenomenon. Cell phones have changed the way we do rescues. In prewireless days, an injured hiker would have to send a friend down the trail who would flag down a car, drive to a pay phone, and call 911. Then the sheriff would call the Crag Rat call-out coordinator, and the phone calls among Crag Rats would start. Thus, by the time rescuers heard about the mission, got their gear, drove to the trailhead, and located the injured person, hours would pass. In some rescues, this meant a long delay at getting help. In other cases, it meant that the injured or stranded person would find a way to get down the trail on his own or with the help of his buddies or bystanders. Now we get a cell phone call from the injured person or from a friend at the scene or from the nearest cell phone reception point. In the case of Mount Hood, where many of the hiking trails are above the tree line and have a clear line of sight to a cell phone tower, hikers often get good cell reception. The good news is that we hear about rescues sooner and obtain detailed information from the victim: injuries, location, supplies available. It is immensely helpful to talk to the injured person because we learn what gear to bring and how fast to hike up the trail: the difference between walking cautiously with a litter or making a risky full-bore sprint with medical gear.

The downside of cell phones is that the injured, ill, stranded, or lost subjects sometimes call 911 reflexively. For example, once a group of teens hiking Starvation Ridge Trail were caught out after dark, and got scared. So they called 911. Jay Sherrerd and a sheriff deputy hiked up the trail only to find the teens were less than a mile from their car. All five were sitting in a patch of poison oak. Jay gave them a kind and pointed "flashlight lecture" on the ten-minute walk back to the parking lot.

Another time we had a cell phone call from Polallie Creek Trail: bee sting with possible allergic reaction. A crew of five raced up the mountain along with volunteer firefighters and a couple of deputies. Sheriff Wampler jumped in the airplane and located a group of three hikers, high on the ridge. We were about to launch a full-scale mission when they called the sheriff back. "That's okay," they said. "We're fine. We can hike down on our own." Apparently one had a bee sting but not an allergic reaction.

When I first joined the Crag Rats, the group was still doing manual call outs, despite the fact that teams across the country had gone to either voice or text pagers. The Crag Rats used manual call outs for years effectively and never bothered to upgrade.

"Why don't we have pagers?" I asked Jay.

"We're Crag Rats," he said simply. Why mess with a system that works?

On the other hand, I grew up in the information age. Electronics come naturally to me. Since cell phones were becoming ubiquitous, I saw an easy way to set up a cell phone paging system. So Penny and I plugged every member's cell phone text message e-mail address into an account at dispatch. Now, when the sheriff activates us, we get text messages on our cell phones with a one-sentence instruction. Usually it says to call Penny or our SAR voice mail box, where Penny leaves a recorded message with directions to the staging area and information about the type of rescue—high angle, medical evacuation, search, body recovery. Penny still does manual call outs as a backup and to reach those who don't carry their cell.

This evening, the weather is spectacular in the mountains; next to dawn, evening is my favorite time of day in the high country. The heat and humidity of the lower valley have given way to crisp, clean alpine air. The sun glows orange-pink on the glaciers, called alpenglow. The forest is serene. We park on the shoulder of the road. Paul's shortcut to the Elk Meadow Trail will save us about a half hour of hiking. Plus the man's cell phone saved us about an hour of searching. We pull out boxes, toss gear on the ground, look it over, and jam pertinent stuff in our packs. If we were on a climbing or backpacking trip, this gear-sorting ritual would take up to an hour: repack, sort group gear, take one last look at food and clothing, and look over the map and route. But on a SAR mission, this dance takes a scant five minutes.

We carry a lot of people out of the mountains, and we have specific mountain rescue equipment to help us perform the task. It's well organized in our SAR pickup. We have a pair of stretchers, or litters. We have a clear plastic cover for the litters to protect the patient's head and face when we are doing a technical extrication. We have the wheel—a fat all-terrain vehicle tire mounted on a steel frame which clips under the litter (and weighs thirty pounds). For each litter we have a lightweight plastic backboard to immobilize a patient's spine. Attached to the backboards are pouches with necessary accessories: a white plastic cervical collar for the neck immobilization and special Velcro spider straps, to fasten the patient to the board. A second set of straps secures the board to the litter.

We have a slew of rescue gear stashed in individual plastic bins: helmets; probes and snow shovels for avalanche rescue; rock-climbing equipment for cliff rescues; extra blankets; radios; boxes of granola bars; bottled water; and AA batteries. Our medical box includes bandages, over-the-counter medicines, malleable aluminum splints to immobilize arms and legs, boxes of gloves and masks to protect rescuers from bodily fluids of victims, among other things. And we have ropes, lots of ropes. We mainly use a 300-foot blue belay rope and two 150-foot red rescue ropes. Rescue is the primary haul line, and belay is the backup line: every high-angle system needs both. We have a half dozen extra 150 footers. We have a bin of multiple lengths and thicknesses of accessory cords and webbing.

Our rope rescue hardware backpack from afar looks like it might weigh twenty pounds, but clocks in at over sixty. It contains specialized carabiners, pulleys, mechanical ascenders to climb ropes, and belay devices to lower and raise ropes.

All this stuff fits in our SAR truck.

For this rescue, like most, we don't know exactly what we need, so we prepare for the most complicated scenario, a rope traverse across a stream. I grab a bulky harness for the patient, a length of rope, and several lengths of webbing. Paul grabs a heavy 150-foot rope. We split up enough carabiners and pulleys to rig a rope rescue and belay system.

"You have a first aid kit?" asks Roger.

"It's in the truck. I wasn't going to bring it," I say.

"Better, just in case."

"There's no injury," I point out.

"What if he falls when we rescue him?" Roger chuckles.

"That would be bad form." I laugh as I stuff my bulky kit back in my pack. I tend to be a minimalist. I try to leave gear in the truck that I'm pretty sure I won't need. Roger prepares for a wide contingency of problems. Still, he's been doing this for a few decades, so I defer to his judgment.

Five minutes after parking we're hoofing it down the trail at a fast trot. It's seven o'clock by now. Our packs weigh fifty pounds each.

"My wife was going to grill steaks at our neighborhood barbeque," I say.

"I never even got to stretch after my ride." says Paul.

"No wedding!" hoots Roger. "By the way, I thought this guy was having a heart attack."

"Me too," I say. I am thoroughly enjoying myself: hiking into the woods in the beautiful summer evening with good partners and feeling somewhat self-important and also indulgent in that I'm enjoying myself. Occasionally, I feel selfish and almost guilty, like I shouldn't be having so much fun when someone's in danger. But, this is part of what keeps me—and all mountain rescuers— motivated and interested in turning out, mission after mission.

After thirty minutes of swatting mosquitoes, we reach Newton Creek. We can see Charlie two hundred feet downstream. He stands with a bright orange space blanket wrapped around his torso. To reach him, we cross a wobbly log to the north side of the creek supporting ourselves with the telescoping hiking poles Paul and Roger brought. Then we hike downstream over loose sand and river-smoothed pumice rocks the size of basketballs. The Newton Creek drainage is about two hundred feet wide, but the stream is a mere twenty feet wide in the center of the drainage. Kyle is perched on an island in the stream.

It's clear immediately that we need only rig a safety line, just in case Kyle or one of us slips on the rocks and splashes into the raging creek. Paul dons a harness. Roger takes a seat on a big boulder to make a body belay, which means he anchors the rope by wrapping it around his lower back while holding the rope in both hands. One end is clipped to Paul's harness, the other end is coiled at Roger's feet. Roger will slowly pay out the rope and, if Paul slips, Roger can use the friction of his body to stop the rope and hold Paul. At the creek's edge, I act as spotter. We gear up quickly, since the sun will soon dip below Cooper Spur, the ridge to the northwest.

Then Paul steps into the raging torrent. On his first step the water is ankle deep. On the second step the water doesn't even cover his boot top. With his third step, he's on the island. Paul, Roger, and I exchange glances, trying not to make Kyle feel ridiculous. The river was probably raging that afternoon and has now significantly abated. As Kyle heaves a sigh of relief, I see the fight-or-flight response that was keeping him tense and alert drain as if a plug was pulled. His features relax, his breathing slows, and he starts talking anxiously.

"That's okay," I say. "We got you."

He's right to be worried: people have died here. A year ago to the month, a twenty-seven-year-old woman died in a similar creek crossing on the same trail. She was a social worker from Portland, who was hiking a four-day solo trip on the entire Timberline Trail. On the evening of day five she was reported missing. On the morning of day six a search was launched. The Crag Rats were enlisted to hike the north sections of the trail. Steve and I were en route when she was found dead. She had hiked the entire trail, save the last two miles. A week of glorious sun had melted the snow and pumped up the rivers. Then a few days of unseasonable rain had caused them to swell further. At the Sandy River, just two miles from her car at the Ramona Falls trailhead, the bridge and culverts had washed out. Her body was found three hundred yards downstream from the trail. She had likely tried to cross, lost her footing, hit her head, and drowned.

It takes Paul ten minutes to get Kyle in a harness, tied to a rope, and set up for a belay—and about ten seconds to guide him across the river. Paul holds Kyle by the belt until he is in the water at which point I grab him by the harness and yank him to shore. Kyle heaves another sigh.

"Good work," I say in encouragement.

"Thank you, guys, for coming out," he says in an anxious, high-pitched voice. "I don't know what I would have done. I could have tried to cross, but it was too dangerous."

"That's okay," I say. "You did the right thing. People have died here before." I reassure him. Leaving Kyle tied to the rope, we walk two hundred feet up river to the wobbly log. Roger crosses the twenty-foot log bridge first, Paul sets up a body belay, and I give Kyle the hiking poles. With Paul belaying and Roger and me spotting him on either side of the log, Paul gives Kyle clear instructions about keeping his poles planted, keeping his feet square, and staying upright so he doesn't lose balance. Kyle starts the crossing, but instantly squats and nearly falls. Roger gently encourages Kyle to keep him moving after he takes a long pause in the middle of the log.

Finally, we hike out as the sky turns to dusk. We illuminate the trail with headlamps and swat a greater number of what seem to be much larger mosquitoes. Kyle's excitement, nervous anxiety and fear has metamorphosed to relief and giddiness. He can't stop talking about his adventure. We keep him sandwiched on the single-file trail between Roger and Paul. Picking up the rear with a relaxed stride, I half listen to Kyle and enjoy the cool night air. Kyle is so excited that, despite following three feet behind Paul, he takes a wrong turn at a trail intersection and steps into the dark forest. We steer him back to the trail. *I hope he's okay to drive home,* I think. Roger and I have a brief discussion, and decide that Kyle is okay to drive home.

"Do you guys know how old I am?" asks Kyle.

"Fifty-eight," says Paul in a good-hearted tone.

"Wow, good guess." We had been briefed by dispatch.

"How old are you, Roger?" asks Paul.

"Sixty-two."

Well after dark we pop out of the woods to the asphalt and our truck. It takes Paul and me a few minutes to find the truck key that we stashed under a bumper. We're swatting away mosquitoes that seem as big as dragonflies now, as if they are getting larger at the expense of our blood. We quickly repack the truck, a second ritual. Rarely do we just toss our packs in and drive home, as we would on a climbing or backpacking trip. We try to get every piece of gear back in place so it's ready to go for the next mission. None of us have time to reorganize it tomorrow. No one would want to show up for a rescue, pop open the back of the truck, and find it muddled from a previous mission. We leave the damp belay rope coiled loosely on top of the rope bin so it can finish drying; otherwise everything goes back in its place. Then we drive Kyle a mile down the road to his car.

At our next meeting we will have a couple laughs over the Newton Creek rescue. With rescues, we almost always find something to chuckle about. To an outsider, laughing at rescued people or situations may seem rude. But it takes the edge off stressful situations. I show Paul the picture of him crossing the stream: he's wearing the Hawaiian shirt, and the water does not even crest his boot top. Roger recounts the story of the guy taking a wrong turn, then telling us his age. We all laugh. Not being able to find the key in the dark while swatting mosquitoes prompts another laugh and a quick discussion about the truck.

"Maybe we should get a magnetic key box for the bumper," says Dennis Klein.

"We left the key in case another Crag Rat showed up and needed gear. But we didn't know where to hide it," says Paul.

"We need some sort of system," I say.

"I can't stand missing all these rescues," says Jim Wells. "My back has been out for a couple weeks."

"I'm always out of town when the call out comes," says Jay Sherrerd on the same note; he's usually willing to drop everything and head to a rescue.

"Don't travel so much," I tell him. "Why don't you just sit around and wait by the phone like the rest of us?"

One from twenty-eight." Back at the truck, the night is black and the stars are in full dress regalia. I fumble for the truck lights, and then flick on the radio. Radio traffic from the fair crackles in the otherwise silent forest: deputies are busting teenagers drinking in the grandstand. The rural country fair is alive with carnival rides, dollar games for chintzy prizes, stinky animal barns, and Juice Newton playing in the bleachers of Wy'East Middle School. It's a bit of Americana I look forward to every year: the orchardists, migrant workers, windsurfers, teachers, telecommuting computer dot-comers, and trust funders all turn out. It is a great equalizer in our small town.

"Twenty-eight," dispatch says, signaling that I can speak.

"We're back at the truck. All clear from Newton Creek. No injuries. We're sending our guy home."

"Copy twenty-eight, all clear Newton Creek, twenty-one thirty." It is 9:30, time to get home.

I crank the starter, juice the gas, and let out the clutch. I point the heavy pickup down the mountain, into the valley, toward home.

CHAPTER 9

Cliff Jumpers

S ame crap, different day," says Jeff Prichar, on yet another cliff jumper rescue. After a few weeks with no rescues except a lackluster ground search, the prospect of a bona fide rescue juices me. Jeff fills me in on the phone as I jump in my truck and hit the road. On the way, Penny calls and says that Devon Wells and Jim Wells are en route. Sheriff Joe is already at Eagle Creek when I arrive.

"Seven volunteer firefighters are heading up the trail about twenty minutes ahead of you," says Sheriff Joe. "Sounds like the patient is out of the water and near the trail. Another cliff jumper. You probably won't be swimming this time." Joe grins.

"Another jumper?" I exclaim incredulously. "Well, I have my wet suit just in case." I smile. At a Crag Rat meeting, Todd Wells had recommended that we pack our gear in dry bags and carry wet suits and life vests to Sunrise Falls. I may have the medical knowledge, but I trust and follow my colleagues' advice when it comes to technical aspects of reaching patients, based on their many years of rescue experience. Jim Wells gave me a suggestion for a rescue-quality life vest. "Nothing fancy. Get lots of flotation. It should be easy to get on and off, especially over bulky clothing. I ordered mine from a fire-rescue Web site," he said. We also talked at the meeting about the recent *Hood River News* story about cliff jumping. It gave locations of popular spots for jumping into pools and encouraged readers to try this new "sport." Our second jumper of the season will not be our last.

In ten minutes, I reach the fire crew, who slowly trudge up the trail with a litter, wheel, and rope. I walk with them at first, but I need to go faster. I don't know what kind of condition the patient is in.

"I'm going to cruise ahead. I'll see you guys up there," I say.

"Yeah, we respond to rescues, and you guys get all the credit," says one firefighter.

Like any small town, we sometimes have minor issues between jurisdictions, especially when it comes to rescues that involve multiple agencies, some consisting of paid personnel and some volunteer. Often the Crag Rats are mentioned in the *Hood River News,* especially when we've completed a difficult rescue. Technically speaking, the sheriff's office is in charge of any search and rescue effort that occurs off a marked road. But because of the size of our town, firefighters perform just as many rescues up some trails, when they are activated by dispatch automatically with a possible medical situation. The fire department does not usually respond to the technical rescues in extreme terrain, but they are quick to head up the trail to bring down a patient with a fractured ankle or sprained knee. Jeff has taken over as fire chief recently and part of his goal is to get the firefighters and mountain rescuers to work better together. This is our turf, but they can respond more quickly to the trailhead, which is a scant five miles from the town.

When I get to the gravel bar, I find a cluster of people at the water's edge.

"Hi. I'm Dr. Van Tilburg, search and rescue," I say as I un-holster my pack. "What happened?"

"He jumped from the cliff, hurt his back," reports his friend.

"How are you feeling?" I ask him.

"My back hurts." The boy is prone on an inflatable rubber raft, half in the water, with a pile of wet towels over him. I quickly check his ABCs. He is, like everyone who gets injured up here, mildly hypothermic and possibly has a spine injury that I can't to-tally access in the field.

"Five from twenty-eight," I call Joe. "I'm at the scene. Male with a back injury at the gravel bar."

"I need a transport recommendation," says Joe.

"He's stable. The litter is five minutes away. I think he's okay to go down the trail," I say, knowing we can get him down the trail in about the same time it would take for a helicopter to ar-rive. If we called in a helicopter every time we had an accident here, they'd be coming every week during the summer. It is costly and, more important, risky. This rescue is so much easier than the last jumper.

The firefighters and I load the boy in the stretcher, cover him with dry blankets, and carry him across the gravel bar. The river rocks are smooth and slippery, so we walk slowly. When we arrive at the Sunrise Falls Trail, we tie a rope to the stretcher, put one rescuer on each rail, and send everyone to the rope. In one com-bined motion, we haul the litter hand over hand up the trail: a dozen rescuers pulling the rope. The trail is steep enough that we need the rope but not so steep that we need to set up a haul sys-tem. At the confluence of the two trails, Crag Rats Devon Wells, Jim Wells, and Brian Hukari show up. I take a step back from the litter and let someone else carry for a time. A paramedic wants to put in an IV.

"What do you think, Doc—should we call the helicopter," he asks, referring to the aeromedical medevac chopper trauma center used for transport from the trailhead parking lot, not the military chopper used for extrication.

"He's stable. I think he's okay to go by ground," I say. We wheel the patient down the trail.

Later, when the *Hood River News* calls me for a report and a photo, I tell them this was a "team response between fire department and Crag Rats." The only picture I send is the one with seven firefighters huddled around the litter. In a small town, everyone needs credit for volunteer work.

We go back to Sunrise Falls a half dozen times every summer. We get four calls in one month, all from cliff jumpers. One page comes while I'm in the middle of my daughter's dance performance. I sneak outside after she takes her turn on stage; I call Penny from the front steps of the school auditorium.

"I can go as soon as Skylar's dance is finished," I say after getting a report from Penny. I'm not leaving a moment sooner.

"I'm at the dance recital too, right out front!" exclaims Penny.

"I'm on the front steps!" I turn around and see Penny ten feet away on a bench under a tree. We smile and hang up our cell phones.

This time, we're looking for a different type of cliff jumper. When the Forest Service noticed a car parked in the same place for a week with three parking tickets on the windshield, they ran the plates. It turned up a missing person. The sheriff then got on the phone, finally reached the man's mom, and we had a possible suicide.

An hour later, John Ingles, Dennis Klein, Paul Crowley, Steve Castagnoli, and I hike up Sunrise Falls Trail along with a sheriff's deputy. On our way up, we meet a dozen Boy Scouts on their way to an overnight at the seven-mile campsite. We ask them to keep an eye out for the man.

"Great job for the Scouts," said Dennis.

It's close to 6 P.M., so we split up to be most efficient. Paul, Dennis, and the deputy hike an old deer trail to the creek bottom and clamber through the thick underbrush at the base of the mile-long cliff. Mostly, the three scamper over huge downed longs and bushwhack through thickets of vine maple and poison oak.

John, Steve, and I take rope rescue gear to the four most likely spots a jumper would choose. At the four main promontories on the cliff-side trails, all of which overlook the creek bottom one hundred feet below, we set up a rappel station. After anchoring webbing around a stout tree, Steve and I lower John over the first cliff to look. John kicks loose dirt and rock. Just because he is tight on a rope doesn't mean he can't get hurt by a falling rock or dirt. No luck.

We hurry to the next promontory, then the next, as we work our way up the trail. Nearing dusk, we have enough time to search Sunrise Falls. Steve hikes around to the top, the spot where most cliff jumpers launch into the pool. John searches the bushes surrounding the pool. After shucking my socks and boots, I wade into the icy cauldron and walk in up to my shorts. I peer into the recesses of the box canyon. I see Steve on the cliff above me and call him by radio.

"I have a good look of most of the pool but can't see the ledge around the corner. Should I keep going?"

"I can see the ledge. It's clear," Steve replies. Thankfully, I don't have to go swimming.

By dusk we have searched all four cliffs and the falls. On the way down, we find one more possible spot a jumper might launch. I quickly set up an anchor on a tree and prepare to lower John off the cliff, first calling Dennis on the radio to make sure they are clear below us. John then drops over, but he can't see much because the canopy is too dense.

It takes twenty minutes to hike down the trail and rendezvous with the team scouring the canyon bottom. We walk back to our cars. No body.

The next day two searchers head up Sunrise Falls Trail to continue the search. They run into a frantic Boy Scout leader, the one we had seen the day before. A young Scout was climbing a log that morning, slipped, fell, hit his head, and died. Two hikers just happened to be passing by, and one was a doctor, who performed CPR for an hour, but the boy did not live. A two-person search team went up looking for the suicide jumper, and ended up carrying out a young boy.

The day following the Boy Scout's death, Roger Nelson hiked all the way to the seven mile campsite looking for the suicidal man. That same day, we had two more calls, one to Skamania County for a missing hiker and a second to a man who had hiked up the Pacific Crest Trail, sprained his ankle, and spent the night on the trail. Five calls in one weekend—our team was maxed.

Five days later, Joe Wampler hikes up the trail to investigate a "foul smell." Right at the base of the cliff, one of those where Steve and I had lowered John, he finds two boots sticking up among the downed logs and thick brush. A searcher would have to be within two feet to see the boots. They are deeply hidden in the thick brush.

Jay Sherrerd, Jeff Prichar, and Don Wiley head down to bring out the body with a rope-raising system. It had been two weeks since the death. Don almost passes out from the bad smell. Afterward Jeff hosed down our litter with a special antimicrobial spray.

"Our litter smelled rather gamey," said Jeff.

A nd, just when we'd had our last call in Sunrise Falls for the summer, I receive another page. Hot August day: another cliff jumper in Sunrise Falls.

It seemed surreal, like déjà vu. I drive to Sunrise Falls, find the sheriff, and grab my pack. I leave my wet suit and life vest in the car: *I can't be swimming again,* I think. I need to go as light as possible since I'm the first Crag Rat here. I run the trail, slip down to the gravel bar on the mud, and climb over the rocks that are strewn across the gravel bay.

"Where is he?" I ask some bystanders. A crowd of people clad in bathing suits linger around the gravel bar.

"In the water," one bystander says.

"Who's with her? Any medical?"

"I think there's two guys over there: a paramedic and a police guy."

"Do they have a radio?"

"Don't know."

"Did they take any gear?"

"Don't know."

I drop my pack, strip my clothes down to my shorts and boots. I shove my radio in a freezer bag and leave my pack at the gravel bar; I'm peeved that I left my wet suit and life vest in the car. The last time I swam here, I couldn't see the patient. This time, I can see a small group huddling around the patient on a rocky ledge above the thundering waterfall. It is a stone's throw from the last water rescue.

I wade into the icy cold water and in ten seconds, I'm swimming. My heavy boots make it hard to kick while I'm trying to hold the radio overhead. I'm only able to do the sidestroke. I make it to a rock wall at one end of the box canyon, toss up my radio, and clamber up the side.

I look up to see the patient is stabilized on a backboard. A guy looks up with bright eyes and a jubilant smile.

"Hi, Doc! Here we are again," says Charlie.

"Hey, same place, same injury, different day. Did you lock your gun in your car this time?"

"Yup!"

"I never expected to see you."

"I was hoping you'd show up."

"Fine day for another water rescue."

Walter, a fire department volunteer is huddled over the patient. I can see Walter's clothes are soaked. He's wearing jeans and a cotton T-shirt.

"What's the story," I ask Walter.

"Jumped off the cliff. Hit the water. Temporarily paralyzed, possibly three minutes. She was found facedown in the water. Probable LOC. Buddies and bystanders dragged her to shore," Walter says as he points to two others on the ledge. It's the patient's son and a Good Samaritan who pulled her to shore.

"Who brought out the backboard?" I ask.

"I did," says Walter. Swimming out wearing jeans and dragging a backboard must have been no easy task.

"Good work," I say to Walter. "Hi," I say to the patient. "I'm the doc. I'm going to do a quick check, but it looks like you're in good hands." I do a rapid exam: patient in full spine immobilization. Alert, oriented, breathing fine. No chest or abdomenal injury. Wiggles toes and fingers. Neurology exam normal.

"Good job, Walter. Not much for me to do," I say, knowing there's no reason for me to take control when Walter did the brunt of the work stabilizing the patient. I walk up to a high point on the ledge, about ten feet above the patient. I reassemble my radio and call Joe.

"We're going to need the floats again."

"Stand by," says someone at SAR base, the parking lot at the trailhead.

In twenty minutes, I hear on the radio that Roger is coming up the trail. We are not getting the floats for the stretcher but rather a floating backboard.

We wait, again, at Sunrise Falls, on the sharp rocky ledge, across the plunge pool from the last water rescue. A fine mist wafts across the bowl from the waterfall. We shiver. In a half hour Roger Nelson shows up with the floating backboard. I see him arrive at the gravel bar. He's fifty yards away but, between the icy cold pool and the thundering waterfall, he seems distant.

I see another rescuer, whom I don't recognize, strip down, don a wet suit, grab the backboard, and head into the pool.

"John," he says as he climbs up to the ledge after swimming over with the backboard. He is from an ambulance crew from a neighboring county, nearly 100 miles away.

"How did you guys get called to respond here?" I say incredulously.

"Dispatch," he says. Then he gruffly attempts to reevaluate the patient. "We need a blood pressure and pulse. We need to transfer this patient to the floating backboard. I'll get my other paramedic out here so we can get her across the pool." I see that this can quickly turn into a turf war. I think John doesn't know who Walter and I are.

"I'm Dr. Van Tilburg, Crag Rats," I say calmly. "This is Walter from the fire department. Our patient's been stable for an hour. We don't need any more people on the ledge. We have four of us who can swim her out. We don't really need a blood pressure. Her radial pulse is strong at ninety," I say referring to the general rule that if a patient has a strong radial pulse, his or her blood pressure is adequate. I also know that if we undress the patient to complete another medical evaluation, we'll loose valuable time.

"Why don't we stack the backboards together so we don't have to transfer her," says Walter. Instantly, the tone changes to cooperation. Turf wars among rescuers can get sticky. It took us several rescues and a month to get a good working relationship with fire department. In addition to the Crag Rats, the fire department, Charlie from the county sheriff, and the paramedics, at the gravel bar we've got Forest Service personnel, and at the trailhead we have a two-person radio crew from Light Wave, a volunteer group of computer guys who provide SAR radio communications. Six agencies—everyone is eager to help, many of us are qualified to take control of the medical situation. Typically, in a rescue, one person is designated medical and another specifically focuses on extrication and evacuation.

"Where do you need me?" says Charlie, cheerily.

"You, Walter, John, and I will swim her out," I say to the crew. I turn to the brother and bystanders and point to the gravel bar, "Can you guys swim out on your own?"

"Sure," they say.

We stack the two backboards, strap the patient to both, and gently lower her into the water. Charlie, submerged to his chest, presses down on the feet to push up the patient's head. Then the four of us start kicking while pushing the double-backboarded patient across the pool. Walter and I are on each side to keep the patient from flipping over, Charlie presses down on the feet, and the paramedic supports the head on his stomach, since the paramedic is the only one who thought to bring a life vest. The water is icy and swimming while wearing boots and trying to keep the patient from tipping is extremely difficult. In addition to the physical demands, it takes mental focus. In five minutes, we can touch the bottom. We slowly emerge from the pool and pass the patient to dry rescuers. Roger and another firefighter lift the patient out of the water and gently set her on the ground. Two more firefighters bring over the stretcher, with the wheel already attached to the bottom. We lift the patient directly onto a stretcher.

Then, the second paramedics starts doing an exam. He wants to undress the patient, put the patient in a sleeping bag, and take vital signs. The paramedic talks with his colleague about transferring the patient in the ambulance or calling a helicopter.

Walter says "We're transferring this patient."

"No, we'll take her," says the paramedic.

"No," says Walter, "this is our call." Clearly we have several medical personnel on the scene and at least two ambulances who can transfer the patient. The patient is listening to the banter. Rarely do I take complete charge. I'm usually the senior medical person on the scene, but I'm never the one with the most rope rescue or evacuation experience. Often I defer to my colleagues on those topics.

But here, we need to move the patient down the trail. One thing I've learned from Jim Wells is that someone in the field needs to take charge every once in a while. At Sunrise Falls, the Crag Rats have ultimate jurisdiction on a wilderness rescue, despite the multiple agencies standing at the gravel bar and despite the adrenaline surging through everyone's blood. I can see this is going to be an issue if I don't step in.

"Look," I say," I'm a doc with Crag Rats. This woman's been stable for two hours. Walter's been with her for the duration. It's about twenty minutes down the trail. We're ready to go. I'd say we don't delay and get going. We do this all the time and so does the fire department," I explain.

"And we'll take the patient in our ambulance," says Walter. What I though was going to be a major scuffle, instantly turns into a cooperative effort.

The patient is large and heavy so it takes an hour to get down the trail.

We haul the stretcher across the gravel bar, and then down the trail. The woman is so heavy Walter expresses concern when we get to the mile-long section of cliffs, the same cliffs we had searched for the man who committed suicide.

"We'd better belay her," says Walter. Walter stays with the patient, and I set up a rope belay on the cliff-side cable. I attach one end of the rope to the stretcher, clip a carabiner to the cable, then thread through the carabiner in such a fashion that it slides through but can be slowed easily by my hand. This carabiner wrap is a quick-break mechanism that will slow the litter or even stop it if a rescuer were to stumble and loose grip.

At the next Crag Rat meeting, we debrief as usual. Sometimes we have a laugh, sometimes we analyze the rescue in depth. This time, we don't spend too much effort trying to figure out why this person launched off a 70-foot cliff into a dark, icy, dangerous plunge pool. We all know the thrill of adventure is captivating, all-encompassing. We discuss there's a dire safety issue at Sunrise Falls; we've had way too many serious injuries here. Maybe a sign, a closure, a fence is needed?

Todd Wells reminds everyone to bring a life jacket and perhaps a wetsuit for Sunrise Falls call outs. Jim Wells tells us to always consider a water evacuation from the falls because the cliff is too dangerous. We discuss buying our own floating backboard and plan a water rescue training for later in the year. Although not typically a discipline of mountain rescue, as of this summer, water rescue becomes another reason to call upon the Crag Rats.

FALL

CHAPTER 10

Disappearance in Gifford Pinchot

On day five in the search for a missing woman, Roger Nelson, Helmut Reidl, and I are tromping amid huckleberry fields and enormous groves of hemlock and fir. I have a ridiculous assortment of electronic gear strapped to my chest, that at sporadic moments make extraterrestrial noises: SAR radio, GPS, cell phone, camera. Every twenty minutes, I call in GPS coordinates; but without the manual, I can't remember how to activate the electronic compass. So Helmut pulls out his trusty old liquid-filled compass and points us to our assigned bearing, 270 degrees.

Ground searches in the forest may not be as exciting as technical rope rescues, but these searches are costly and they take much more time. The three of us are helping a neighboring county in Washington State with this search for a missing woman. More than a hundred rescuers have gathered from Washington and Oregon. We are ground pounding, or searching by foot, the thick woods around Steamboat Lake, a remote area of Gifford Pinchot National Forest. One of the oldest national forests, it was originally part of the Mount Rainier Forest Reserve, established in 1897, and renamed after Gifford Pinchot in 1949 after the United States Forest Services first chief, an environmentalist and conservationist who thought the forest should be used for "the greatest good of the greatest number in the long run."

The 1,312,000 acre forest includes the Mount St. Helens National Volcanic Monument and seven wilderness areas including Mount Adams and Indian Heaven Wilderness, where the kids and I go backpacking. The area abounds with campers, backpackers, fishers, hunters, mushroom gatherers, huckleberry pickers, and in winter, snowshoers, backcountry skiers, and snowmobilers.

The subject, a forty-nine-year-old woman, was camping near Steamboat Lake with her family. On her way home, she turned off the gravel road. Her family, following in another car, said they thought she was stopping for a bathroom break or to collect some wood. The family also said that she had left home unexpectedly in the past, so when she didn't show up at home they didn't report her missing for five days. When deputies found the car—full tank of gas, no flat tires, and her cigarettes on the seat—it started right up. Now we are ten days removed from the last sighting and five days into the search. After driving up Forest Road 88 in a daze, having just worked the night shift at the hospital, I find Roger and Helmut.

"Doughnuts," Roger offers with a smile. "Help yourself. I've already signed you in."

"Thanks, might have one."

"I've already had a couple." Helmut smiles. A native of Austria and our current Big Squeak, or president, he is a jovial and organized man who speaks with a thick accent. He has brought the deep love and rich culture of European ski mountaineering and ski instruction to our group.

"Anyone else show up?" I ask, noticing only three Crag Rats amid a dozen searchers gathering for the morning briefing.

"Three's pretty good for a weekday morning, don't you think?"

says Roger. "People don't get too excited over a ground search, especially when it is day five."

Today Helmut, Roger, and I are assigned, along with three other searchers, to an area dubbed Priority Area 7, about a half mile from the dirt road where the woman's car was found. We start a search line heading southwest through the thick forest and dense underbrush. The right-hand border of our search area is flagged by hunter-orange surveyor's ribbon from yesterday. It is my job to keep the ribbon and border in sight. The six in our team fan out twenty feet apart. On our left-hand border, another searcher ties surveyor's ribbon to trees for the next group. We stay in voice and visual contact, but the foliage is so thick, we could easily miss the subject, unless we walk right into her. Everywhere I look I see twenty places a body could be lying. This is not the most effective search, but without a thousand rescuers to cover the 200-acre search area, this is as good as we can do.

We bushwhack through a mix of huckleberry, salal, Oregon grape, and vine maple. The dense brush is further thickened by large downed logs, rocks, depressions, and hillocks. It takes twenty minutes to hike to an abandoned logging road, the end of our assigned search area. We call in our last coordinates. A sheriff's vehicle picks us up, and we are shuttled back to the top of the slope. We make a pass through Area 8, following our south flag line from Area 7. It takes another half hour. Then we hike through Area 9 in the same way. After two hours of searching, we wait at the top of Area 10 and open brown-bag lunches brought up by a deputy. Just as we are about to eat, the radio cracks to life.

"I thought I heard a hello," says a rescuer from team 5. Immediately SAR base kicks into high gear. Following instructions from SAR base, three members of team 5 speedily search the surrounding area. When that turns up nothing, several members start doing circle searches around the point they heard the voice. Meanwhile, a deputy drives our team to the Steamboat Mountain trailhead. Our heart rates are pumped up from the excitement and the physical effort of clambering up the trail. At the top of Area 5 we peer down a steep slope about two hundred feet above team 5, but the thickly tangled brush is so dense we can't see or hear them.

Helmut, Roger, the two other searchers, and I quickly fan out through the brush, alternately yelling and whistling, then stopping and listening. Helmut lets loose a beautiful yodel.

Of the two dozen or so call outs we do every year, about a third will be for a lost person. Missing-person searches sometimes take several days to complete and are costly. In 2005, 730 SAR missions were launched in Oregon. Most commonly, searches are for hikers, motor vehicles, or hunters. Only thirty of the 730 were for mountain climbers. Our small rural county of 20,000 residents typically spends between $1,000 to $4,000 for vehicles, deputies' pay, and equipment for each rescue, somewhere between one and two dozen annually. Fortunately most missions only last a few hours and mainly require volunteers. But sometimes missions can be lengthy and rack up significant costs. We tend to hear about the rare and expensive rescues, like the two-week search for a downed plane in Arizona in 2003 that cost an estimated $2 million. Or the 2006 search for two missing climbers on Mount Foraker in Denali National Park that ran up $127,000. In an extreme example, one of the most expensive SAR mission in the United States occurred on Mount Hood when the climbers slid into a crevasse and the $7 million Air Force Reserve Pave Hawk crashed, as discussed in chapter three. Fortunately, these costly rescues are not the norm.

In addition to sheriff's deputies and volunteers, fire-rescue crews and Forest Service personnel often respond to rescues. In a rural county like ours, firefighters are both paid and volunteers; and both agencies are funded by local, state, or federal taxes. Only an ambulance-transport bill can be billed to a patient's health insurance.

A helicopter can run up the price of a rescue. If a helicopter from the military is used, as is done a half dozen times a year in Hood River County, federal taxpayers pay $2,800 per hour for a Black Hawk, and $7,500 per hour for a much larger twin-rotor Chinook. Often the military budgets for "training exercises" and sees real-world rescues as experience for combat missions.

Volunteer time is difficult to quantify. In a typical busy year of twenty rescues, a Crag Rat may donate thirty hours on actual rescues and another fifty on maintaining equipment and training. Crag Rats spend their own money for their equipment: boots, clothing, climbing helmet, headlamp, and such.

Rescue cost is usually the hottest topic in outdoor Web forums that follow big rescue missions: should the rescued person bear any of the financial burden?

User fees, in the form of permits for hiking and climbing, offset some costs. In Mount Rainier National Park, for example, climbers who attempt the peak pay a $30 fee, and McKinley climbers in Denali National Park pay $150. Mounts Adams and St. Helens have climbing fees as well. The fees pay for protecting the environment, managing human waste, and rangers who respond to rescues among other duties. In Colorado, hikers can voluntarily buy a Colorado Outdoor Recreation Search and Rescue, or CORSAR, card. The $3 annual fee goes into a state SAR fund. This way, users of the outdoors help contribute to the cost of rescues.

Climbers who are members of the national American Alpine Club, the Portland-based Mazamas, or other climbing groups, have SAR insurance. The policy covers members up to $3,000 after a deductible for backcountry rescues up to 6,000 meters in elevation. Although climbing Everest is not covered, it can be added with an optional per-trip rider. Generally, the sheriff's department does not bill the insurance for these missions.

In certain cases, private companies provide SAR services and bill health insurance. American Medical Response, an ambulance company contracted by Clackamas County on Mount Hood's popular south side, has a reach-and-treat team. Outfitted with winter clothing, medical backpacks, and snowshoes, they can climb up the mountain to respond to an injured person. They do not specifically bill for the search and rescue, but they can charge the patient's health insurance for medical transport by ambulance to the hospital.

Debate has raged for a long time about whether a rescuing agency should be allowed to send the bill to the rescued. The National Forest and National Park Services sometimes bill patients for damage to property or give citations with fines for those who "create or maintain a hazardous or physically offensive condition." But they cannot specifically charge for SAR services. Privately owned ski resorts, on the other hand, have been known to bill reckless skiers who require rescues when they break laws or duck ropes.

In 1995, Oregon legislators passed a law allowing the county sheriff to send a bill to a rescued person. It was inspired by a group of climbers on Mount Hood who were caught in a storm. Lawmakers did not feel taxpayers should pay for "those jokers on the mountain," referring to lost climbers. The first-of-its-kind law allowed reimbursement to up to $500 if "reasonable care was not exercised" and "applicable laws were violated." In other words, someone would have to be grossly negligent or knowingly break the law. (Paradoxically, the "jokers on the mountain" were actually prepared. They waited three days on the mountain until the weather cleared. They climbed down on their own, without needing rescue.)

Our sheriff has sent a bill twice. In 1995, a man who was leading a youth group up a creek jumped into a plunge pool and died. Because of the high blood alcohol level found during his postmortem exam, the sheriff felt the man was at fault. The family received a bill but did not pay. Similarly, when an intoxicated hiker fell on a trail and sustained a leg injury, he was sent a bill for the costly rescue. Again, he did not pay. However, one sheriff's office in Oregon did get paid. In May 1996, Deschutes County, in central Oregon, was called to rescue a group of boaters who knowingly had proceeded past Closed signs, where bystanders shouted warnings, and drifted downriver to the class VI rapids of Benham Falls, required help, and verbally abused the rescuers. The five boaters split a $1,560 bill.

Four other states now have laws similar to Oregon's. In Idaho, you can be billed up to $4,000 for entering closed areas. In New Hampshire, you can be fined up to $10,000 for recklessly or intentionally creating a situation causing an emergency response. This law has been used eight times, mostly when hikers have been lost or caught in foul weather, have no experience or equipment, and call 911 on a cell phone. In California, the limit is $12,000 and one has to be guilty of "gross negligence" and willfully entering a closed area. Thus simple negligence, like forgetting proper shoes, or natural hazards, like lightning, does not apply. Hawaii has legislated no reimbursement limit if the rescued violated trespass laws, disregarded warnings, and failed to exercise reasonable care.

One concern of groups like the Mountain Rescue Association and American Alpine Club is that if people know they could be billed for a rescue, they could delay calling for help, thus making their predicament more dire. In a few anecdotal cases, people in crisis have delayed calling for help because they feared paying for it.

A second argument against sending a bill is that we use tax dollars to pay for police and fire services. Why not for search and rescue?

And, third, some government and volunteer agencies feel that charging for rescues also mandates rescue, thus opening public agencies to lawsuits. In 1991, the Tenth Circuit Court of Appeals ruled in favor of rescuers in *Johnson* v. *Department of Interior*. The court declared that a dead climber's estate could not sue the National Park Service in Grand Teton for the way a rescue was performed because no regulations or formal policies outlined conduct for SAR and thus there is no "duty to rescue." Many people believe that if a person can be charged for the cost of a rescue, agencies would have a duty to rescue. One major lawsuit for an allegedly bungled rescue would instantly deplete years of recouped costs from sending the bills to rescued persons. People felt so strongly about this shield that in 1994, when Denali National Park proposed a mountaineering fee of $200 to include SAR reimbursement, the Park Service dropped the SAR coverage and lowered the fee to $150. The Park Service did not want to directly charge climbers in advance for search and rescue, because they would then create a duty to rescue and thus be liable every time someone called for help.

Instead of charging for rescue, the Park Service decided to be proactive in preventing accidents. Education is, fortunately, effective in limiting the number of people who get into trouble. For example, Denali National Park requires a climbing-safety class before a person is issued a permit to ascend Mount McKinley. In the class, rangers inform climbers they can die, and that rescue is often neither immediate nor even possible. Although the number of climbers on Mount McKinley has continued to rise, the number of accidents, deaths, and rescues has dropped since the climbing-safety program started in 1995.

Something similar needs to be implemented with the Sunrise Falls cliff jumpers.

After an hour of scouring the Area 5 for the source of the "help" noise, we surmise the voice was perhaps the wind or someone's imagination. Our team asks for a shuttle back to base camp. Helmut, Roger, and I eat our lunch. It's two o'clock and I must look terrible.

"Go home, Chris," says Helmut. "You need rest."

"Yeah, get out of here," says Roger. He and Helmut will be out until dusk. At the day's end, the search will be suspended after five days. Three days later, I'm at work when the Crag Rats are paged again, for the same mission: the search is resuming for one day after the sheriff obtained new information. I need to spend the weekend with my girls, but Jim Wells plans to help.

Four months later, two elk hunters in the Steamboat Lake area stumble upon human remains at Mosquito Creek, in what was Priority Area 3, a heavily searched area. The body is upright, a mile from where the woman's car was parked and a mere 150 feet from a search ribbon. Searchers may have walked within thirty feet without spotting her. There is a good chance she was dead before the search even began.

Sometimes we never find the lost. Sometimes they appear in a few days, beat up but walking. Sometimes they are dead and turn up many months later. Longest we've had in these parts was twenty-one years. On November 13, 1980, two Mount Adams climbers, Gary Claeys and Matt Larson, were reported missing. A full-scale search operation was initiated, although a brutal storm raged for a week and hindered search efforts. A tent was located at False Summit, at 11,000 feet, and tracks were seen heading east. Rescuers suspected the lost climbers tried to descend the Mazama Glacier, fell into a crevasse, and perished.

In 2001, an unusually low snow year with the lowest snow-pack in seventy years, many glaciers and snowfields receded to the lowest levels in decades. On October 9, a recreational climber on a routine ascent of Mount Adams found a rope, chipped away some ice, and discovered frozen feet in the Crescent Glacier. Rescuers climbed up to the glacier and found the body. It was wedged in a melting crack of the glacier. It took all day to excavate the rope, the body, and, a second body, found attached to the other end of the rope. The sun had finally opened the twenty-one-year-old tomb of Claeys and Larson.

CHAPTER 11

Dead Man on Suksdorf Ridge

People die in the mountains, but it is not always doom and gloom. Today on Mount Adams we're called to a rescue *and* recovery: the dual mission of finding the living and retrieving the dead. I have a lot of respect for these peaks, especially the remote, wild terrain of Mount Adams, which I've climbed, skied, and snowboarded more times than I've bothered to count. At 12,276 feet high, this volcano was first called Pahto, or son of the Great Spirit, by the Klickitat and Yakima tribes. Because it is tucked deeper into the Cascades, Mount Adams was hidden from the view of British explorers sailing up the Columbia's hundred-mile estuary and thus not immediately "discovered." The peak was named by Thomas Farnham in 1843, after President John Adams. Local mountaineers A. G. Aiken, Edward J. Allen, and Andrew Burge reported the first ascent in 1854.

This mission call out was first sent to our colleagues at Central Washington Mountain Rescue (CWMR) late on Saturday night, since Mount Adams is in Yakima County, Washington. Overdue climbers are a regular occurrence in the mountains. Often they are found on their way back down, having taken an extra day for any number of reasons, such as poor weather or difficult climbing conditions. This search, however, came on the heels of an uncharacteristic four-day August blizzard: snow up high, torrential rain in the valley. To make matters more complicated, a lightning strike from the storm started a forest fire on the access road to the South Climb trailhead, thus closing the mountain for climbing. On a busy summer weekend up to two hundred climbers can use this route.

After searching all Sunday morning, a three-person CWMR team found a lone tent at midday at 9,500 feet. Inside they found a seventy-year-old man and his dead partner, who'd had a heart attack two days earlier. Both men had climbed the mountain more than a dozen times. After his partner died of a heart attack and the storm rolled in, the other man did what years of mountaineering had taught him: stay put, wait out the storm. So despite being holed up in a tent for several days with his dead partner, the man was in good shape when rescuers located him: hydrated, nourished, warm, dry, and able to summon a weak smile.

That was several hours ago. The three-person crew faces a daunting series of tasks: bring the man down, haul his dead partner's body down, try to find their way with a thick cloud cap settling over the volcano, avoid the wildfire in the thick woods below the timberline, and beat the sun which is descending to the horizon. So on a Sunday at noon, late in the climbing season, I rally to head to the mountains. I dig glacier travel gear out of the garage—ice ax, crampons, winter clothing—and hit the road with Jay and Steve.

"I brought everything," says Jay, not knowing exactly what he will need.

"I packed light," says Steve.

We drive across the Hood River Toll Bridge, up State Route 141, past the tiny rural farming community of Trout Lake, into the dense old-growth forest of Mount Adams Wilderness, and up the gravel road to Morrison Creek Horse Camp. A few miles up the gravel road, a Forest Service truck blocks further passage.

"Fire, no entrance," says a ranger.

"We're mountain rescue. We're helping with the climbing accident."

"Oh, okay. Be careful—there are fire crews all over the road."

We lumber up the dirt track in four-wheel drive, creep past big earthmovers trenching a fire line, and almost get stuck in a mud hole where a tanker truck is filling a small water-tender pickup. As we drive higher and deeper into the mountains, the road becomes rocky and rutted. The road ends at Cold Springs camp, 5,500 feet elevation. A slew of cars are jammed in the small dirt parking area but it looks abandoned of humans. We get a brief report from the sole CWMR volunteer staffing the base, load up our packs, and set off at a brisk trot. It's a beautiful Indian summer evening, and it reminds me of my first climb on this snow-clad peak.

On a windless weekend toward the end of June two decades ago, my brother Pete and I decided to climb Mount Adams. It had been good windsurfing all week, but the crowds at the brew pub where I worked for five summers during medical school were making me edgy. I was so sick of drunken tourists and measly tips and "I'll have another pint" yells, I needed to get away and climb into the mountains. I had worked, night after night, on slow-motion autopilot like an ameba. The sun dodged behind Underwood Mountain, and the sky turned from bright blue to dark blue-green to aqua, a shade that matched the river. Pete and I had our sights set on the Southwest Chute, a narrow avalanche gully that is the best ski and snowboard descent on the mountain.

"I hope I have everything," I said.

"Me, too. Come on," said Pete. Pete's old blue and white Toyota Land Cruiser FJ-55 ran noisily as we headed north on Highway 141. The tires buzzed on the asphalt and warm air rushed in the windows. It was too loud to talk. After twenty miles, we stopped at the Mount Adams Ranger Station and signed the climber's register.

"It's going to be crowded. Look at the list. We've got to get an early start tomorrow," I said.

"I was counting on crowds," said Pete. I signed our names, and went through the checklist: map, compass, first aid kit, sleeping bags, ice axes, crampons, extra food, extra clothing, stove, candles, matches. We had no rope and no tent.

"What CB channel are we on, Pete?" This was back before cell phones and Family Radio Service.

"Seventeen." I wrote it on the register.

We continued north and turned on Forest Road 80. CAUTION: ONE LANE WITH TURNOUTS, said a bright yellow sign. The one-lane paved soon turned to one-lane gravel then dirt, rocks, and deep ruts. At Cold Springs Camp, we put on our boots, humped up our packs, and started walking. The warm evening air was adulterated with fragrance of subalpine fir. The quiet was sparked with the occasional wisp of helicopter seed pods and bushwhacking squirrels, magpies, pine martens, and chipmunks. The sky glowed yellow and orange. We came to a patch of snow every few hundred yards and welcomed the coolness on our bare sweaty legs.

At dusk the sky turned to pink and purple. Stars appeared. Gaining altitude, we stopped to pull on fleece, eat trail mix, and guzzle water. A bit later we came to the first snowfield and put on gaiters. The hardening snow crunched under foot. The sky darkened and the mountain loomed above us, towering like the Great Pyramid of Cheops. We continued north past the timberline where the trees got smaller, more wiry, and windblown with tiny needles pointing southeast, a process called flagging, in which the persistent high-altitude wind shapes the trees. We arrived at Crescent Glacier by dark. My pack was heavy with my snowboard lashed on, and I was carrying a new ice ax Pete had bought me for my birthday.

We kept a good pace with Pete in the lead. He plodded along rhythmically. I struggled, sometimes stepping awkwardly trying to match his cadence. The snow got progressively firmer and easier to hike on as the evening cooled and we gained elevation. A chilly wind blew down the glacier.

After an hour hiking on snow, we reached the first bivouacs around 8,000 feet. Scores of past climbers had built a series of four-foot-high half circle rock shelters blocking the west wind. The ground had been cleared of rocks so that climbers could sleep on remnants of volcanic ash. We saw many dome tents silhouetted against the sky, most darkened. In one tent I saw a flickering headlamp of someone rearranging their gear. Two people higher up brushed their teeth. As they spit, toothpaste was illuminated by the moon and splat on the rocks in white-blue sparks. With the moon up and the glacier lit brightly, I felt like I was inside a lit house at night and the people on the rocks could see me better than I could see them. I felt exposed. Pete and I hiked past most of the tents, going faster now that the snow was hard. We filled our bottles from the runoff above Crescent Glacier, and I dropped a few iodine purification tablets into my bottle. We rested again briefly. My feet got cold, and I put on my fleece jacket.

"We could stop and find a bivouac. But there are too many

people here. It may take a while to find a shelter," said Pete. "I know of one higher up if you want to keep going. We can camp in the snow if we can't find it."

"Sure," I said, knowing if we made it to the large flat area at 9,500 feet called the Lunch Counter, we would be on Suksdorf Ridge, just below the long snowfield leading to False Summit. The hardest part of the climb would come at the top of the morning.

At 11:00 P.M. we gained the ridge. With a small search of the rocky island that was perhaps fifty yards in diameter, Pete located the last bivouac, a tiny shelter only two feet high. Different from the others, it blocked the north wind because it was on Suksdorf Ridge. My toes were very cold: I took off my boots and massaged my feet. We unrolled our bags. I stayed awake for a while, looking at the stars, a billion more than I saw all year in medical school.

When my watch alarm rang at five, Pete was already up boiling water for an instant hot chocolate and coffee mixture. Boots of the first climbers chirped by on the snowfield next to us. I heard their heavy breathing and saw steam rising from their nostrils. We drank mocha while packing our gear. We set off on Suksdorf Ridge to False Summit.

On the way, I felt like was climbing an escalator running backward, making no progress. The white snowfield seemed to never end. My pack was heavy, so I had a sensation that the pack was pulling me outward. I didn't stop to look back at the rising yellow sun, fearing the weight might pull me into a long slide down the snowfield. It took ninety long minutes to reach False Summit, and along the way, I hated the climb. I wanted to turn back. It wasn't fun or even remotely enjoyable. But we finally reached False Summit, and the sun lifted high into the morning

sky. We sat on the rocks sticking out of the snow with still another hour's climb to go—across the saddle and up the final pitch
to the summit.

"That was tough," I said, not admitting I wanted to quit.

"Yeah, but it's not so bad now, huh." We ate trail mix and put
on sunglasses. A long string of fifty climbers dotted the snow on
the route below us. The walk across the saddle was easy, but the
last pitch to the summit was steep. I got dizzy at 12,000 feet. My
head pounded, and I felt my pulse in my temples. I walked three
steps, rested. Three steps, rested. Three steps, heavy steps, rested.

At 7:15 A.M. I finally crested the last sun cup, which are large
depressions in the snow formed by radiant heat of the sun over
the summer. I was ten minutes behind Pete, not knowing that I
was really on the summit until I spied Mount Rainier and Goat
Rocks to the north; Mount St. Helens stood to the west, a burnt,
dusty, snowless top. Low clouds to the southwest covered Portland
and the lower gorge up to Bonneville Dam.

Ahead was a smooth, silky descent on creamy snow. I anticipated the tight centripetal force pulling me in and the edge of the
snowboard pushing me out. I'd catch air off the sun cups. But on
the summit, Pete and I basked in the summer sun for an hour.
The top of a mountain: 12,276 feet high.

Now, years later, I'm hoofing it up the trail on an identical
evening to my first climb: warm yellow glow in the sky,
good company, crisp clean air. Unlike my first ascent on a recreational climb, I have a sense of urgency. I recall how tired I was on
my first climb; I imagine the old man was in outstanding shape.
About 500 feet above the timberline, we meet the dead man's
partner walking down with two rescuers.

"We're Crag Rats. Do you need any help?" I ask.

"We're okay," says a rescuer.

The dead man's partner smiles. It is a content, relaxed, comforting smile.

"He died. And it was stormy. I couldn't come down. I didn't want to risk it. I just stayed there," he says, obviously needing to tell his story. He starts rambling on about what happened. Jay and I stop to listen. That happens often after someone is rescued. They are so tense and tight during the fight for survival that when they are rescued, adrenaline pours out of the system and a full relaxation sets in. That's why someone can be near death for an entire day, but when the rescuers show up, they go into shock.

With my doctor's habit of assessing a patient, I deduce that the man is okay. He is alert, talking, and smiling, with no visible signs of shock. He's walking down, albeit slowly and without his pack, under his own power. He needs to process the experience of being stranded in a tent with his dead partner. Psychological trauma is perhaps the chief concern. Jay quickly picks up on the fact that he needs reassurance. Jay's good with direct questions, bringing his lawyer skills into the wilds.

"You did the right thing." Jay's done this so many times he knows just what to say.

"Good job, guys," I tell the other rescuers.

"I left my tent up there," says the man. The years of mountaineering has taught him well: never leave your gear. His experience and love of these mountains is evident in his smile. He will return for another climb, I'm sure of it. I see the old man's worn pack and ice ax; my own pack and ice ax are worn, too, but not to the extent of his. I still remember when mine were shiny and new, like the old man's must have been, many decades ago. We peel away and keep climbing.

"We'll get it," Jay says, hoping that someone grabbed it. All

of a sudden, I don't want to stand around and chat. My doctor in-
stincts tell me the man needs help coping with the emotions of
fear and loss and the tragic experience, but the rescuer in me urges
me to provide assistance where it is most needed. Others are still
high on the mountain, with a difficult and dangerous task.

"I hope I'm still climbing these mountains when I'm that
age," says Jay.

"Me, too." I think of my first ascent with Pete, the many
times since then I've climbed this peak, and the deep desire I have
to bring my kids up here. On the ascent, Jay and I discuss our
daughters' school, the biking we've been doing this summer with
and without kids, and our family trips to the coast. Steve, true to
his personality, is quiet but powering alongside us in a steady
rhythm. We meet up with Peter Garland, the Klickitat County
sheriff's deputy in charge of SARs.

"Glad to see you guys," he says. "We have no one in the
county with mountain experience. Thanks for coming."

"We're here to help," says Jay, smiling. He never misses a rescue if he can help it.

"You could have called us this morning," I say. "We could
have been here earlier."

"Well, that is a bit of a problem," explains Peter. "I would
have liked to call you. But the rules of SAR in Washington man-
date that I call the nearest state agency first, even though they are
four hours away in Yakima and you guys are one hour away. But
if you guys sign up as a Klickitat County SAR group, I can call
you earlier. But you have to be officially registered with the
state." That's a discussion Crag Rats need to have at a meeting.

"Oh," I say, knowing that persuading the Crag Rats to fill out
forms might be a chore.

"I think it's a good idea," says Jay.

"Let's bring it up at a meeting." I chuckle.

At last we reach the snow of Crescent Glacier, out of breath because we've been climbing quickly and chatting. The glacial ice is filthy from the last three months of blowing sand and dirt. Three-foot-deep sun cups and three inches of slush make walking very difficult.

We're about halfway up the glacier, when I look up and realize the blue sky has abruptly vanished. Cloud cap, a lenticular cloud atop the peak, has formed in the past half hour. It descended as we ascended. We meet the warm, moist fog at 8,500 feet and enter a white out: the sky and snow are the same color so it is difficult to see where one ends and the other starts. Then three rescuers from CWMR appear from the white fog dragging a body wrapped haphazardly in a tarp. Hunched over with heavy packs, they look tired. They can't slide the body down the snow because of the thick slush and deep sun cups.

"We're so glad to see you guys. We've been at this all day," says a rescuer.

"If we can get the body down to the foot of the glacier, a crew is following us up the trail," says Jay. The glacier terminus is a thousand feet below. With four fresh rescuers, the descent speeds up considerably. Jay takes over on the belay, the trailing rope that is used to tether the body so it doesn't go careening down the steep slope. Steve and I take another rope and fashion handles. We are able to walk ten feet ahead of the body and drag it over the sun cups.

In a half hour we reach the basin at the foot of the glacier. Abruptly the snow stops at the terminal moraine. Here the drainage from the glacier down to timberline is littered with basalt boulders, rocks, gravel, and sand. Rescuers from several adjacent counties in Washington are waiting with a body bag, stretcher, and a wheel. We hear on the radio that the uninjured partner has made it back to base, more rescuers are heading up the trail to help us, and the victim's family waits at the ranger station, anxious for the return of the body of their beloved, who had died on the mountain he had climbed two dozen times. *A good way to die,* I think. I've seen people endure a slow, painful death from cancer. I've seen bloody deaths from car crashes. But a painless death on a mountain you love in your eighth decade of life, with your best friend seems pretty high on the list for good ways to go.

At the glacier's terminus, Steve and I gently place the body in a heavy black vinyl body bag, then hoist it onto the litter. I suppress the urge to unwrap the tarp because of my desire to confirm the man is dead. Then we start the long task of carrying out the dead man down the rocky primitive trail. It meanders through basalt lava flows, over huge boulders, through a rocky stream drainage, and finally back down the approach trail to Cold Springs.

A month later, Peter Garland will attend a Crag Rat meeting to explain the laws and needs of Klickitat County. It would be much easier if we signed up as an official Klickitat County SAR team: they could call us earlier instead of using neighboring counties first. The Local SAR group is having trouble recruiting members, he explains. Ambulance crews now perform rope rescues with minimal training. The helicopters are all leaving for Iraq and Afghanistan. All we have to do is fill out a one-page form. When he leaves the meeting, we have our usual spirited discussion and some reluctance is voiced with good reason. Tradition, control, and the okay from our sheriff are all concerns.

"If they need me, they can call me," says Kirk Worrill. "We've done rescue over there for years without filling out some form."

"They could use us, but they can't call us," I try to explain. "The mission for the body recovery started at dawn, but we didn't get a call until noon."

"Plus their SAR insurance is much better if we get hurt or lose gear," says Jim.

"I think it is a good idea," says Devon Wells, Jim's Wells son and assistant fire chief for Hood River fire and rescue and a long-respected member of our unit.

"I'll do it," says Jay matter-of-factly.

Eventually we vote to participate in Klickitat County missions, contingent on getting it okayed with Dwayne Troxell, the deputy sheriff. But still, only a handful of members fill out the forms. I accept that change comes slowly with a group that is eight decades old and has a long, rich history and powerful traditions. It doesn't seem to make sense to me, since as a doctor I'm used to following rules and filling out paperwork. But Crag Rats would rather be saving lives in the mountains, and many of the guys don't see the need to fill out a form to do so.

In a few weeks we receive a thank-you and a small donation from the family. The Crag Rats are called for more rescues in Washington and respond, with or without official documentation.

CHAPTER 12

Mount Rainier

Late in the climbing season, Jay Sherrerd and I decide to climb Mount Rainier. We have an opportunity because of three key ingredients: good weather, great climbing conditions, and our schedules that align to give us both the time off.

But this is no ordinary weekend ascent of a snowcapped peak.

I spend a good portion of my time in the mountain wilderness and have climbed, skied, snowboarded, canyoneered, kayaked, surfed, and windsurfed around the world. I worry about getting injured in the wilds and nowhere is this fear more powerful than at the gnarliest peak of them all, the volcano that is synonymous with Pacific Northwest mountaineering: Rainier. It is so gargantuan that it is used as a training climb for Everest and McKinley. At 14,410 feet, it's a skosh shorter than California's Whitney (14,491 feet), but much more difficult. It contains more glacier ice than any other mountain in the United States outside Alaska. Massive glaciers with huge crevasses are only one hazard. The stormy Pacific Northwest climate another. It is a long, long climb to a very high summit. Rocks, ice, and seracs can crash, and avalanches can slide down the entire mountain.

The massive volcano jutting out from an endless sea of green conifers was first called Tahoma by natives (also Takhoma or Ta-co-bet), meaning "big mountain," "snowy peak," or "place where water begins." British explorer Captain George Vancouver named the volcano after Rear Admiral Peter Rainier when Vancouver spied the mountain in 1792 from Puget Sound. It was first climbed in 1870 by Hazard Stevens and Philemon Van Trump. Their Yakima guide reportedly refused to ascend to the summit, as the natives thought it a sacrilege. In 1899 this land became our fifth national park. Now, about ten thousand people attempt the mountain every year; roughly half make it to the top.

After several prior attempts and canceled opportunities due to lack of a partner, conflicting schedules, poor route conditions, or weather, Jay and I seize a chance to ascend the behemoth. The weather is predicted to be stable high pressure, which means it will be clear for a few days. The route is in excellent condition (translation: safe). Jay and I line up our schedules and find two open days during the week. Matt Ryan, a former ski patroller and avalanche-control expert who now works as a nurse, completes a quorum for a rope team.

As with any climbing trip, I start laying out gear in my garage a week before. It is not just my compulsive nature but a proven habit that gives me plenty of time to see if I need additional equipment or repairs on my existing gear. And it helps me mentally preparing for such an adventure. By e-mail, Matt, Jay and I coordinate who will drive and who will bring community gear: stove, tents, climbing rope.

I lay out three stacks of clothing. One set I will wear in the car, consisting of comfortable but "useless in the mountains" cotton. A second stack I will wear on the approach to our bivouac, Camp Sherman, elevation 10,000 feet: lightweight polyester shirt and underwear, nylon shorts, heavy synthetic socks, climbing boots, cap. A third stack goes in my pack: winter clothing. Even in warm weather, I prepare for the cold. I pack a long-sleeve zippered turtleneck and long underwear made from high-tech polyester, windproof fleece pants, down vest, high-tech PrimaLoft down-substitute sweater, Gore-Tex winter pants and parka, extra socks, lightweight gloves, heavy gloves, a fleece hat, and gaiters, which are heavy nylon cuffs that attach to my boots and pull up to just below my knees to keep snow out of my boot tops. I have double plastic climbing boots which I will wear from the car to the top of the mountain.

I assemble two caches of food: one for driving to and from the mountain and another for the climb. I pack the nonperishable food for climbing in two one-gallon freezer bags: trail mix, energy bars, dried fruit, lemon drops, and peanut butter and jelly sandwiches. The climb will take twenty-four hours and roughly 4,000 calories. But because weight and space are at a premium, I can only take a limited amount of food.

I organize food, water, stove, sleeping bag, sleeping pad, helmet, goggles, sunglasses, headlamp, survival and first aid gear, map and compass, cell phone. And then there is the climbing gear, which is heavy: crampons, ice ax, a picket, rope, harness, carabiners, a belay device, pulley, and Prusik cords for crevasse rescue, just in case one of us three falls into one. We leave skis at home after getting a route report from a climbing ranger. It is too late in the season for a smooth glide down. The snow is hard, the crevasses are wide open, and the sun cups are like inverted moguls on a ski slope. My gear for the big ascent of this big mountain forms a large pile.

The night before, I don't sleep much. I'm nervous about the crevasses: the deep, dark cracks in the volcano. I'm hoping

the weather holds. I obsess about my daughters. I can't get injured for the sake of Skylar and Avrie. My wife would be dev-
astated, too, but the kids weigh heavier on my mind than my
spouse.

But this is an opportunity to climb to the top of the world
for mortal climbers; it takes a rare breed to climb higher, such as
the peaks in Alaska and Nepal.

Tahoma beckons.

Jay, Matt, and I leave Hood River at 5 A.M., drive the windy
forest roads for three hours, and get a permit at the White
River Ranger District. The landscape is much different than in
the south Cascades. Around my home, the large trio of snow-clad
volcanoes—Adams, St. Helens, and Hood—dominate the endless
rolling foothills. Rainier's surrounds are more like the Alps.
Crags, rocky outcrops, and spires pop from the thick green forest
in all directions. The valleys are deep, with passes so high that you
drive two thousand feet higher just to get fifteen miles across the
park. The trees are gigantic and ancient: Douglas fir, western
hemlock, and western red cedar are a thousand years old, as tall as
a high-rise, and as wide as a bus.

We chose the Emmons/Winthrop Glacier route; it is longer
than the dog route up Disappointment Cleaver on the South
Side. But the Emmons/Winthrop is safer. It has less people, less
rock and ice fall, less traversing between glaciers, and fewer exposed slopes. When we first spy the mountain from the park entrance, the huge glaciers resemble bestial claws and the yawning
crevasses look like fingers holding rings of danger and fear.

Climbing for recreation is entirely different from a mountain
rescue mission. There is no urgency. In fact, we can turn back at
any time, which is the reason I'm climbing with Jay and Matt.

They have no problem turning around if conditions look bad. Both are safe, smart climbers. Once the three of us were skiing and snowboarding the Bathhouse Couloir in the remote Steens Mountain, a rocky mountain range in the middle of southeast Oregon's Alvord Desert. About halfway up the couloir, I was post-holing, or sinking to my knees, when climbing up a steep, narrow chute. Despite cold temperatures all that week, a warm front had moved in overnight. The snow was too slushy for my comfort level. I was worried about an avalanche. I told the guys I was turning around for safer turns on the apron, the gentle slopes leading up to a cliff. No one gave me a hard time. They climbed for another fifteen minutes and also decided to turn around before the top.

But Rainier is another level in the adventure-sports realm. It's not like a mountain bike or hike in the forest. With this big mountain, the risks are magnified: more and larger avalanches, rock slides, crevasses, steep slopes, cliffs. The weather and altitude alone are daunting. So why, exactly, am I doing this, with two young daughters at home? (I would later find out Jay had the same reservations.) The endorphin high and adrenaline rush you know about. The mental and physical challenge: figuring out the route and setting up equipment for rope belays. The thrill of ascent, going somewhere new, doing something extraordinary, and reaching a place that few can go to, one which takes both brain and brawn. And the beauty of the alpine wilds.

We leave the car at White River Trailhead, 4,000 feet elevation, and hike through the cusp of timberline, where the old-growth groves slowly thin to sparse, stunted, wiry alpine fir. I stop to take a picture of a hoary marmot, as big as a medium-sized dog, standing on its hind legs about ten feet from the trail. *My girls will love this picture.*

We pop out of the woods at Glacier Basin, a huge bowl of snow-covered slopes spreading in all directions. The snow fingers touch an alpine meadow and create the headwaters of White River. We start the long hike up Inter Glacier. In seven hours or so, roughly a little more than one hour per thousand vertical feet, we arrive at Camp Sherman, at 10,000 feet. Camp Sherman is a patch of rocks tucked above Inter Glacier and wedged between Emmons and Winthrop Glaciers. It's about half the size of a football field where a tiny ranger shack, a self-composting solar pit toilet, and two dozen tents rest on the rocks and snow.

It is more of a way station than a camp; we'll spend barely eight hours here. We arrive at four o'clock and set about our high camp chores: set up tents, fill water bottles from a spring seeping from a nearby crack in the Emmons Glacier, heat up instant dinners, and arrange our bedrolls and climbing gear. Jay realizes he forgot his headlamp. So he barters with a climber who is returning from the summit and heading home. He learns that a $45 headlamp goes for $100 at Camp Sherman, and I tease him to no end about his bad deal.

By 6:00 P.M., with the sun still high in the sky, we crawl under Matt's tarp, a floorless shelter that is held up by a single pole in the middle. Wind skirts under the edge and ruffles the nylon noisily so that none of us can sleep.

At midnight my watch alarm beeps and we get up. Instead of making a real cup of drip coffee, I slug down some instant espresso that I've dissolved into a cup of lukewarm water heated on a camp stove. It tastes horrible. Then I slug a Starbucks Double Shot, a canned coffee drink that I'd bought earlier in the week. It, too, tastes horrible.

When we set off, I look at my altimeter watch: it reads 10,030 feet and 1:09 A.M.. Most of the camp is still preparing to leave, but I see lights bobbing just above us on the Emmons from early risers. It is very dark without a moon, but the stars brilliantly spangle the black sky. We step off the rocks of Camp Sherman and begin to climb a trail in the snow. The route is a well-worn path three feet deep in the snow pack, so deep that I can use the snowbanks on either side as handrails. Every few hundred feet we see a ranger's wand, a four-foot bamboo trail marker. Every so often we step over a crevasse, a foot or two wide. I shine my light down the caverns, and they appear bottomless. My high-powered xenon bulb headlamp does not touch anything but blackness.

I suck on the water tube attached to a reservoir in my pack, not because I'm thirsty but because I know I need to drink. I get hungry in an hour, take a bite of an energy bar, chew it to a dry paste, and choke it down with water. It doesn't taste good. After three hours, I have three energy bars in my pocket, each with one bite taken.

A gentle breeze keeps us cool in the dark night despite working up a sweat. More important, the slight wind keeps the snow cold and thus firm for easy climbing with crampons. With the first glow of light at dawn, sun cups and sastrugi, tiny snow ridges formed by wind, sparkle across the vast expanse of glacial ice. They have been forming all summer but look as if they magically appeared. The texture looks like wind stippling the waves and swells in the ocean.

At 13,000 feet and sometime after 5 A.M. the sun peeks over the foothills in a yellow glow. We glance back at the sunrise occasionally but don't stop moving upward, toward the summit. I feel ill abruptly. Altitude illness? I hope not. This could mean turning around. But I think maybe the dehydrated food from last night, something I eat about once every other year, has settled wrong. Along with that, the caffeine is working in my gut. I tell Matt and

Jay I need to stop. I pick a spot on the upper Emmons, untie from the rope, hike down my harness, hike down my pants, and hike down my long underwear. I let loose and instantly feel better. Afterwards, I scoop up my business with a "blue bag," supplied by climbing rangers to keep the route clean. I put the blue bag into a freezer bag, and strap the package to the outside of my pack. I tie back into the rope, suck down more water, and feel renewed strength.

Several years previously, I did have a mild case of Acute Mountain Sickness while climbing Mount Adams. Just 500 feet from the summit, I had a sudden piercing headache. I climbed to the summit with the nagging headache, lingered on top for a scant ten minutes, then quickly headed down. The headache disappeared when I returned to 10,000 feet. Descent nearly always resolves mild altitude illness. So now on the giant Rainier, I know to stay hydrated, nourished, and oxygenated. I suck in lungfuls of air: increasing the rate and volume of my breathing to increase the oxygen availability for my blood. This is too short of a trip to acclimatize. Get up and down as quickly as possible.

Acute Mountain Sickness (AMS) is not the only illness I've had in the wilderness. On a three-day canyoneering descent of Long Canyon in Southern Utah in 110-degree summer desert, I experienced a sudden wave of dizziness, vertigo, nausea, and fatigue. It might not have been a big deal at home; I could have ended my bike ride or stopped my hike. But in this remote area of the southern Utah slickrock desert, we were a long way from our car, and I was worried and scared. I thought maybe I had heat exhaustion, when the body overheats, core temperature climbs over 100° F, and one has identical symptoms to the ones I was experiencing. (*Heatstroke*—commonly used but often incorrectly— is heat exhaustion coupled with mental-status changes and a dangerous temperature of 104° F or higher. That is a medical emergency, because the body goes into shock.) But I wasn't too hot: we'd been careful to hike in the cooler morning hours, and when the thermometer climbed to its midday high of 110, we hiked as much as possible in shade and stopped at every pothole full of stagnant, muddy water to douse ourselves. Using these techniques, despite the high ambient temperature, we were able to keep the natural cooling process of our bodies in check with the environment. I knew I was not dehydrated: I'd been guzzling water constantly. The nausea was wicked and frightening, and I was worried I would pass out. Finally we made it back to the car and drove to a local diner. I scarfed four grilled cheese sandwiches and the symptoms disappeared. Only then did it dawn on me that I had water intoxication, caused by drinking too much water and not replacing lost electrolytes. Sodium, vital for many bodily functions from muscle to brain function, was critically low. The salty, grilled cheese sandwiches solved the problem

I've also had a slew of minor injuries, like any outdoor sports enthusiast. From mountain biking, I've cut my leg and arms plenty of times. I have had a dozen cases of poison oak, when the oil from the plant causes an itchy red rash that lasts for a week. I've bonked my head falling off my bike and broken two helmets. I've sprained my ankle while trail running in Mount Hood National Forest and hiking in the Maroon Bells Wilderness in Colorado, among other places. I've crashed once on my road bike and another time was hit by a car. I have not, fortunately, been bit by a shark surfing or suffered major injury from climbing, skiing, or snowboarding.

If I am going to get hurt badly now, it may most likely occur from an avalanche, because I spend so much time in the mountains on snow. Avalanches are perhaps the most ubiquitous and romantic mountain hazards and they come in all types. The most common is a slab, when the mountain snowpack collapses and slides. Usually a thick, strong layer—new snow, for example—has not bonded to a weaker layer—such as a hard crust from rain followed by cold weather. A weak layer can be buried a few inches or a few feet down, and the strong layer looses its grip on the weak layer, and slides. In the summer in the Pacific Northwest volcanoes, we have many point-release avalanches. These occur when the warm summer sun turns the snowpack to slush, thus loosening bonds and causing the top few inches to slide. Even a small slough can knock you off your feet and drag you down a slope into rocks and trees or over a cliff. I am cautious when I ski, snowboard, and climb. I choose good weather and a stable snowpack. I choose routes that are the safest possible during ascent and I have trusted partners. I minimize these dangers at all costs.

I have come to be more cautious when sporting of late because of Skylar and Avrie. I have a heightened sense of safety that I never had when I was single, or even when I was married without kids. Sometimes my wife says I'm a worrier or a pessimist. I admit, when I look at a landscape or participate in an outdoor activity, I'm always thinking *How can I get hurt?* or rather, *How can I avoid getting hurt?* I don't see myself as a pessimist but as a cautious, reserved participant in the world around me. Understand, I have a skewed version of the world of adventure sports because I see bloodied bikers, kayakers, windsurfers, snowboarders, and skiers in the emergency room, at the ski clinic, and in the mountains. I've seen paralyzed athletes and severely debilitating head injuries. I've seen car crashes on mountain roads and my share of dead bodies in the wild. I don't want to be a casualty. This realistic albeit morbid view is part of being a doctor and a mountain rescuer.

Early summer alpenglow on the treacherous north side of Mount Hood.

In the mountains, every second counts, especially when evacuating a critical patient from a deep canyon.

One of many difficult rope rescues in the Columbia River Gorge. (Jim Wells)

A heart attack up Newton Creek became a stream evacuation with no injury, on a beautiful midsummer's eve.

Extricating the patient from a deep canyon is often only half the battle; here we race down the trail to an awaiting ambulance.

The rescue and recovery mission on Mount Adams was particularly challenging, with the lightning-sparked wildfire and a thick Harry Potter-esque fog descending from the peak.

Even after years working as an emergency doctor, the scene of the Viento Ridge plane crash was grisly, and one of the most emotionally challenging missions of all.

Testifying in the court-
room for the Svitek
snowboard death was
both fascinating and
frustrating; above, the
tree well she died in,
and below, the slope
she was last seen on.

The Mount Hood mission in December 2006 was the biggest search in decades. Jim Wells was incident commander at an advance search base, Cloud Cap Inn, accessible only via snowcat.

As Team 1, we skied to 9,000 feet in cold but clear skies.

Another midnight storm on Mount Hood, we struggle through fifty mph winds and a raging snowstorm.

Jeff Pricher (right) and me using the Mountain Locating Unit at midnight on Mount Hood. (Richard Hallman)

Atop Dad's skis, careening down the cow pasture in rural Washington State. (Eleanor Van Tilburg)

In the mountains with my daughters on a three-day backpack trip to Mount Rainier National Park.

It all boils down to what I call it the fun-to-injury ratio—how much fun I am having versus the amount of risk I am taking. I know the risks and possible consequences of pushing the limit close to the edge. I have a comfort zone, and I like to stay within it most of the time. So when Jay, Matt, and I climb the big mountain, I am scared, no doubt about it. But I'm cautious: safe route, safe partners, good equipment, clear weather. We are in good shape, skilled, well nourished, and well hydrated. I constantly reevaluate the conditions of the snow, weather, and route. The lure of these peaks is too strong to let them go unclimbed.

Today is a spectacular day on Tahoma/Rainier, Snowy Peak, the Place Where Water Starts. Superb weather, excellent route conditions, and the best partners lead up to one place: the top of the world. It is cold, clear, and windy. Snow and ice coats the summit crater, which is bigger than a football field. Rocks on the rim are bare, scoured by winds. Heavy chunks of volcanic debris shift under the spikes of our crampons. The rocks give me a sense of comfort: a small patch of terra firma without the risk of avalanche, ice fall, or crevasse. I can see the Pacific Ocean.

At 14,410 feet high, the air is thin. After ten minutes, even without climbing, I am breathing hard. I am tired but I feel strong: no headache, no nausea, no dizziness. I am actually hungry for the first time since leaving the car yesterday. Every twenty seconds I consciously take in a deep breath and increase my breathing rate, to keep my head clear and my muscles supplied. It is a long way down, same way we came up, but it will be unfamiliar as we are now about to descend during daylight.

I am sick of energy bars, but I need energy, so I eat my sandwich: peanut butter, honey, sliced bananas. The food drops into my gut and I can feel the calories soak into my blood, coursing through my arteries, and nurturing my brain and muscles. I wake up from a daze I didn't really know I was in. I guzzle more water, devour the rest of my sandwich, and wolf down handfuls of trail mix. I am clearheaded and euphoric. I made it to the summit of this behemoth. We smile for pictures, raising our ice axes over head as every climber does.

After a short fifteen minutes, we agree to head down: the more dangerous part of climbing a mountain. We would love to linger for an hour on the summit, but instinct makes all three of us want to start down while we are strong, while the weather is good, and while the glacier is still firm. We pass scores of climbers on their way up. When the sun melts the glacier later in the day, they will have a more difficult descent in slush.

On the way down, I see all the crevasses that we either jumped or climbed around; they were shadowed by darkness on our way up. They are gargantuan and chilling. At the Winthrop Glacier bergschrund, the name for the large crevasse at the head of a glacier, a snowbridge two feet wide spans a crevasse eight feet wide. We'd crossed it on the way up, but it was not fully light so I did not recognize the magnitude of the giant fissure. Halfway across, I slow briefly for a picture, too scared to completely stop. The crevasse widens immediately below the bridge, opening to a thirty-foot-wide, one-hundred, two-hundred, maybe three-hundred feet deep cavern. I can't even see the bottom, only the spot where the blue ice walls become dark shadows. We set up a boot ax belay, in which Jay drives an ice ax into the snow, wraps the rope around his ax, stabilizes the ax with his boot, and gently pays out the rope as Matt crosses, and then I cross. Once across, I set up a belay for Jay.

At another crevasse farther down, where the Winthrop meets

the Emmons Glacier, we easily jump across the two-foot span after first clipping our rope with a carabiner to a picket, an aluminum snow stake that serves as an anchor. Again I look down:
no bottom to the black hole. If I had seen this abyss on the way
up, I would have had trouble resisting the urge to turn back.

I know what it is like to be inside a crevasse. On a crevasse
rescue training one year, Jay lowered me into the gaping dark void
of a gargantuan Eliot Glacier crack. Deep in the crevasse I was
oddly warm, out of the wind and drifting snow. The eerie quiet-
ness was punctuated by claustrophobia. I had to gather my com-
posure and climb back out. I tried to keep the front point of my
crampons on the ice wall while I swung my ice ax high overhead.
Instead of sinking, my ax let loose a dinner plate, a large flat disk
of ice, which popped off the wall and crashed on my helmet. I
swung again in the same spot. That time I buried the pick deep
and climbed out of the ice.

Jay, Matt, and I descend the mountain quickly but carefully.
I'm in the middle of the rope team. I have to walk fast enough
not to step on the rope behind me, but if I go too fast, I step on
the rope in front of me. Not until we arrive at Camp Sherman,
do I heave a sigh of relief. We left the tarp set up, but I had packed
up my pad and sleeping bag early that morning. I am completely
exhausted, hungry, and thirsty. I need food and fluids, but I have
no appetite. In addition to the long and brutal fifteen hours of
climbing to the summit and back to Camp Sherman, I am working on two nights of little sleep. At camp, I lie down on the gravel
underneath the shade of the shelter and fall asleep.

I count rescues as time away from kids and the family. After a
busy year doing rescues this summer, I cancel a climbing trip
to Mount Shasta and put a two-week Baja surf trip on hold for

another year. I guard my free time cautiously. I can't plan SAR call outs, but I can plan the rest of my life. Soon enough my kids will grow up, and I want to be here for them. Jay and I manage to do both: spend time with the kids and attend a Crag Rats outing.

I would love nothing more than for the kids to love the outdoors and even to become Crag Rats when they are older. But I have learned to balance gently coaxing them to participate in the avocations that I love, while still encouraging them to try a broad range of activities so they can find their own passions. Roger Nelson's words from the Newton Creek rescue keep replaying in the forefront of my mind: *keep dragging them out in the wilds. You'll thank yourself for it later.* It reassures me that I'm at least following a well-trod path. Skylar and Avrie have been exposed to more outdoor experiences than most kids who are five and seven years old: they mountain bike, hike, backpack, ski, rock climb in the gym, swim laps in the pool, and surf on their knees. Not even eight years old, Skylar has backpacked on three overnight trips near Mount Rainier, Mount Adams, and Mount St. Helens. Although she likes fluid and graceful action like swimming, gymnastics, and dance, Skylar gave me an unequivocal yes to another backpack trip this coming summer. She is fretting over which friend to bring, though. Avrie first backpacked at age five too, up near Rainier. She loves almost any form of motion: from bowling to biking, skiing to hiking. Next year, we might climb St. Helens.

Matt, Jay, and I sleep for an hour. I'm sprawled on the rocks and dirt without removing my boots, without unrolling my sleeping bag or pad, without even a jacket under my head. I awake suddenly, gobble a bag of lemon drops, and guzzle water to wash down a mouthful of the tart candy. I feel the mass of sugar drop into my stomach and sink into my tissues. In five minutes, I am rejuvenated with the bolt of sugar and fluids. I suck down another liter of water and prepare for the last descent, six thousand feet down Inter Glacier, back to the car. I feel euphoric knowing I've made the summit and the most dangerous part of the mountain is behind me. I feel accomplished. I feel strong. I feel relieved. And I miss my daughters.

CHAPTER 13

Rattlesnake Bite on Dog Mountain

I often miss rescues when I'm with Skylar and Avrie or when I'm at work. When a rescue is needed, and I can't go, I get anxious and frustrated. I'm so eager to help, employ my skills and aid a lost or injured person, that I have trouble focusing on anything else. I want to help every possible chance I can. Jay Sherrerd, I know, has the same reaction when he misses a rescue.

Sometimes I respond to a rescue, but there's nothing to do, which also can be frustrating, but I have learned it is part of volunteering. Just before dinner with the neighbors one rainy Sunday, I'm paged for a "car off a cliff" on Lost Lake Road. I drive up to the community of Dee, ten miles from my house. I find the volunteer firefighters huddled around their truck, looking into the dark void of a canyon. Jim Wells and Devon Wells, father and son Crag Rats, have rappelled fifty feet down a steep, muddy embankment to a rather smashed-up pickup truck. They cautiously poke around the truck but find no one inside. Meanwhile, a sheriff deputy follows footprints that lead to a house and the driver of the truck, who had climbed out of the truck after rolling off the road and hiked to the house up the road. Once the pickup is cleared and the man is located, there's nothing to do, so we all drive home.

Another time I participated in a rescue from the hospital. I was in the emergency room, working. "Rattlesnake bite on Dog Mountain," the ambulance radio crackles to life and announces. I listen attentively. The team has responded to Dog Mountain, a popular hiking trail in the Columbia River Gorge. A woman had been hiking in sandals when she stumbled upon a rattlesnake sunning itself on the trail and got bitten on her big toe.

The first firefighter on the scene called me, medical control at the hospital, for advice. He remembers reading about suction and a tourniquet.

"Splint her, put her in a litter, and bring her in," I tell him over the radio. Immobilizing the leg and the patient will minimize circulation of the toxin. Suction doesn't really work for snakebites: it can damage the local tissue and is ineffective at removing venom. A tourniquet, though it does slow circulation of the toxin, also impedes blood flow to the limb, which can also damage tissues. A light compression bandage is useful for keeping the toxin at the wound site, so long as it is not applied so tightly that it impedes blood flow.

Fortunately only about a quarter of all snakes inject venom when they bite. And of those that do, only another 25 percent inject enough venom to have any systemic effect on the victim. Most of the time, good wound care—cleaning and bandaging—is all that is necessary. We may send the patient home after a quick exam. But we cannot take any chances.

When the patient arrives thirty minutes later, she is critically ill from the snake venom. She is dizzy, anxious, and sweating. Her entire leg is swollen. The two tiny puncture wounds on the top of her toe are surrounded by purple bruising. The patient is in shock: rapid pulse, low blood pressure, slurred speech, disorientation. The rattlesnake venom is taking its toll.

Immediately I ask the nurse to pump the patient full of intravenous normal saline, a solution with the same salt concentration as blood. Extra saline will increase fluid volume, which in turn improves delivery of oxygen to the tissues and removal of toxic carbon dioxide. I order a battery of tests, but the one I'm most concerned about is the platelet level, the single best indicator for how much venom the patient has received. The lower the level of platelets, the more venom is circulating in the patient's bloodstream. If the platelet count drops too low, the blood cannot clot, and internal bleeding can occur. My decision is based partly on the results of this platelet test. The other part is based on judgment and initial treatment: how ill does the patient appear and how quickly can I reverse the shock. I don't really want to give her the antivenom unless I need to.

Although antivenom can be lifesaving, it can be life-taking as well. The protein that binds the snake venom and removes it from the body is made from horse serum. The human body sees it as a foreign invader and often mounts an immediate, overwhelming immune response called anaphylaxis, the same allergic reaction that can cause death after a bee sting. I don't know if the patient is allergic to the antivenom, but I don't want to take the risk unless she is critically ill. Unfortunately the woman was likely bitten by a baby rattler, the paramedics report. Juvenile rattlers have more concentrated venom and often inject more of it because they are unable to control their venom sacs.

In fifteen minutes I get the platelet test result. This patient is barely over the level. I call the state toxicologist at poison control to consult. The toxicologist agrees: no antivenom for now, but watch the platelets carefully.

In the hospital we have multitudes of blood and urine tests

and X-ray, ultrasound, computed tomography, magnetic resonance imaging, and positron emission scanning to help us diagnose patients. We have high-powered medicines like rattlesnake antivenom, antibiotics for infections, blood thinners, hormones, pain relievers, and chemotherapeutics. In today's medical world, doctors are aggressive with diagnosis and treatment. I tend to be cautious, concerned, and concise: I was once called a minimalist by a professor. I follow my instinct but at the same time trust science. Sometimes these conflict, but today I am reassured. The patient's swelling reaches her groin but goes no farther. Her shock is quickly reversed. Her platelet number are stable, then begin to rise. She stays in the hospital two days.

I've always worked part-time practicing medicine. It used to be so I could spend many days climbing, backpacking, biking, snowboarding, and writing my books. The last five years, though, it has been to focus on my kids: volunteer in school, meet the bus, shuttle them to dance, swimming, or drama class. In order to be more available to the kids, I've found a niche in consulting and teaching, so maybe it's time to stop working in the emergency room and follow a new path. In this undecided state of mind, when everything changes, I head to where I find the most solace and surround myself with those with whom I am most comfortable.

I take my kids to Cloud Cap Inn. In October the Crag Rats have a business meeting there. The kids and I drive up to attend. This is the last venture up the rutty, rocky road before the gate goes up for the winter. The morning air is so cold and clear this time of year that it is intoxicating. The fall leaves are peaking: the big leaf and vine maples are in various stages of yellow, orange, and red. Bright yellow larches stand out like lighthouse beacons in a sea of green. A fresh layer of snow on the mountain covers all the brown of summer; it glistens and shines in the morning sun like fresh white frosting. This October weekend is called the Wood Party, because after the Friday night business meeting we spend Saturday restocking the cabin with firewood. Jay Sherrerd and Penny Hunting come up with their daughter Casey.

I make a mental note to change over my pack. Instead of being ready with poison oak clothing, summer hiking boots, and rope-rescue gear, I need to prepare my winter ski bag and rescue pack. In winter, I need a full set of warm winter clothing; avalanche-rescue equipment, including a shovel, probe, and beacon; skis with climbing skins to ascend the mountain on snow; and glacier-travel equipment, such as crampons, an ice ax, and snow anchors.

This beautiful autumn afternoon metamorphoses slowly to a spectacular evening. The warm yellow summer sun reflects my genuine good feeling for excellent friends and my daughters. We make a huge dinner for a dozen, smiling, filthy-faced kids who nicely fill up the long picnic table in the front room. I'm on cleanup duty. After dinner we walk to a nearby viewpoint, parents strolling and kids running among the boulders and timbers. Brownies for dessert. Brush teeth. Pajamas. Potty. Everyone got a headlamp? Sleep buddy? Pillow? We gather on the back deck to watch the pink alpenglow fade to a crimson, carrot, and indigo sunset. We roll out our sleeping bags, cuddle, and tell stories.

There is a good one about these mountains that are so dear to me. Tyhee Saghalie, the great chief of all gods, came down to the Columbia River from far north. Hi-Yu Skookum Chuck, plenty strong water, the stream was called, and Nch'i-wana, big river. When Tyhee Saghalie came to the land with his sons, Pahto and Wy'East, everything was majestic, perhaps like Heaven or Nirvana or Olympus. He gave Pahto the land north of the great river and Wy'East the land to the south. They created Tahmahnawis, a great stone bridge between the two.

One day Loowit, a wandering hag who smelled of rotten rats and combed her hair with pinesap, discovered how to make fire. She built Tyhee Saghalie a roaring-hot fire as a gift. He roasted salmon for the first time in his life and felt the fire's warm glow against his face. He granted Loowit a wish in return and she chose to be beautiful, with long wavy hair; bright green and gold eyes; soft lips; and a happy, soothing smile.

Pahto and Wy'East fell in love with her and fought as only brothers can. They caused wind, rain, lightning, thunder; falling rocks and trees; and avalanches of snow and mud. In a great explosion, Tahmahnawis cracked, broke, tumbled into the great river, dammed the flow, and formed a great cascade of water.

Tyhee Saghalie woke from a warm nap in front of his fire and saw the great battle. In penance, he turned Pahto into Mount Adams and Wy'East became Mount Hood. Some say Loowit became Mount St. Helens. Others led me to believe she escaped the torrent and began her life anew. Maybe when Mount St. Helens erupted in 1980 her spirit was dispersed to every woman on earth.

Loowit aptly has two personas: her name translates as Fair Maiden for the Klickitat Indians and as the Smoking One to the Salish. One is beautiful, spunky, and sparkly; the other wild, spirited, and free. The first European to see this volcano was British Captain George Vancouver on April 10, 1792, when he sailed up the Columbia River. He named it after Britain's ambassador to Madrid,

Baron Alleyne Fitzherbert, Baron St. Helens. It was the first of the Cascade volcanoes climbed by modern-day mountaineers: Thomas Dryer reached the summit in 1853 when it was 9,686 feet high.

I saw Mount St. Helens explode. The mountain burped and rumbled for a year until the cataclysmic eruption of May 18, 1980, lopped off the top 1,321 feet. We cleaned out our gutters three times that year and had school canceled several times because of ash fallout. I remember when playing outside, raindrops would leave tiny specs of gray ash deposits on my shirt. The mountain was closed for climbing for almost a decade. Then my first year living in the Columbia River Gorge, just before entering medical school, I made the two-hour drive to the trailhead. Back then, it was a huge climb—four thousand feet up the mountain—and it looked like the moon: broad pumice plains; huge lava beds; ash slopes as fine as beach sand varied in multitudes of gray; and sparse tiny plants, no more than a few inches high. The volcanic rock was jagged. On the ash slopes, I slid two steps back for every one up; my boots filled with the fine grit. Finally, at the summit, I gazed into the crater. Steam rose from a crack in the mountain and created a warm mist on the rim.

That was my first major mountain climb. It probably will be Skylar and Avrie's first mountain, too when they are old enough. They have done more outdoor sports than most kids their age: they rock climb, camp, bike, swim. This summer we spent many days canoeing; to prepare them I took them to the local pool fully clothed and pushed them in. We spent an hour practicing water survival in case they fell overboard; I had trouble teaching them through all the laughter. We spent many days geocaching, a sport in which you search for treasures hidden in waterproof boxes in the community using a GPS receiver. It's good practice for me with a GPS and great fun for the kids. In fact, it's a good excuse to drag them on hikes. They have a few years before they climb mountains; if they don't want to, I'm not worried. Skylar passed on sports this fall to enroll in drama. Avrie excels at every sport but needs a good deal of quiet time in her room.

In the twilight, a few stars sparkle in the indigo sky, and the soft pink and purple alpenglow kisses the Snowdome and Coe Glacier on Mount Hood. It is here, I realize, that my daughters will find their path. It doesn't have to be the Crag Rat path or one of doctoring or rescuing. My girls fall asleep on the deck. I lie down in my down sleeping bag between them. We are warm and cuddly, squished together, outside.

WINTER

CHAPTER 14

Storm Warning on Zigzag Glacier

Dinner interrupted, I leave home at 7 P.M. in a wild wind-
and rainstorm.

I am at home with my family eating at the kitchen table,
when the phone rings; my wife instantly knows from my terse
words and strained face that something is wrong. She first thought
I am being summoned to the hospital on my night off. But it is a
search and rescue call out at night in the mountains in the middle
of a raging storm. We have been asked to help find a lost snowboarder at a ski area on Mount Hood. I hastily load my pack,
cram extra gear into my truck, grab a plateful of dessert, kiss my
family, and speed off into the night.

Driving alone, I try to listen to music, but it's too distracting.
Instead, I go through a mental checklist of what gear to bring up
the mountain from the mound in my truck. Headlamp, water,
food are givens. Will I need a stove to melt snow for water? Will I
need my bivy sack, my single-person tube tent used for an unexpected night on the mountain? Medical gear? Should I dress light,
because I'll be hiking all night, working up a sweat? Or dress
warm for a slower search?

Raindrops glare in the oncoming headlights of other cars. Rain is falling faster than the windshield wipers can slap it away. I try to heap apple crisp into my mouth while watching the road, but a spoonful plops in my lap. When I zoom around a corner, the whole plate slides across the passenger seat of my truck and disappears into the unreachable crevice by the passenger door. I feel nervous about the rescue, my first in my mountain rescue career. I am stretching my limits, pushing my medical and outdoor skills into the unknown. I've been preparing, in some ways, for this moment my whole life.

As I drive into the mountains, the rain turns to snow. Thick heavy flakes pile on the windshield. My wipers now struggle beneath the heavy slush, and the wet pavement quickly becomes snow covered. I shift into four-wheel drive and slow down. On a dark stretch near Government Camp, a lone snowplow appears suddenly out of the darkness. Lit up like a Christmas tree, it passes me in the opposite direction, giving me bit of comfort.

When I turn up the pass road, the driving becomes treacherous. I shift into compound low, and the steady hum of my truck motor changes to a deep growl. The twisting mountain access road rises three thousand feet in six miles. It has not been plowed, and the drifts have reduced the width to one lane. I slide around the corners, even in four-wheel-drive with snow tires. The blinding snow comes straight at my windshield. I can't see much farther than ten feet.

Finally, at the ski area, blowing snow obliterates all sense of order. Spindrifts dance eerily beneath outdoor lamps. Snowbanks have climbed to the eaves and hide the old lodge, which looks mysteriously foreboding. Lights are on, but the lodge looks vacant. *Good night for a rescue,* I think. *Darkness, wind, snow, ice, and cold all add up to danger in the mountains by anyone's terms. Anyone here?*

It is bitter cold, black dark, superstormy, and waxing toward

10 P.M. on this night. I'm not so much nervous but anxious, eager, and thrilled to be finally on a rescue. Did I hear the message correctly? Had the rescue been aborted? Had the victim been found? A snowplow drives through the parking lot, but it is too dark to see the driver; it is almost as if the giant machine has none. I grab my pack and run inside to ski patrol headquarters. The tiny room is packed with at least twenty bustling people. It reminds me of a cardiac arrest code in the hospital. The equipment, clothes, and language are highly technical and specialized; but the buzz is not medical parlance but search and rescue speak. I sign the search and rescue register, turn in my keys so my truck can be moved during the night for the snowplow, and check out a radio. A corner table is the makeshift search and rescue HQ. A Forest Service ranger; a county deputy sheriff; and Don, mountain rescue leader, discuss the next course of action looking over a map. Earlier that evening, a teenage boy had been reported missing by his friends. The last seen point was the chairlift at 4:30 P.M. The boy wore only snowboarding clothes. He carried no food, water, or survival gear.

There are several likely possibilities. He could be upside down in a tree well, suffering from deep snow submersion asphyxiation. This occurs when someone falls headfirst into deep snow and can't get upright because the snow is too soft and they have no leverage. The person suffocates. In that case, we may not find the snowboarder tonight, next week, or perhaps even next month.

He could be buried in an avalanche. The snow from even a small ravine could slide and bury him. He could be buried a mere six inches deep and be impossible to find.

He could be huddled and hypothermic under a tree or in a snowbank awaiting rescue. In that case, we would have to pass within twenty feet to see or hear him in the dark night, howling wind, and whirling snow.

Or, best case, he might have snowboarded down one of two backcountry ski trails, which are old roads that connect ski area with the nearby town. In that case he would either turn up in town or he'd be found waiting in the middle of one of the trails.

"Chris, do you think this guy would head down a Ski Trail without knowing where they were?" Don asks me, since I am one of the few snowboarders on our team.

"I don't think so," I say after studying the last-seen point on the map and the ski trails. "Snowboarders don't like to hike, and that would be out of the natural fall line of the ski resort. The fall line would put him in Black Ax Canyon. That's my bet."

Four ground teams of four members each have been searching for an hour. Team one is searching high on the mountain up near the last-seen point. Team two is working the trail. Team three is following a set of quickly disappearing footprints at the bottom of the chairlift. Team four was skiing toward Black Ax Canyon, the edge of the ski area and the direction the footprints appeared to be headed.

Team five, my group, is instructed to sweep the Ski Trail. We pile rescuers and gear into the utility compartment of the maintenance snowcat and head off to the start of the trail. The diesel machine is filthy and stinky. Our expensive Gore-Tex jackets become covered with soot. The roar of the vehicle is so loud, we can hear neither our rescue radios nor each other.

We are out for thirty minutes when the call comes in: the snowboarder had been found. The boy had been huddled, perhaps sleeping, in a tree well. He wandered back to the ski resort by following the lights he'd seen when the clouds lifted. A snowplow almost ran him over when he stumbled from the trees.

The snowboarder had been in the ski patrol room for fifteen minutes by the time I return. He holds a cup of steaming cocoa, too hot to drink, and has a blanket wrapped around his soaked clothes. He looks about twenty years old. His face is ashen; he shivers uncontrollably. The sheriff is trying to reach the boy's parents. Other rescuers are drying out, getting food and water.

As a doctor, my first instinct is to evaluate the patient. My anxiety, nervousness, and apprehension melt. This is familiar territory. I know what to do.

"What's your name?" I ask.

"Jack," he mumbles through the shivers.

"Where do you live?"

"Portland."

"Look me in the eye," I say. He complies.

I make my initial diagnosis. Hypothermia: mild. Dehydration: mild. He's embarrassed and greatly relieved. The fight-or-flight adrenaline response that had been keeping him alive and focused on getting back to the lodge has abruptly ceased. Shock is setting in, and I need to reverse it quickly. I have a momentary pause, suddenly realizing I have the skills to help this boy.

Hypothermia is when the core body temperature, which averages 98.6° F in humans, cools. The core can lose heat in many ways in the cold. Heat evaporates through perspiration. Heat escapes from the lungs during exhalation. Valuable heat is used to warm the cold air during inhalation. Convection heat loss occurs when the skin warms the air next to it, and conduction heat loss is when the skin heats up objects it is in contact with such as a jacket or a rock. Radiation heat loss is direct heat loss from the body to the environment.

Mild hypothermia, between 91 and 95 degrees, begins with shivering and cool, pale skin. As hypothermia progresses, a patient can have slurred speech, poor coordination, poor judgment, rapid heart rate, and rapid breathing. The symptoms occur because the body is trying to conserve heat; it constricts blood vessels in the arms and legs and preserves blood flow to vital organs: heart, lungs, brain. The body attempts to generate heat by involuntary muscle movement like shivering. It also begins to break down fat and carbohydrates stored in the liver, muscle, and fat tissue to generate heat.

Moderate hypothermia, at 80 to 90 degrees, becomes extremely dangerous. Shivering stops, and disorientation and confusion occur. People at this stage often start undressing in the middle of a storm because all blood is diverted from the extremities to the core, so the brain tricks people into a feeling of warmth. In this more-advanced stage of hypothermia, dramatic decrease in core temperature causes the heart to slow, breathing to slow, and blood flow to the brain to slow. The vital organs of the body—heart, lungs, and brain—go into a power save mode like a computer and shut down to a bare minimum to preserve energy and prevent cellular damage. Hypothermia at this moderate stage is sometimes reversible.

When severe hypothermia sets in, body temperature below 80° F, people go into irreversible shock: the heart stops, the lungs stop, brain damage occurs. A patient usually cannot recover, even if warmed up. Occasionally, if one has no detectable pulse and appears dead, he may still have a chance. One axiom of wilderness medicine is: "A patient is not dead until he or she is warm and dead."

Prevention and treatment for mild hypothermia are fairly simple. Adequate nutrition supplies calories for heat. Adequate hydration ensures blood flow to deliver the calories. Exercise generates heat. Clothing minimizes heat loss through convection, conduction, and radiation. Shelter from the elements and external heat sources like a fire or chemical heat packs help, too. In short: we feed patients, give them water, and warm them up by any means available.

In the hospital, I treat patients with advanced hypothermia with sophisticated techniques. We strip the patient's wet clothes and cover him or her with a special blanket that blows warm air. We pump the patient full of warm intravenous fluids. I can do a bladder lavage: put warm water in the bladder via a catheter. I can do the same warm-water lavage in the gut via a tube down the throat to the stomach and up the rectum to the colon. We can do peritoneal lavage, which involves piercing the abdominal wall with a catheter and infusing warm water into the cavity. In extreme cases, as a last-ditch effort to save a life, an extracorporeal bypass can be done, in which the blood is removed by a heart-lung machine (the same device used to keep a patient alive during open-heart surgery), warmed, then replaced.

This snowboarder's hypothermia is not so severe. But we are a long way from a hospital. There's no way an ambulance can drive up the road safely at this time of night in this storm.

"I need some help," I say to a couple of my partners. "We need to get him warmed up and dried off. Can someone bring a large cup of lukewarm water?" I am afraid if we don't get him warmed up quickly, he will go deeper into shock or perhaps even have a seizure from hypothermia and dehydration. His blood was rapidly reinfusing his arms and legs. This was cooling his core because the blood previously close to his core was now circulating in his extremities.

The boy's dehydration compounds the hypothermia, because his blood does not have the volume to adequately deliver calories to his organs and tissues. Dehydration often coexists with hypothermia and has a similar, equally debilitating, set of symptoms: headache, restlessness, irritability, rapid heart rate, rapid breathing, dry mouth, and thirst. The hot chocolate, although supplied with good intentions, was too hot for the kid to drink. And it's not the heat of the cocoa he needs but the water to treat dehydration and calories in the form of sugar so he can generate heat.

I remove his boots and socks. His toes are cold and red, but I find no blistering, whiteness, or blackening that would suggest major frostbite. Frostbite is when the skin actually freezes (not to be confused with frostnip, which is when the skin cools, becomes numb, but does not freeze).

In this case, the boy had been well-covered by his snowboard boots and gloves. If he had frostbite, it would have led to a major medical ordeal, as the treatment is rapid rewarming in 140-degree water. This extremely painful process is difficult to do at midnight in a ski-patrol room without pain medicines and a nursing staff. Imagine stepping into a hot shower with numb feet after a cold bike ride or run: the pins and needles pain is hugely magnified during frostbite treatment. But early treatment can minimize permanent tissue damage in the most commonly afflicted areas: fingers, toes, nose, and ears. The hypothermic, dehydrated boy guzzles the warm water and asks for more. I turn to his three friends, waiting on the bunk nearby.

"Please get him some dry clothes," I say.

This is going to be a long night, I think.

We finish sometime around three in the morning. The boy is revitalized: warm and hydrated. The deputy, after discussing the boy's health with his friends and parents, lets the boys drive home down the pass, sandwiched between a snowplow and a sheriff's truck.

I unroll my sleeping bag and pad in the cafeteria of the lodge and try to sleep despite the exhilaration of the rescue and my first real patient outside a hospital. Not to mention the storm is still whooshing through the eaves of the lodge and rattling the windows. My two lives in sports and science have fused in the middle of the night in the middle of a storm high on a mountain.

CHAPTER 15

Midnight at Bennett Pass

Tonight is a school night for Skylar and Avrie, so Jennifer and I start the all-important bedtime routine: bath, brushing teeth, reading books. When our home phone rings, I'm sure it's a friend calling to ski. It is supposed to start snowing sometime after midnight: powder day tomorrow. I spent the morning at Mount Hood Meadows Ski Resort with the kids. On arrival, we stopped in the mountain clinic where I work ten shifts a season as the mountain doctor. We usually score a cup of hot chocolate from the nurse and go potty. While we were there today, we saw a patient on a gurney who was bleeding from a small nose laceration. The cut would require only one simple stitch, but it looked worse because he had blood all over his face: face injuries always bleed a lot. Skylar was fascinated by the blood. My youngest, Avrie, was itching to get on the hill.

We spend a good portion of the winter in the mountains skiing. For me, teaching the kids to ski entails teaching them about much more than just having fun on the ski slope: the pure air, mountain beauty, wild weather, and staying mentally and physically fit.

"Yum," said Avrie with a smile when I brought out hot

chocolate and French fries from the cafeteria on our mid-morning break.

"You guys want to head back out for another run?" I asked enthusiastically.

"Yeah." Avrie's eyes lit up. "Let's go!"

"I want to go see that man bleed," said Skylar. "Will he be all right? How did he fall? Will he keep bleeding?" She always has many questions.

Now, at bedtime, we're pleasantly fatigued from the day on the mountain when the phone rings.

"Hey, Jay, going up to the hill tomorrow?" I ask into the phone. "Storm warning tonight, powder."

"I'm going up right now. We got a call out. You available?"

"I'm just getting the kids to bed. I didn't get a page."

"Okay, I'm paging you now, *Doctor*," he quips in his smart-alecky, good-natured tone.

A jolt of adrenaline surges in my blood. It has been a long time since we had a call out. My winter pack has been ready for months. The much bulkier winter pack includes an avalanche transceiver that transmits a radio signal with a range of fifty meters. If a person wearing a beacon is caught in an avalanche, I can switch mine to Receive and home in on their signal. The winter pack also contains a compact aluminum-blade shovel for digging through cement-hard avalanche debris and a collapsible probe that, when assembled, becomes a six-foot-long pencil-thin aluminum rod used to poke through the snow to locate a buried person. I'm also testing a new avalanche safety device called an AvaLung, technically called an artificial air pocket device. It is a snorkel-type tube worn like a sling around the chest. If a person is buried by an avalanche, the tube lets him or her breathe under the snow. Using a series of one-way valves, the tube allows one to suck in air from the front of him or her, then shunts carbon-dioxide laden expired air out behind him or her, where its less likely to be breathed in.

I head into the mountain winter with specialized moun-taineering skis, also called alpine touring skis, the most efficient mode of travel in winter. They are a faster means of travel com-pared to snowshoes and cross-country skis. When I clip into just the toe binding, my heel can move up and down. I attach adhesive climbing skins on the bottom of the ski; the skins have one-way hairs like scales that allow the ski to slide up the slope but not down. Thus with the mobile heel and skins, I can easily ski *up* a mountain slope. Then, once atop, I remove the skins, lock down the heel of my boot to the ski, and schuss down.

Tonight, I dress in ski clothes for the second time that day, grab my gear, and zip out the door. Thirty minutes later, Jay Sherrerd, Todd Wells, and I are heading up the mountains at 9:30 P.M. in my Suburban, heat cranked up. The report is that a man in his thirties and his father set out snowshoeing at noon from Bennett Pass. The men were supposed to meet their wives at five o'clock at the Tim-berline Lodge bar for drinks. When they didn't show, the women drove ten miles down the hill to the Bennett Pass parking lot, where they found the empty, frosty car. In the city, not showing up for cocktails is no big worry. But in the mountains, when it is pitch-black, below freezing, and windy in January, it could mean death. A rescue call out was initiated immediately. Tonight hap-pens to be really dark and really cold. Despite the urgency, I drive slowly on the twisting mountain road because a fog has settled on the ground. I open my thermos of echinacea tea, take a sip, then spill it on my lap.

"Shouldn't you save that for the snowshoers?" asks Todd. Having done this countless times, he's thinking ahead.

"Oh, sure," I say, though I really wanted a cup of the warm, bland tea. We round the corner at the Teacup Lake, three miles from the pass. The thick fog disappears abruptly and the stars pop out. We exit Highway 35 at Bennett Pass and spy three sheriff's vehicles lighting up the parking lot. Sheriff Joe sits in his truck while two reserve deputies unload snowmobiles from a trailer.

"Thanks for coming, guys," says Joe in his unhurried, unflustered way. "Just hang out a few minutes. We're going to have the snowmobiles sweep the trail first. Let's hope it will be an easy night," Joe smiles, an eternal optimist. He wants to get home to his family after a long day's work, whereas Jay, Todd, and I are yearning to head out on a midnight ski search in the mountains. After all, we've come all this way, we're packed, we're ready.

"Where are the wives?" asks Jay.

"Good thinking," I say to Jay and give him an elbow in the ribs. "I knew there was a reason to bring along a lawyer." Jay succinctly interviews the wives of both men. He's done this countless times and knows just what to ask. I watch and learn. I've interviewed patients in the emergency room many times. Out here, the key questions are very different.

New snowshoes, say the wives, first day out, no experience.

No, they don't have survival gear or extra clothes.

Water? Not sure.

Food? Doubt it.

Flashlight? Don't think so.

Map and compass? No and no.

Oh, and by the way, they brought along a puppy.

We wait in the warmth of my truck, engine running to blast

the heat. On Joe's extra radio we listen to him and the deputies on snowmobiles communicate.

"Why don't we have decent radios?" I ask Jay and Todd. They've been members much longer than me. "All the other search and rescue groups show up with good radios."

"We just haven't bothered," says Jay. "I'd like to have one. Maybe we should bring it up at a meeting." He smiles.

"For a dozen rescues a year, it might be hard to justify the cost," Todd points out.

"Maybe the sheriff has smaller ones?" I ask. When I brought the question up at a Crag Rat meeting earlier in the year with Kirk Worril—a weather-wizened, twenty-year rescue veteran, horse enthusiast, and paramedic firefighter—he brought me a brick-sized radio from the sheriff's basement stash of unused gear. "I can do bicep curls with this," I said. "Can we buy some radios?" This was the radio I'd carried all summer.

"We'll have to talk about it at a meeting," Kirk answered.

Here in the warmth of my truck, Todd studies the topographic map of the pass and muses about the likely location of the two missing snowshoers. Todd figures the two probably followed the cross-country ski trail due south, then at some point veered off the trail and got lost. They either traveled west down a gentle slope into White River Canyon drainage or they headed northeast, in which case they would end up at the Pocket Creek cross-country ski area. The sheriff already sent a deputy to drive through Pocket Creek. In either case, if they didn't make it to a road by dark, they were likely lost. It is easy enough to get turned around on these trails, even on a midsummer day. In the winter, when everything is white, with no visual reference point to find the trail, it only takes a few seconds after darkness falls to become disoriented. The only trail markers are blazes, three-inch blue metal diamonds hammered onto trees every so often to delineate the cross-country ski trail. Inexperienced and ill-equipped, these two were not prepared for a night with temperatures that will dip to the single digits. They are probably lost. They might be dead.

Anyone—no matter what skill level, preparation, or physical fitness—can get into life-threatening trouble in the wilderness. Outdoor enthusiasts can get caught in foul weather, become lost, or get injured. It happens to those with only basic outdoor skill as well to as extreme athletes. Survival in the wilderness depends on physical and mental stamina, the situation, and often pure luck.

In a survival situation, people act in wildly different patterns. Some stop thinking logically. Some are stubborn and don't want to admit they are lost. A few panic or slip into depression, worry, despair, and hopelessness. More than one subject has been found with an unopened backpack of food, water, and clothing. Others, by contrast, employ a positive mental attitude and determination—often called the will to survive—to make it through the crisis. Highly motivated individuals often have strong reasons back home to live: children or a spouse.

The likelihood of survival rises dramatically when people are fit; maintain good nutrition and adequate hydration; are not fatigued; have the mental capacity to handle a crisis; and, above all, have a deep respect for Mother Nature. Of course, survival equipment and skills help, too. And so does training, practicing, and experience in survival skills.

Sometimes, though, no matter how prepared or skilled a person is, nature unleashes a fury and works against survival. That may be pure luck: if a storm passes or just weakens a bit, one may survive; if it strengthens, one may die. Luck does favor the prepared, for sure: a person with honed survival skills and equipment has a better chance in equal conditions than someone without. Wilderness survival often depends on what one does before getting in a dangerous situation.

Just how do you prepare for adversity in the mountains? For years mountaineers and outdoor aficionados have promoted the ten essentials, vital equipment you should always carry when in the outdoors.

The single most important item to keep from getting lost is a good topographic map of the area, showing roads, trails, geography, and elevation. With this kind of map you can look at the land, spy a ridge or valley, and find the corresponding feature on the map. A compass should accompany your map, so you can find your position on a map and then determine a route to travel.

Many hikers now carry GPS devices into the outdoors. These devices are about the size of a large cell phone and log on to U.S. government navigation satellites and can locate your exact point on Earth. As long as the GPS has a map of your particular hiking area loaded into its database, if you are lost, you can use a GPS to find your way. However, it takes some time to learn to use GPS units. The manuals are thick. The unit can tell you your longitude and latitude. But if you don't know the location of your car, the GPS cannot point you in the proper direction. You need a map, too. And these electronic devices don't always work: extreme cold can make them malfunction; their batteries die; the housings and screens break when dropped. In deep canyons, sometimes they can't receive a signal.

The list of survival essentials also includes extra food, water, and clothing. Sometimes this is an energy bar, windbreaker, and bottle of water. Other times it may be bulky winter clothing, a stove to melt snow, and freeze-dried meals. You should carry a means to start a fire: matches or a lighter and fire starter. Other essential items include a flashlight with extra batteries; a first aid kit and sunscreen; emergency shelter like a tarp; and a means of communication, such as a whistle, cell phone, radio, and signal mirror.

In addition to essential gear, a partner is vitally important. We conduct multiple rescues every year that would never be needed if a person were hiking with a partner. When Crag Rats like Jay educate outdoor enthusiasts, we recommend they attend a survival class, which includes learning skills on building a shelter, navigating, signaling, procuring water, and building a fire.

If you do get lost, injured, or otherwise stuck in a survival situation, you can follow a method for getting help. First, stop and calmly survey the situation—take stock of your equipment and supplies and assess the environment around you. This may take as little as thirty seconds if you simply took a wrong turn on a biking trail or sprained your ankle on a solo hike. Or it can be a major undertaking if you've capsized a raft in the rapids on a river trip.

Next, prioritize survival tasks, make a plan, act decisively, and follow through. Sometimes survival may be as simple as turning around and hiking back to your car. Or making a cell phone call. Or setting up a temporary shelter in a thunderstorm. Many people get into trouble because they are unwilling to recognize a potential disaster and take that simple conscious step, like turning around. They continue a trip in the wrong direction or they hike deeper into a storm or they get colder, wetter, and more tired. Above all, one needs to keep a positive attitude, never give up, perhaps even smile. This last bit is not something you can buy or be taught. But it is vital.

We've learned that the snowshoers lost on Bennett Pass have neither map nor compass. They don't have emergency shelter like a tarp or even a plastic bag. No fire starter or lighter to build a fire. They had no headlamp or flashlight. They don't even have spare clothing. And they have the dog.

"Why," I say while sneaking a cupful of tea, "would they bring the dog?"

Todd shrugs without looking up from the map, "People like their dogs."

The snowmobiles set off on the trail but quickly find that the snow is too soft; they can't ride farther than a few miles. The sun has melted the snow to slush, so the machines have difficulty plowing through on a narrow trail in thick trees. The deputies pick up snowshoe tracks with accompanying dog prints that head south, then southwest. If the prints were left by the lost men, they have apparently headed into White River Canyon. We're in our truck listening to the radio when Joe talks it over with the deputies.

"Okay, head back this way. We've got some Crag Rats on skis for you to pick up," says Joe. That's our cue, so we jump out of my truck and strap on our packs.

The loud machines roar back into the parking lot. We climb aboard and head into the woods. The throaty mechanical growl and bright headlights are alien intrusions into the forest. Trees, logs, and snowbanks zip by. The heavy machine doesn't fit in the rolling cross-country ski track. It bounces and bumps against the snowbank on the narrow trail. I am tossed around and thankful when we slow down to creep over a downed tree. This snowmobile shuttle is like a dark, electrifying ride at Disneyland.

After fifteen minutes riding on the snowmobile, the heavy

apparatus grinds to a halt. Word has come from Joe that the lost men have turned up back at the parking lot. It's midnight.

Apparently they had indeed followed some ski tracks into White River Canyon not knowing that they were leaving the trail. Once down in the drainage, they turned around. But instead of climbing back over the hill they came in on, they hiked north and could not locate the parking lot or cross-country ski trail. At four o'clock they decided to head back downhill, exactly in the opposite direction of their car. At dusk they came across an old snowmobile track. The two snowshoers now had a choice: go right, which meant uphill, or left, downhill.

If they had a map, they would have known that right, or north, was the proper choice. In two miles they would have hit Highway 35, about a mile west of the Bennett Pass snow park. They really didn't even need a compass to tell them which way was north, as they could have seen the setting sun in the west. A map would have showed them it was only a half hour hike. They would have arrived back at their car about the time their wives showed up at the parking lot.

But they went downhill because it was easier. They hiked and hiked and hiked. And carried the puppy. At least they stayed on the snowmobile track. Well after dark they came upon a sign that said HIGHWAY 26, 9 MILES, so they kept going. And at least they didn't stop. They would have quickly become cold and— combined with their thirst, hunger, inexperience, and lack of equipment—possibly would have succumbed to hypothermia. Luckily they formed a plan, stuck to it, and had the will to keep going. Exhausted, dehydrated, and hungry, the two came out on the highway fifteen miles south of Bennet Pass, around midnight, where a motorist gave them a ride.

Later, Jay will talk to the snowshoers in his lawyerly voice: kind but stern. Jay always makes a point to educate people in a polite, direct, calm way.

But now, in the black forest, when our snowmobile drivers turn around, Jay tells them to head back without us. Above us stars speckle the black sky and emit a faint glow on the mountain. The shadow is barely visible against the sky. Jay, Todd, and I watch the snow machines disappear down the trail. The foul exhaust smell dissipates, leaving us in the purity of the mountains. Clear, cold, dark. Quiet and serene.

This is a fringe benefit of mountain rescue that cannot be calculated, valued, expected, or taken for granted. We ski down the trail, one run home, in the frosty dark night.

CHAPTER 16

Plane Missing, Presumed Down

Viento Ridge, midwinter, midnight. Although I'm only five miles from my house by county roads, this is a place I would never go otherwise. Up Binns Hill Road, the potholed asphalt turns to heavy, logging-grade gravel. Beyond a locked county gate the gravel turns to mud, not the backyard variety but deep, wheel-sucking sludge. We pass a clear-cut in a saddle between two ridges and the confluence of five primitive dirt roads, all in various stages of being overgrown. The road we want, if you can call it a road, is covered by a blanket of snow. But the six inches of slush is like icing on thick brown muck. Our wheels spin and churn the snow and mud into a brown glop. It is so deep and slippery that a sheriff's pickup gets stuck, winched out, and nearly stuck again.

Finally we pull over into some weeds at the side of the road. The glow of our GPS says this is the location. Jim Wells and I strap on packs and start walking northeast in the dark with Sean, a local pilot who logged the GPS coordinates earlier that day from the air.

The beam of my xenon-bulb headlamp creates a cone-shaped funnel of light that the dense fog reflects at me. Jim's lamp, which is powered by a belt pack of batteries, is much brighter. We're tramping in snow and mud in plastic mountaineering boots that keep our feet dry and ankles protected. The forest atop Viento Ridge is strewn with large boulders, dense shrubs, and huge downed trees. It's cool and very dark. My plastic boots squeak in tune with Jim's.

After ten minutes of following the GPS we realize that we are walking parallel to the road. We huddle for a conference and decide to go back to the car, drive a mile back down the road to where the first team is parked, and start hiking from there. The GPS coordinates are accurate; we need to trust the instrument. In the pitch-black night, the GPS doesn't show ridges or canyons, only the direct line to the accident. We need to take the most direct route. We jump in the truck, our boots caked with snow and mud, four-wheel through the snow and mud-track to the first sheriff's pickup, park, and strap on our packs again. This time we are headed due north, directly down a ridge to the accident site.

The crisis started twenty-four hours previously when a Cirrus SR22 airplane was reported missing at 1:30 A.M. on Friday by a worried wife. All three men in the missing airplane are local, young family guys. Everyone in the community has some connection to them.

On Thursday evening the trio buzzed home in the Cirrus after a business trip to Salem, a hundred miles away. A dense fog settled over the Hood River Valley and the entire Columbia River Gorge. At night in foul weather, pilots have several approaches to our mountain town, which is nestled between two giant snow-capped volcanoes, smack on the crest of the Cascade Range. One approach is to come in high and safe at 7,000 feet, well above the tallest point in the valley, Mount Defiance. If you can spot the airfield, you can land; if you can't, you divert to the Dalles, Oregon, twenty miles east of Hood River. The second approach is to fly twenty miles east, duck below the fog, and follow the river west to Hood River. Sheriff Wampler, an experienced pilot, said if you fly at 2,000 feet over the river, you're safe in the gorge. The third means of arrival is to duck under the clouds at Troutdale and follow the river east, again staying at 2,000 feet and over water. When you see the bright-red neon signpost of the Meredith Hotel, hang a right.

But the route the Cirrus SR22 took was none of those. The plane ducked under the clouds at Troutdale, Oregon, and followed the river east a few miles. The last radar transmission suggested the Cirrus turned right above the town of Stevenson, Washington, at 8:30 P.M. on Thursday and made a beeline for home, twenty miles *before* the Meredith sign, up and over the south wall of the 2,000-foot basalt cliffs. My friend Doug, a local pilot, later told me this is called scud running, flying just under the clouds and just above the treetops.

A large-scale air search was launched at dawn on Friday, hampered by the continued thick fog and occasional drizzle. The search included Sheriff Wampler in the department's Piper Cub, a half dozen local pilots, Portland's Civil Air Patrol (an auxiliary of the U.S. Air Force made up of former pilots that volunteer for such occasions), and the Army National Guard from Salem. The sky above the gorge buzzed with aircraft. They searched the airwaves for signals from an emergency position indicating radio beacon, or EPIRB, but none was found. They searched up and down the Willamette Valley near Salem. Spotters looked for a bright orange and white parachute, the latest technology with which the plane was equipped. If it lost power during flight, the parachute could have been deployed to ease the plane to the ground.

Finally, about dusk, when most aircraft were making their final passes before calling it a day, a keen-eyed Army National Guard spotter in a Black Hawk spied the wreckage high on

Viento Ridge, five miles from the Hood River airfield. The chopper crew spied two dead bodies, but could not see the third. Sean, the local pilot now hiking with us, flew quickly over the site and marked the GPS coordinates. He then flew up the ridge, found a logging road, and logged another GPS reading. He traced a network of primitive forest roads until he found pavement and the airport. His alert thinking located vehicle access to the crash just before dark, at which time the Crag Rats were paged.

Until all three bodies were confirmed dead, this was a search and *rescue* mission.

So on this dark night, Jim, Sean, and I tramp through the woods using the GPS unit to locate the crash site. Even though we try to follow the GPS bearing, we have to detour because of giant downed trees, massive piles of basalt boulders, deep depressions in the natural fall line of the ridge, and vine maple thickets too dense to walk through. We proceed slowly: we can't afford even a minor ankle sprain. An advance team is twenty minutes ahead of us on the ridge. It is so dark, we are unsure if either team is on the right ridge. We could be thirty feet from the crash site and walk right by. So Sheriff Wampler fires up the Piper Cub again and flies laps up and down the ridge above the treetops to give us a reference point. With every pass of the plane, we point our headlamps at the sky. Joe can see both teams. Yes, he says on the radio, we are headed to the crash. I'm not sure if there is a name for this navigation technique, but it works.

"Stand by," I hear on the radio, as do several hundred people listening on scanners at the Hood River airfield and around the gorge. The advance team has made it to the crash site. Jim, Sean, and I pause in the dark forest. The search is over, the plane located. Now we have to wait, a familiar function of SAR missions. We turn off our headlamps to save the batteries. We are immediately chilled by the frigid night air that we didn't notice while hiking. I have a light sweat on my body and feel a wicked coldness seep into my bones. We pile on every layer from our packs: hat, gloves, coats.

In ten minutes the call comes in.

"Twelve fifty-nine times three." All three dead. In that instant, rescue becomes recovery.

Body recoveries can be nasty. Unlike in a search for a lost person in which we don't know the extent of injuries, or the rescue of an injured person in which we are racing daylight to save a life or limb, body recoveries have little sense of urgency. We know the job has to be done, but there are no lives to save. No golden hour of trauma. Certainly we need not risk a difficult extrication in the middle of a dark, cold winter night.

With a body recovery, especially in a horrific plane crash, the emotional response of rescuers is first and foremost in my mind. As a doctor, I am familiar with blood and injury, and, unfortunately, death. I see minor injuries like cuts and scrapes. I see major injuries, like broken bones and large lacerations. In my training, I've seen severe car accidents and gunshot wounds.

My first inspection of a dead body was while dissecting a cadaver in medical school. It was much less human, more of a learning device. "Keep the head covered," we were instructed, "until next semester." Our team of four students—indeed the entire class—worked with scientific chatter and the occasional chuckle, necessary coping mechanisms for dealing with bodies. I was fascinated by the science of dissection, ever since reading about Michelangelo and da Vinci unlawfully dissecting by candlelight in the catacombs of Florence and Rome.

I vividly remember the first time I had to pronounce a patient dead, years later, when I was a newbie intern at a busy university hospital in Salt Lake City, barely four months after graduating from medical school. At midnight the nurse told me a patient on my partner's service had expired. I had to pronounce him dead and sign the death certificate. "Before two A.M., please," the nurse asked, "so I can release the body to the morgue." The death was expected, following a long battle with a chronic disease. The family had already come to view the body. The nurses had done all their paperwork. I was the last one called. I had never been taught this skill in medical school, not even forewarned it would come. The room was dark and quiet. The body was cool and waxy, with a slight hint of an unpleasant musty odor, like old wet wool. I placed my stethoscope on the chest: silence. I felt for a pulse: nothing. I checked again, signed the chart, went back to bed— and stayed awake the rest of the night wondering if the man was really dead. I had heard stories of bodies falling into a hibernation state, having no detectable pulse or respiration, then waking in the morgue. I had no idea if they were true.

Death does strange things to one's emotions, more so if it is someone you know, not an anonymous body showing up in the morgue or cadaver lab. If it is a loved one, expected and unexpected deaths trigger typical grief reactions. But to rescuers, the emotional response is much different, especially for those who have no medical or rescue experience. Rescuers may feel sad, depressed, anxious, worried, or even, sometimes, without emotions. Rescuers may wonder about the deceased's wife, kids, job, home. Or they may think about their own lives and families: *What if I were to die in a plane crash?* Some rescuers feel they should suppress these emotions so that they can get the job done.

All emergency personnel—rescuers, paramedics, doctors, nurses, firefighters, and police—have a variety of coping mechanisms for dealing with death. Often laughter eases the gruesome nature of a body recovery. Sometimes we default to the business approach: just get the job done. Sometimes people have to look up close, to determine what happened from a scientific point of view. Sometimes rescuers avoid looking directly at the body, linger in the background, or choose mundane tasks that do not involve direct contact with the bodies.

In severe cases, rescuers succumb to more poignant emotions, such as critical incident stress syndrome. This condition, similar to post-traumatic stress disorder, involves minor behavior and emotional problems that can develop into life-changing stressors. Body recovery in mountain rescue can cause such a state. It is normal to feel withdrawn during a body recovery. It can be normal to feel queasy, sad, and even anxious. Sometimes with a more prolonged and severe reaction, a rescuer can feel separation, depression, and fear. Rescuers can have physical reactions to emotional stress like nausea, muscle spasms, increased pulse or breathing rates, problems with vision or hearing, insomnia, sexual dysfunction, and poor appetite. Most people can rebound and recover after a few days or a week. But it is normal to mull over the case, feel vulnerable and sad for a short time. When a rescuer experiences a prolonged period of having problems resuming to normal emotional equilibrium, his or her entire life can go awry. Feelings of emotional withdrawal, dislocation, horror, flashbacks, nightmares, grief, anger, despair, sadness, and hopelessness may be natural, as long as the feelings are short-lived and the person recognizes them, comes to terms with them, and moves on. The worst situation is when rescuers experience cognitive dysfunctions due to a body recovery that cause problems with work and family, like disorientation; impaired decision-making; and difficulty with judgment, memory, comprehension, and concentration.

The best rescuers—the ones that keep coming out time and again—are able to handle difficult situations, like a plane crash, as part of the job. They separate the thorny emotions of mountain rescue from their home life. They approach situations in a businesslike way: *Let's roll up our sleeves and get to work. If I don't do it, someone else will have to.* Professionals like firefighters, police, paramedics, nurses, and doctors often do this routinely and automatically: often they can forget about a death five minutes into the next call or patient. Volunteers, however, who don't encounter death routinely, may have a more difficult time.

I ponder this catastrophic and tragic trio of deaths as we wait for team one to climb back up the ridge. I'm feeling rather businesslike; instantly I start planning to devote tomorrow, Saturday, to help with this recovery. While Jim and I wait on the cold, windy ridge for the advance team to hike back out, my phone rings.

"Chris, we have a body recovery tomorrow," says Bill Pattison, a five-decade veteran of the Crag Rats. He is a cheery, fit, septuagenarian who runs the Cloud Cap Restoration Committee, comes to most meetings, and is always willing to roll up his sleeves for the group. For instance, he thinks nothing of spending hours on the phone to figure out why the propane lanterns in Cloud Cap are not burning brightly. Then he will drop everything to drive to Portland, pick up special high-altitude lamp mantles, drive to Cloud Cap, and install them. He knows more about the history of the group than anyone and will talk your ear off about it. "Can you make it?" asks Bill.

"I think so. I'm on Viento Ridge right now. I will check with my wife."

"Good. You make eight. I have eight Rats," says Bill.

"Eight—that's great!" I am surprised and happy that we will

have a good crew for tomorrow. At the same time, I'm reorganizing my day in my head so I can be available. I'll have to call home tonight.

"How are things? What should I tell them?" asks Bill.

"Well, I'm not at the crash site, but it sounds bad. We'll need some people with experience. Everyone will need hiking boots, rain gear, and gloves. There's not much snow, but it is wet and muddy. Rain gear is probably more important than snow gear."

"Great. I will let everyone know."

As we grow colder, Jim is worried about the advance team becoming lost. They are not mountain rescuers but volunteer reserve deputies. He calls them on the radio as they hike back up the ridge. From his many years of experience, he decides to supplement his directions: he digs out his whistle and blows it loudly every five minutes.

"Oh, we hear you," says one of the deputies on the radio.

"Great," says Jim. He continues the blasts every few minutes. Finally we see the sole flashlight of the trio walking up the ridge. When the advance team reaches our perch, they take a quick break, and we give them some food and water.

"Let's keep the break short," says Jim. "I don't want you guys to get as chilled as we are."

"We found them. All dead," said one of the deputies. I can read his face: all business, clear and concise, matter-of-fact. "And it's bad."

"How bad?"

"Really, really bad."

I say, "Are we able to reach the crash on foot? Any cliffs?" If we need technical-rescue gear, it would be better to know tonight.

"No, it is accessible. It's steep, but you can get to it."

We climb out to the vehicles together, marking the route with bright pink and orange surveyor's tape.

An hour later, I pull into my driveway. I methodically organize my gear for tomorrow, jump in the shower, and crawl into bed.

The next morning, the weather is cold and clear at the airport; clouds have settled over Viento Ridge. I return to the staging area after a few hours sleep, feeling rather emotionally neutral. We've got a job to do; I'm going to help. I think little of the dead, their families, and the loss to the community. I focus on the task at hand: hiking into the mountains to bring back three bodies. It's cold, the weather is marginal, and we've got a large crew of varying levels of experience in dealing with body recoveries. Crag Rats arrive. A crew from Wind River Search and Rescue shows up with all-terrain vehicles and four-wheel-drive pickups. Many of the local pilots who helped with the air search come back. The families drive up, too, recognizable by their grief. I take Dwayne Troxell aside.

"I think we should limit the people headed to the crash site," I say.

Dwayne says, "We can't use a helicopter. It's too tight with the big trees, and the military won't authorize one for body recoveries anyway."

"Once we have the bodies packaged, we can get a few groups of people to help us haul them out."

"We'll let Wind River help us with the hard part," Dwayne jokes. The Crag Rats have a long-standing mutual aid agreement with Wind River: they are not mountain rescuers but do primarily ground SAR, below the timberline. We like to give them some of the grunt work, in a good-natured, sibling rivalry sort of way.

At the briefing, Dwayne takes charge. "I will lead in the Crag Rats. We'll shuttle everyone up so we can limit vehicles. When we've packaged the bodies, we'll need everyone to help us carry them out." He looks around to make sure he's got everyone's attention. "This next announcement is really important. I've had about ten calls from the company that built this plane. This plane was equipped with a parachute and has an explosive on board to deploy it. If the chute has not deployed, the explosive is extremely dangerous. Doc, you got anything?"

"I've got medical gloves for everyone in the truck," I say. I restocked all the medical gear last summer. "And if anyone feels queasy, just sit down and take a break. No big deal."

Even I am not quite prepared for the extent of the wreckage and the condition of the bodies when we approach the crash site this dull gray morning. I am expecting to see a small plane in several pieces and the three bodies strewn about. But the Cirrus was completely and totally obliterated. Upon contact with the ground, it was pulverized. Only a dozen chunks of wreckage are bigger than a kitchen table: everything else was reduced to small fragments of metal, glass, plastic, carbon, foam, and wires. I spy the main chunk of twisted metal and wire that was the cockpit. The motor block is twenty feet away. Downslope fifty yards lie two sections of wing and the propeller. The parachute is completely fanned out with its two dozen lines in neat rows. It is the only thing that looks orderly in a sea of chaos.

Dwayne asks me to record the crash, and so I take a hundred images with my digital camera. Meanwhile, Dwayne surveys the scene and picks up what personal effects he can find for the wives. Paul Crowley and John Harlin locate the rocket canister; it looks like it has detonated, but we defer to Dwayne. Paul marks the spent canister with yellow sheriff's tape—no need to take chances.

We find a small oxygen canister; Paul marks that, too, so that this potentially flammable device is clearly visible. We find the EPIRB smashed with the batteries strewn nearby: no wonder it did not emit a signal. We mark it, too, for the Federal Aviation Administration and National Transportation Safety Board officials who will come to the wreckage later today.

The first body is lying facedown in the dirt. Several Crag Rats load him in a body bag, a major chore on the steep slope and amid the wreckage.

The second body is strapped into the seat in the remnants of the fuselage, tilting upside down and to the side. We tie the hunk of tangled metal and wires to a tree with the rope that John had keenly thought to bring. The seat belt is cut with tree-trimming shears. The body drops to the ground, and the guys load him into a second body bag.

The third body we also package quickly. Once in body bags, we realize we need more rope to make them easier to carry. We have a long haul out. Dwayne radios the FAA and NTSB officials. Yes, it's okay to cut the parachute lines they say. Take pictures first. Only cut what you need. It most likely is not a crime scene, but they still need to survey the crash. When we tie up the body bags, one zipper rips. Obviously, it's not meant for the rigors of a mountain environment. I duct tape it together. The bodies smell foul, even when sealed in the black vinyl bags.

"I need to order some of those heavy-duty body bags for the truck," says Dwayne. "These I got this morning from the funeral home." As a veteran military pararescue jumper and seasoned lawman he has seen more than his share of dead, too.

We take a half hour to package the bodies. Then we spend another thirty minutes scouring the scene, searching for personal effects, and dangerous items. The extra time helps us process and reflect on the crash and the bodies. We try to determine the flight path. This scientific approach helps us all cope with what is a visually overpowering scene. Too ghastly for levity, too compelling to ignore.

Dwayne points out a sheared six-foot-diameter Douglas fir about sixty feet off the ground and a second severed trunk about thirty feet off the ground. "Probably didn't know what hit them," The FAA and NTSB would later determine this was a controlled flight into terrain at roughly 200 miles per hour. In lay terms, this means they basically flew full speed into the side of a mountain.

Eventually we start the long trek out. The eight of us can haul only two bags. Dwayne stays to supervise the scene. A half dozen Wind River volunteers come to take out the third bag. When Paul, Steve Castagnoli, Brian Hukari, and I reach the crest of the road, we find a flurry of volunteers and media. Paul asks them to turn their cameras away before we bring the body out from the trees into the back of a sheriff's office pickup. Paul and Brian immediately slam the tailgate to hide the body bag.

I spy white bread, convenience store cold cuts, processed cheese, and powdered doughnuts on the tailgate of another truck. I remove my leather gloves, then peel off the medical gloves I wear underneath. After I clean my hands with an antibacterial wipe, I scarf two doughnuts and inhale a sandwich, as do my partners.

A guy in a government-type navy windbreaker asks me about the explosive and the EPIRB. Eager to help, I play back my digital photos, but my battery power is dwindling. I tell him we saw the smashed EPIRB and the detonated canisters of the parachute deployer.

"I'll need copies of those pictures," he says. I'm taken aback.

I want to help, but since I recorded the scene on behalf of the sheriff's office, I don't feel at liberty to pass out pictures, especially images of mutilated bodies. Then I instantly wonder who I'm showing these pictures to: a member of the press possibly?

"You'll have to ask the sheriff. I'll give him a CD," I say, hoping it's the right answer.

"FAA," he says, flashing an ID card and a badge. "I *will* need copies of those pictures." This is my first mission involving the federal government. I'm confused about the legality and I'm also disturbed by the request. Especially considering the situation and the brutal task we just completed carrying out the first body bag. Fortunately, Paul's standing next to me.

"Make him get a warrant," whispers Paul, loud enough for the guy to hear. As a judge, Paul has a keen sense of proper procedure.

"Okay. You'll have to ask the sheriff," I say again, hoping that's the end of the conversation.

Paul and I quickly walk away, stuff more processed food down our gullets, and wash it down with bottled water. In ten minutes, we have a conference and decide we should head back down the ridge. Back through the brambles and thickets, in fifteen minutes we meet up with another team. It's the Wind River guys. They are fatigued and faltering. Paul and I grab hold of the package at the front. Paul has them walk in sync. I follow his lead. We get another package up the hill to the truck.

Later that week I attend the services for Paul and Chris. Mourners pack a local church and the high school auditorium.

"Mrs. Stein says you guys are heroes," says Skylar after school that week. None of us think of ourself as a hero. Rather, we are members of the community, and this is a way we help the community. Many people help in other ways: volunteering at school, for the fire department, or for the city council, or other types of activities. We are no more heroes than the group at the food bank or someone who delivers Christmas presents to the poor. I explain that to my daughters, but with the massive press coverage and the buzz around town, it is difficult to put this in perspective to a child.

Paul organizes a debriefing the next week in the basement room of the courthouse. Mostly the Crag Rats who were near the crash site show up. In our causal style, we discuss the likely cause of the crash but not our emotions dealing with the body recovery. I wasn't too worried about our guys, but I was a bit disappointed we didn't discuss our emotional responses to the dead.

"I didn't expect to sing 'Kumbaya' around the table," Paul would later say with his dry humor when I asked him what he thought of the hour we spent in the basement room in the courthouse. "But it would have been nice to talk a bit more about our feelings."

We talk about the crash at the next meeting. The Crag Rats go over rescues as a process and try to find something to be learned. We critique ourselves at every juncture. This mission was particularly horrible, yet we still focus on the details of our actions. We decide that we should have had a Crag Rat at the top of the ridge, writing down the names of everyone going into the forest. We also should have made sure at least one Crag Rat was assigned to each package: employees of one dead man carried out one bag. We learn something from every rescue, even this most gruemost one.

The recovery, it turns out, is not over for me. Four months later, one of the wives asks me to meet with her and the other two widows to see my pictures. I put her off three times, thinking that if she really wants to see the details, she will keep calling me. And she does. So finally I acquiesce. Like many family members in similar situations, the wives first want to determine exactly "what happened." I sit down with the two of the wives for an hour. I show them the least graphic pictures first, then move on at their behest to more difficult ones. But after seeing the digital images, they come to realize that their husbands' deaths were instantaneous: the men never suffered.

"It's not as bad as I thought," they both say afterward. "Thank you. That helped."

Later that summer, my neighbor, who had trained the pilot on flying the Cirrus and who was good friends with one passenger, asks me to take him back to the crash site. He asks me repeatedly, and I run out of excuses.

"You need to do this," says Jen.

"I know."

My neighbor and I set off to the crash site on a cold, foggy, drizzly fall morning, weather not unlike the day the plane went down. The sun cannot find a hole through the clouds. We drive up the road, make a wrong turn, find the staging area, and set off in a downpour. My raincoat keeps me dry, but my pants quickly soak up water from brushing against knee-high ferns and Oregon grape. We can see clumps of vine maple and thick groves of fir trees thirty yards all around us. But the fog gives them a backdrop of white and the scenery is unchanging, creating the sensation that we are hiking down the ridge but never going anywhere. There is no trail: we hike over logs, around big rocks, and scramble through thickets of shrubs and trees. The leaves dump buckets of water on our heads as we push through the branches. Bits of orange and pink surveyor's tape are still on the tree branches, reassuring me of the route.

Finally we find the crash site. I point out the fractured trees and the locations of the wreckage and bodies. We find tiny bits and pieces of metal and glass, but for the most part, the slope has been cleaned by a salvage crew. My friend erects a small plaque.

I did have one nightmare after the mission, but I never told anyone. Usually my sleep is so deep that I never remember my dreams. But I remembered this one: I saw a bloody unrecognizable head with a floating severed arm. It appeared only for a split second. Then I jolted awake.

CHAPTER 17

Svitek v. Nidecker and Mount Bachelor

The snow came, dumping more than two feet that week and at least twelve inches overnight. High winds loaded gullies, chutes, and couloirs with fat white flakes. After the week-long storm, the sun appeared at dawn and the cool temperatures continued. That day at 5 A.M. it was eleven degrees, clear, and calm. Like a big swell lining up heavy rollers for that once-a-year dream surf session, all elements were in place at Mount Bachelor, Oregon, on February 9, 2002. It was a magical, deep-powder day.

If you ski or snowboard, you know that deep, dry, light powder is pure euphoria. Skis and snowboards float and glide in powder, especially when it is so deep that it feels like you are not touching the bottom of the slope. Long, high-speed swooping turns infuse you with an endorphin and adrenaline high. Light snow billows overhead and engulfs you—called the white room. The centripetal force zings your belly as a roller coaster does, but it is smooth and quiet, nonmechanical and natural. Gliding into a turn you float weightless for an instant, then your speed slingshots you into the wide-open field of white.

A deep-powder day doesn't happen very often; when it does, if you have work or family duties, you may miss it. Many feel it's why we ski and snowboard in the first place; the whole season culminates in that one epic day or that one spectacular run in deep, dry, untracked powder. It is a thrill rarely equaled in this world. As the day goes on, you forget about everything else. This is as good as life can get. You have tapped the source.

Of course, people fall when they ski or snowboard. Maybe you catch an edge, or pearl, when the tip of your snowboard dives under the snow, or endo, when you tumble head over heels. Maybe you slide to a stop and lose your balance just in the wrong place. Maybe you even push the limits: try slopes a little too steep and a little too deep for your skill level.

And then, catastrophe. Kate Svitek, a twenty-two-year-old off-duty lift operator, college graduate, and adventure-sports enthusiast, fell. But she didn't fall in a pile of snow or on a wide-open slope. She fell on a steep slope in a dense forest in the most remote part of the ski resort on Mount Bachelor. She fell alone, as she earlier chose to separate from her friends at the top of the run. She landed upside down in a deep tree well in deep snow. Immediately, she probably had an overwhelming sense of claustrophobia and dread. She was boxed in by the light, dry powder snow with no way to right herself.

Tree wells are the deep holes in the snow that lie around the trunk of a big conifer. On heavy snow years these holes can be up to ten feet deep. After a storm, they can often be filled with powder snow, loose, dry, and deep. Thus, if you fall in a hole, especially if you fall headfirst, it is extremely difficult to extricate yourself. There is nothing to grab onto or with which to push yourself right side up. It's much like being trapped in a well.

At 4:45 P.M., Kate was reported missing by friends, after they had cruised around the mountain looking for her. When a missing person report occurs on a subzero evening at a large ski resort, everyone takes it seriously. One of the largest, most costly, and most labor intensive searches in Oregon history was launched.

Ski patrol immediately fanned out to sweep the slopes. The lodges were searched, the bars and the restaurants, too. At 9:30 P.M., the Deschutes County sheriff was notified, and at 10:22 P.M. a page went out to search and rescue. Volunteers showed up at midnight. More than two dozen searched all night. They searched all the next day and for the next ten days. The search involved twenty crews from four states. The Army National Guard sent Black Hawks. Ski patrollers scoured the mountain by snowmobile. Search dogs came from California.

Nights got colder. Days got longer. No Kate. The likelihood of survival plummeted with the below-freezing night temperatures.

That cold February day my phone rang when the kids and I were assembling puzzles on the floor of the living room.

"Hey, Chris," said Jay, in a casual tone, "a couple of us are heading down to Bend tomorrow in a sheriff's truck to help with the search for that missing snowboarder. Want to go?" Work the next day kept me from going.

The search was never officially suspended, only scaled back after two weeks. Deputies investigated the possibility of foul play. Ski patrol ran regular runs on the remote ski run called Northwest Territories West Bowls, starting with the last-seen point, the spot on the upper slopes where Svitek separated from her friends. Everybody essentially lost hope of finding Kate Svitek alive. The chances of surviving for two days were good, one week slim, but after two weeks extremely low.

Three weeks later, on March 4, ski patrollers Ray Irvine and David Prather set out on what had become a routine West Bowl search. They started at the top of Northwest Territories chairlift, which is close to the 9,064-foot summit of the dormant volcano. The wide-open snowfields were beginning to melt in the spring sun. Irvine and Prather followed the fall line from the last-seen point, just above timberline, and skied into the thick glades below. They were in a chute that had been searched several times before. But this time, up to a foot of snow had melted, compacted, and consolidated.

Irvine's eye was caught by something that didn't look like it belonged in nature. In search and rescue, experts often teach newcomers not to look for a missing person, but look for something that doesn't belong. Irvine skied over to a tree, brushed aside some snow, and realized it was a boot. They found Kate at 12:53 P.M., one day after Kate's parents had held a memorial in her home town of Spring House, Pennsylvania, and twenty-three days after she disappeared.

Kate had died of asphyxiation, most likely immediately after falling. She was buried nine feet deep, about 370 yards downhill from the last-seen point, in a tree well in a thick clump of trees. The young college graduate, who moved out West to live the dream, who ripped one of the best powder days of the season, was dead.

Tree wells form in midwinter, mostly in the Western United States. Deep depressions in the snow form at the base of trees initially because the large, low-lying branches of conifers collect snow and shed it away from the trunk. As winter progresses, the branches droop, take up space, and further keep snow from gathering around the trunk. Thus where the snowpack may be seven or eight feet deep on open slopes, the tree wells may have only three or four feet of snow, leaving a five-foot hole.

After a big storm, the snow-loaded branches create a second hazard: branches dump snow on top of a victim who falls in.

The steepness of the slope creates a third hazard: fresh snow can spill on top of a person falling, further burying him or her.

Initially Kate's airway was probably obstructed, her mouth and throat jammed full of snow. (Trauma was possible but not likely, I decided, after reviewing the autopsy and sheriff's reports. Although she wasn't wearing a helmet, there were no cuts or scrapes on her body.) If she had an obstructed airway, death came rather quickly. After a few minutes without air, a person falls unconscious; in five minutes she is at risk for permanent brain damage; in a few more, the heart and lungs begin to stop working; in ten, death occurs.

If Kate's airway was clear, then she almost certainly died from carbon dioxide displacement asphyxia. In normal respiration, a person breathes in to draw oxygen, and then breathes out to expel toxic carbon dioxide. When buried in snow, one can draw in oxygen from the snow pack, but eventually the area around the face becomes saturated with carbon dioxide. When one keeps rebreathing the same air, it eventually becomes filled up with carbon dioxide and no oxygen. Rebreathing expired air rapidly causes suffocation. If a person has a large air pocket in front of his or her face, sometimes he or she can live for thirty minutes or longer when upside down in a tree well.

Even if Kate didn't die instantly, she certainly became disoriented right away. Her ability to right herself would have been extremely limited. First, she would have to push against the snow, but the light dry powder would have been like trying to swim in feathers. She'd push against it but wouldn't have been able to get any purchase to flip over. Grabbing a branch may have been impossible. She was upside down with her back to the tree. She would have had to reach way up and behind, contorting her arm, provided there was even a branch to grab.

We have up to five deaths a year due to tree-well and deep-snow suffocation. Almost every skier and snowboarder has a near miss at some point.

There are means to prevent getting stuck in a tree well. First, you need to ride terrain and snow conditions within your skill level and stay in control. You need to have the right skis or snowboard: for deep powder you need longer and wider skis or snowboards, so you have more surface area, float better, and have better control. You need to stay in voice and visual contact with your partner; ride slopes one at a time so you can use a spotter. If you go down, you can try to grab the tree, land feet first, or roll upright. If you fall into a tree well, you can try to make an air pocket in front of your face to give your partner more time to dig you out.

Certain tools may help. A whistle is louder than the human voice if you need to alert your partner. An avalanche beacon may help speed recovery. An AvaLung, also called an artificial air pocket device, may improve survival time. The AvaLung was primarily designed for avalanches, hence the name.

Kate did not have survival and rescue equipment. She was an intermediate snowboarder, but she was riding some of the most difficult terrain in one of the most challenging snow conditions on Mount Bachelor. Her board was designed for all-purpose riding, not deep snow and steep slopes. And she voluntarily separated from her partners. When her riding buddies headed straight down the fall line from the last-seen point, she decided to take a chute to her left. Although the chutes are separated by fifty yards near the top of the conical volcano, as riders descend slopes, the two chutes get farther and farther apart. By the time Kate fell, she was several hundred yards away from her friends, well out of voice and visual contact.

After the massive rescue and recovery of Kate's body, Kate's parents filed a lawsuit against both Mount Bachelor Ski Resort and Nidecker snowboards, the brand of snowboard and bindings Kate used.

Mount Bachelor, as it turned out, was dismissed from the case. Kate had signed a liability document, sometimes called a release or waiver, to get her complimentary employee season pass. With the document, she had acknowledged the inherent risk (that which is inseparable from the sport like the risk of hypothermia when snowboarding), released Mount Bachelor from legal responsibility, and waived her right to sue in cases of simple negligence, or when someone fails to act reasonably. Whether or not Bachelor was negligent, Kate forfeited the right to sue. Such a document does not release the resort from gross negligence, or willful, wanton, intentional wrongs. If ski patrollers did not repair a safety gate in a timely fashion, that may be simple negligence. A patroller would be grossly negligent if he or she showed up to work intoxicated. But gross negligence was not substantiated in this case. So Mount Bachelor was off the hook.

Nidecker Snowboards, however, was on the line for $15 million for manufacturing defective bear-trap bindings that were "unreasonably dangerous" and for negligently failing to make bindings that spontaneously release upon a fall. The two-strap highback bindings are what almost every snowboarder uses, and thus if Nidecker was liable, so was almost every snowboard binding manufacturer.

Nidecker has an unusual, lengthy history. Henri Nidecker started the company in 1887 in Vaud, Switzerland. Originally, he built cart wheels, ladders, and wheelbarrows. In 1912, he hand-crafted ash and hickory skis, then moved to plywood in 1946 and fiberglass in 1963. The company is still run by Henri Nidecker, Jr., who declined to offer a settlement. Nidecker had weathered lawsuits before, and it would face this one.

I have laced up my boots and buckled into bindings hundreds of times since first riding a Burton Backhill in 1985 on Mount Hood. But now I am riding in Multnomah County, Oregon, Courtroom 734, in front of twelve jurors and a judge. This is the first jury trial against a snowboard company. If Nidecker loses, it could be a blow to snowboard companies across the globe. Because of my background in snowboarding and mountain safety, I was hired to provide expert testimony on behalf of Nidecker. Over the course of the previous six months, I spent many hours re-viewing documents, searching the literature, calling wilderness-medicine colleagues with experience in snow submersion, and viewing pictures of the scene and the body. I traveled to Bend, strapped on my snowboard, and traced Kate's run from where she was last seen to the tree well where she died.

The exhausting two-week trial centered on one issue: would snowboard bindings that spontaneously release during a fall, like those on skis, have saved Kate's life? Nearly every snowboard binding available today *does not* spontaneously release, unlike alpine ski bindings which automatically pop off with a fall. With snowboard bindings, the rider is strapped or clipped into the bindings: they do not come off unless the rider takes them off.

Meyer releasable snowboard bindings were marketed in Eu-rope as early as 1989. In fact, they were distributed by Nidecker. But poor sales ended production after three years: very few riders bought the bindings and, many of those that did returned them.

They simply did not work well, and snowboarders quickly learned that riding with both feet fixed to the board was much safer. Earl Miller, inventor of the ski brake, designed releasable snowboard bindings around 1993, which for many years were produced by Revolution Manufacturing of Utah, a company run by his son. They are not commercially available to consumers, however. I know this because before the trial, I tried for six months to purchase a set.

Although potentially useful in an avalanche, in which you would want to release your board so you are not dragged down deep into the sliding snow, for all other aspects of snowboarding one primary worry exists: if only one binding were to release during a fall, a disastrous injury could result to the leg still attached to the board. Unlike snowboards, alpine skis release from feet to protect the knees and ankles from injuries from torque, or twisting forces. Since a snowboard is three times heavier than a ski, it can yield about three times the force—and three times the damage—if the snowboard were connected to only one foot, which could happen if a rider had releasable bindings and only one foot popped out. As it is now, a snowboarder falls with both feet fixed to a single board; this is much safer because injuries are usually impact, unlike the twisting injuries of skiers.

Even if releasable bindings were available, it still would have been nearly impossible for Kate to have ejected from the bindings either spontaneously or manually. If the bindings were tight enough to withstand the force of snowboarding, they would have been too tight to simply kick off. She was buried upside down and most likely could not have reached the bindings to manually remove them.

During extensive research on the topic, I found it really doesn't matter what snow tools one chooses, skis or a snowboard.

Of forty-seven cases of nonavalanche related snow immersion death (NARSID) cases in the United States, thirty-one have been skiers with releasable bindings. What's more, former Whistler ski patroller Dr. Robert Cadman buried six skiers and four snowboarders to study NARSID; when the skiers and snowboarders kicked off their planks, they sank deeper. Avalanche expert Paul Baugher also ran tests of buried skiers and snowboarders and got the same results.

Other lawsuits have been filed regarding tree well–submersion deaths. Burton Snowboards, Homewood Mountain Resort in California, and a Lake Tahoe sports shop were sued after snowboarder Isaac Goodkind died of NARSID on January 2, 1993. In addition to suing Burton for not making releasable bindings, the plaintiffs blamed Burton for not making a bright fluorescent base that is visible in a search and for using advertising that encourages the use of intoxicants. The judge dismissed the case against Burton, the sports shop, and the employee because Goodkind signed a "Retail Snowboard Equipment Purchase, Release of Liability, Waiver of Claims and Assumption of Risk Agreement" upon purchase of his snowboard equipment. The case against Homewood, however, was not dismissed, because the lawsuit claimed the ski area should have closed the area of the accident and that they negligently conducted the search. It took them five hours to find and dig out Isaac, who was buried in an eighteen-foot snowbank. The case was settled out of court.

This distinction between gross negligence and simple negligence is the crux of outdoor law because of releases or waivers of liability for the former. It is this issue that drives up the liability insurance and thus the prices of lift tickets, guide fees, equipment, and other costs that are transferred to consumers.

The outdoor-adventure sports standard was first set in 1929

when James Murphy sued Steeplechase Amusement Company on Coney Island because a ride called the Flopper flopped him. Because the inherent risk in riding the Flopper is being flopped, the New York State Court of Appeals dismissed the claim. This common law principle is called *volenti non fit injuria*, or those consenting cannot be injured. This held until 1974 when James Sunday sued Stratton Mountain Resort in Vermont after he fell skiing and became paralyzed. In *Sunday v. Stratton Corp.*, the courts awarded the man $1.5 million, reversing the ideal of inherent risk. The court said that the ski resort had a heightened duty for safety. In other words, although the inherent risk of skiing includes falling, it may not be the responsibility of the skier to prevent a fall.

Rising insurance premiums and expensive lawsuits threatened the entire industry, and drove up costs that were transferred to consumers. As a result, many states passed recreation safety acts to protect businesses from frivolous lawsuits. Even so, outdoor-recreation companies retain costly insurance and aggressive risk-management programs.

The biggest lawsuit in years to challenge outdoor liability laws sent chills through the outdoor industry. On January 17, 2001, Pete Ro took an ice climbing course from the famed mountaineer Jeff Lowe at the Ouray, Colorado, Ice Park, a box canyon loaded with beautiful frozen waterfalls. Another student was belaying Ro. After Ro reached the top of the route, he was instructed to unclip from the rope and wait for a vehicle to pick him up. Lowe and other climbers heard Ro yell "off belay" a universal signal that he was at the top and unhooked from the rope. So the other student then unhooked the rope, as was customary. However, Ro leaned back, likely thinking he was still attached to the rope. He fell 135 feet and died on impact. A year later, Ro's widow sued.

Neither of the two waivers Ro signed would allow dismissal of the suit against Lowe and his parent company, San Juan Mountain Guides. Ro had signed one waiver when he booked the trip and another when arriving in Colorado the day before. Although they might have held against simple negligence, the plaintiff argued that Lowe had bronchitis, could not effectively communicate, and thus was grossly negligent. Again, the case was settled out of court.

This buzz about outdoor liability sends chills down my spine because as a doctor, *getting sued* is an ugly risk of my profession.

Mountain rescuers, fortunately, are protected from lawsuits in several ways. First we act under the authority of the county sheriff. On every rescue mission, we are backed by the sheriff's office. In addition, the federal government passed the Volunteer Protection Act in 1997. Volunteers working in a nonprofit capacity are provided immunity from tort claims. Although the nonprofit organization may be liable, the volunteers are not personally responsible.

But then, because I'm a doctor, I have an extraspecial threat that looms over my head every time the pager buzzes. It is the ugly beast called medical malpractice.

To help defray the burden of medical malpractice suits, most states have a Good Samaritan law. In Oregon, a volunteer or bystander is protected from lawsuits for acts when providing emergency medical care in good faith without compensation in a location where medical care is usually not rendered. In Washington, the Good Samaritan law is much clearer. It particularly states that an emergency response organization volunteer, who may get minor reimbursement for expenses, is covered under the Good Samaritan Law.

After a two-week trial, two and a half hours of which I was on the stand, the Svitek jury came back. They voted in favor of Nidecker on both complaints: nine to two for product liability and eight to three on negligence. Despite our favorable verdict, I still think many jurors missed the point. Some who voted in favor of Nidecker suggested that they thought the snowboard company was guilty but didn't want to punish one company for a practice the industry follows as a whole. Jurors felt snowboarding needs to be safer. But they missed the greater issue, the issue of inherent risk. If you are riding the edge, you could fall. Tapping the source is dangerous.

In the end, Nidecker, snowboarders, and outdoor enthusiasts did not really win. Snowboard resorts, manufacturers, and shops carry insurance to cover liability and negligence claims. This cost, in turn, is passed on to consumers in the form of higher prices.

At least two issues are unambiguous. A well-crafted "release of liability" is often upheld by the courts, especially in cases of simple negligence. And prevention of NARSID is primarily the responsibility of the outdoor winter sports enthusiast. Although new technologies will likely make snowboarding safer, prevention of tree well and deep snow immersion asphyxiation rests primarily with snowboarders and skiers themselves. It is the inherent risk of winter sports: without mountains, trees, powder snow, and steep slopes, there would be no snowboarding or skiing.

Two seasons later we would have a big snow year, and six skiers and snowboarders would die from deep snow submersion. A seventh person, an off-duty ski patroller making backcountry runs in Washington's Crystal Mountain, fell deep.

"It all happened extremely fast," she said. "I lost a ski, started sliding, then stuck into a tree well like a lawn dart." She tried rocking to get loose and reaching for a branch but couldn't do either. "It was absolutely tight instantly—I couldn't move at all. Everything iced up very quickly and I could only move my hands three or four inches."

When her husband pulled her out a few minutes later, she was unconscious, blue, and her eyes were open. He revived her with immediate CPR, further demonstrating rescue by your partner is your most likely chance of survival.

We all tend to push our limits; some go closer to the edge than others. But the thrill of risk is an inseparable aspect of adventure sport. Sometimes it leads to death of a young healthy woman; sometimes another survives.

CHAPTER 18

Anatomy of a Search: Tragedy on Mount Hood

On Sunday, December 10, Skylar, Avrie, and I drive to Portland through a blustery, rainy, frigid storm, en route to see Disney's *High School Musical*; not my first choice for a Sunday. I'd rather be skiing with the kids.

My phone vibrates and beeps once on the dash.

"What's that?" says Skylar, her eyes light up.

"Probably a Crag Rat call out," I say, knowing no one else text messages me.

"Who's hurt?" Avrie sets down her book and perks up with interest.

I read aloud: "North Side search of the mountain, call voice mail."

Midwinter call outs never come at a good time. Often these missions are for lost or injured skiers, snowboarders, or snowshoers. Once a cross-country skier with a broken leg was stuck on the Bennett Pass cross-country ski trail. We hauled her out with the Crag Rat snowcat. Another time, Crag Rats responded for two lost snowshoers, only to find them a quarter mile from the White River parking lot.

Instead of ignoring the page, I call the voice mail, and put

Penny's smooth, calm voice on speaker: "Crag Rats, hello. It's Sunday and we've got three missing climbers on the North Side. Call Penny if you can respond to a search tomorrow morning."

Then I reach Jay Sherrerd at home.

"Three climbers were reported missing on the north side," says Jay. "We're trying to get a crew for the morning."

"Not today?" I ask.

"It's too late to get anyone up on the mountain today. Sheriff Joe and Crag Rat Bernie are headed up this afternoon in the snow-cat to open Cloud Cap."

"Okay. I have to work tomorrow," I say.

"I'm leaving on the red-eye tonight to visit my dad," says Jay. "Tom Scully's a maybe if he can get child care. It's his only day off this week. Todd Wells and Dave Wagg are a go. Don Pattison is taking the day off work."

Jay says he is reading the e-mails from the climbers, which have been forwarded from one of the wives. Jay's trying to determine which route they'd chosen. The e-mails discussed the Eliot Glacier gullies, two narrow, steep couloirs that are among the most dangerous routes on the mountain. Jay and I both know that a winter rescue on the north side of Mount Hood requires as many Crag Rats as we can muster. I may be able to get time off work if I can trade a shift with another doc in my group, but I won't let the rescue interfere with my time with the kids. The storm, which started Saturday, is still going strong. It's now pelting us with rain as I drive to the city, away from the mountain. For all we know the climbers took an extra day on the mountain and are on their way down. Or maybe they are having lunch in Government Camp and plan to call home as soon as they finish, which has happened in the past.

Because I can't go, I'm anxious and agitated.

———

The fateful trip started Thursday, December 7, three days prior. The three mountaineers set off to climb the rugged, remote, extremely technical north face of Mount Hood: Jerry Cooke, thirty-six, a New York attorney; Brian Hall, thirty-seven, a personal trainer from Dallas, Texas; and Kelly James, forty-eight, a Dallas landscape architect and father of four. The two gullies above the Eliot Glacier are the most difficult routes on the mountain, along with Yocum Ridge on the northwest flank. These 2,500-foot, 60 percentage-grade, near-vertical chutes are what mountaineers call "mixed climbing," that which blends distinct technique and equipment for three media: rock, ice, snow. To the east lies the difficult and dangerous Cooper Spur Route. To the west is our beloved Snowdome, a snowfield that leads to Cathedral Ridge, a climb called the Sunshine Route because it's in the sun all day. In addition to the technical difficulty of these north face gullies, objective dangers abound, including crevasses, seracs, rock falls, ice falls, avalanches, impassible cliffs, and lack of an easy escape route if a climber gets in trouble halfway up the climb. The danger is magnified with winter weather. December is among the most unpredictable and dangerous times of year. Storms roll in off the Pacific Ocean and can last for days, creating poor visibility and freezing temperatures. Even if the sky is cloud free, the air is extremely cold up high in December, and rarely is the sky windless. But then, even in summer, rock falls abound: the gullies are treacherous no matter what the conditions.

As recommended by the Forest Service climbing regulations, the three climbers signed in at the Mount Hood Ranger Station in the community of Mount Hood, fifteen miles south of the town of Hood River. They also left a note on their car, which was parked at the Tilly Jane trailhead adjacent to Cooper Spur Ski Resort. The three climbers prepared for an alpine-style ascent, also known as "light and fast" in climbing circles. Traditional mountaineering techniques involve a climber carrying a large, heavy backpack with equipment for a gradual ascent of the mountain and a wide variety of contingencies. This often means mountaineers will bring a tent and sleeping bag, extra food and clothing, a small stove with fuel to melt water, and extra equipment. Contrarily, alpine style, like what James, Hall, and Cooke employed, involves taking small packs with much less gear. This allows climbers to climb quickly. The idea is that without a massive backpack, you can get up and down the mountain in half the time.

The notes left by Hall, Cooke, and James listed equipment, including bivouac sacks, called bivy sacks for short, which are emergency, one-person tube shelters. They apparently did not have a tent or sleeping bags. They did have food and a stove to melt water, although it was unknown if they carried enough fuel to melt snow for drinking water for one day or one week. Although they had never climbed Mount Hood, they came with experience of summiting other big mountains, like Mount Rainier in Washington and Mount McKinley in Alaska.

According to their e-mails and the note left on their car windshield, they were to climb one of the north gullies in one day and descend the mountain via the south climb route, the easiest way down. They were to meet friends at Timberline Lodge on Friday or Saturday, and would get a ride back to their car. If they got into trouble they would descend the Cooper Spur Route.

On Thursday, December 7, the three left their car and climbed two hours to spend the night at the Tilly Jane ski hut, an unstaffed backcountry ski cabin at 5,500 feet elevation. In the hut, they lit a fire, signed the log book, and left a $20 donation to the Nordic club that maintains the cabin. "Thanks for your hard work on this great shelter. We did not plan on staying but the warmth of the fire changed our minds. We climb as a group of 3 and we left a $20 bill. We will leave tomorrow for the north face! Wish us luck."

On Friday, December 8, the sun was out in the morning. The trio began to climb the Eliot Glacier and began ascending one of the gullies. That afternoon, the weather changed and a storm rolled in: snow began falling, the wind picked up, the temperature fell. By dark, the storm was fully blasting. It was a classic Pacific Northwest blizzard: wet, windy, cold, and huge. It was so gigantic that later in the week, it would leave 1.5 million homes without power.

On Saturday, December 9, probably sometime in the wee hours of the morning, the three climbers either achieved the summit, or came within 300 feet of the mountaintop. But the morning was a whiteout: blowing snow, thick clouds, and high winds created essentially no visibility. The climbers either could not find the Pearly Gates, the name of the chute that leads down the south climb to Timberline Lodge, or they were not quite on the top of the mountain and felt they couldn't continue the last 300 feet up. In either case, they were in trouble.

They dug in and hunkered down in a snow cave.

Early on Sunday, December 10, the climbers were reported overdue, and Sheriff Wampler initiated the call out. On Sunday afternoon, at 3:30 P.M., Kelly James called home on his cell phone. He talked to his family for four minutes, explained that he was stuck in a snow cave and that his two friends went for help early that morning. He was disorientated slightly, speaking in jangled words, not exactly making sense. It was unclear if he was injured. He was probably hypothermic. That was the last anyone heard from the three climbers.

————

On Monday, December 11, more than a dozen searchers catch a 5:00 A.M. snowcat at the Tilly Jane Trailhead: Crag Rats, sheriff's deputies, Portland Mountain Rescue members, and the elite 304th Rescue Squadron based at the Portland Air Force Reserve. Snow is falling, the sky is pitch-black, and the air is blustery and bitterly cold.

The rescue crew is cramped in the back of the snowcat; the top of the rig is laden with gear. The snowcat stops on the way up to cut away branches and remove downed trees. The beast lumbers up the six-mile, 2,000-foot ascent to advance search base, Cloud Cap Inn.

By first light, the teams set out on skis and snowshoes, despite the blinding snowstorm. High wind, freezing temperature, and poor visibility makes searching both treacherous and nearly impossible. The thermometer dips into the teens, and the wind jacks up to 80 miles per hour.

"The searchers are so focused on staying warm and surviving the elements, they have little time or spare concentration to actually search," Jim Wells explains. "The number one priority is *not* to search but to stay safe," he says. Survival takes complete focus and total effort.

At the same time the Crag Rats leave from Cloud Cap on the north side of Mount Hood, Clackamas County and establish a second search base at Timberline Lodge on the south side. Another half dozen teams of searchers set out to comb the south climb and attempt to reach the summit via the easiest route to the top. Although the phone call from Kelly James suggested he was near the summit, we don't know on which side. Searchers need to cover the planned climbing route, the planned descent route, and the emergency escape descent route: both sides of the massive volcano. Despite the notes and Kelly James's cell phone call, no clues help narrow the search area.

Crag Rat Dave Wagg reports the wind is so strong in the Eliot, gusting up to eighty miles per hour, that at one point it blew him over. Don Pattison jokes, "That's the advantage of weighing more." He outweighs Dave significantly. Then Don gets blown over, too.

"The weather is pretty gnarly," says Tom Scully in the newspaper, who is maintenance manager at the ski resort and used to being on the mountain more than half the days of the year. "Visibility was horrendous and the wind just kept knocking us over. We had to hold onto rocks." At one point, it is so windy, the searchers clamber on all fours to keep from being blown off a ridge. Every time they stop, the searchers become cold, so they can't afford any rest breaks. Despite the raging storm, Wagg, Pattison, Scully, Todd Wells, and two Mount Hood Meadows ski patrollers, including Dennis's son Paul Klein, ski to 8,500 feet up to the Eliot Glacier and the area called the Chisholm Trail. This route is not so much a climbing route, but it's the line everyone takes when they fall off the summit or off Cooper Spur climbing route. Other teams search Elk Meadows to the west and the Newton Clark Glacier to the east. All searchers are recalled at 2:30 P.M., the turnaround time to get safely off the mountain by dark: no climbers were found, not even a clue.

The south side teams retreated even earlier, at 1:30 P.M., from high wind, cold temperatures, and zero visibility.

At the Tilly Jane parking lot, the staging area, Joe Wampler fields questions from media. Two Black Hawk helicopters arrive from the Salem National Guard 1042nd Air Ambulance Company. The choppers wait on standby at the Hood River Airfield. It's too stormy for helicopters to fly.

T-Mobile cell phone technicians, along with help from the

FBI, use a computer algorithm to attempt to pinpoint the approximate location of the cell phone call that Kelly James made two days previously. They use Sunday's cell phone call from Kelly James as well as the cell phone pings. Even when not being used for a call, a cell phone, essentially a sophisticated radio, regularly communicates with the nearest cell tower every few minutes. This way, incoming phone and voice messages can be routed to the correct tower and thus forwarded immediately to the phone. By reviewing records, the phone company can tell which towers the phone *pinged* and thus the approximate location within 500 meters. The techs estimate the latitude at 45.285537, longitude 121.619467. This places James between 10,000 and 11,000 feet high on the north side, on the Cooper Spur climbing route, very near the summit.

Penny begins the call out all over. *More searches needed for tomorrow 12/12 for N side climbers—call voice mail,* reads the page.

Word of the search becomes the top story in the local news. Media trucks and journalists clog the staging area. Joe lets a few select journalists ride the snowcat to Cloud Cap Inn.

Rescuers come down via snowcat at dark to return to family and work duties. No team today is able to search higher than 8,500 feet from the north or south. No team sees anything resembling climbers, climbing equipment, or traces of either. To call it searching is rather euphemistic. It's really survival. If a search team did not come within ten feet of the climbers, it would not have been able to spot them. Jay and I, with family and work commitments, both feel frustrated and anxious that we can't help with the search. We have the skills, equipment, knowledge, and desire to help. We want to be on the mountain, in the thick of the search, helping. It gnaws at both of us.

By nightfall, the mountain is consumed by the raging blizzard.

while the first day of searching comes to a close, the climbers begin their fifth night in the wilderness.

Tuesday, December 12, the weather is no different. Actually worse. The wind is now gusting over 80 miles per hour. Thick gray clouds dump at least a foot of snow, and the howling wind creates drifts five times deeper. The temperature barely reaches double digits.

A fresh crew catches a 6:00 A.M. snowcat, driven by Crag Rat Dick Arnold. The track is compacted now from multiple trips via the Crag Rats' and sheriff's snowcats. Searchers leave Cloud Cap Inn at first light to search the crevasses, avalanche zones, and ridges. Similarly, on the south side, teams leave Timberline to hunt on the upper mountain, Palmer Glacier, and Illumination Saddle, and the lower flanks including Sand Canyon and Zigzag Glacier. If Cooke and Hall made the summit and descended the south, they may have hiked off route, a common occurrence due to the Mount Hood Triangle. When a climber descends the south side to Timberline Lodge, he or she follows due south on the compass. But this is not the natural fall line, rather a subtle side hill traverse and descent. Inattentive climbers following the fall line, or just stomping directly downhill, can end up in Zigzag Glacier or Sand Canyon. One south side team reaches 8,500 feet but retreats due to severe conditions.

The lower drainages, gullies, roads, and trails in the woods on both the north and south are scoured by skis, snowshoes, snowcat, and snowmobile. Obvious catch paths that a climber might take are checked first. So many sheriff's deputies are searching on the north side that Joe Wampler arranges the Hood River City Police and the Oregon State Patrol to help with normal county deputy duties. Searchers from Eugene Mountain Rescue and Corvallis

Mountain Rescue, both about four hours away by car, show up to aid in the search. Pacific Northwest Search and Rescue, a ground based team turns, out in force to help the south side mission.

But the storm overpowers search efforts. All field volunteers are recalled again at 2:30 P.M. Since it takes at least two hours to ski or snowshoe to a team's search zone, and because the teams are then recalled at 2:30 P.M., the searchers have a very short window during the day to actually search. Plus, they can't see much, and most searchers are engrossed in trying to stay warm, ski through thick snowdrifts, keep an eye on their partners, stay hydrated and nourished, and other necessities of survival in the winter mountain wilderness that preempt actually looking around for the lost climbers.

"Those are the strongest winds I've ever been in—knock you down, hands and knees," reports Lindsay Clunes of Corvallis Mountain Rescue in the newspapers. And in addition to the cold and wind, there is no visibility.

No team today can get a good look at the north face. No team ascends higher than 7,500 feet on the north side or 9,000 feet on the south side. No team today can reach the summit. No clues are found in the lower zones below the timberline.

Suddenly, at 3:30 P.M., the clouds lift from the valley a skosh. It's enough clearing for the two Black Hawks to fly for an hour before darkness falls. The choppers cannot rise above the tree line, 6,000 feet, due to the excessive winds, a raging storm, and thick gray mat of clouds. But they are able to make several passes on the lower treed flanks of the mountain between Tilly Jane and Cloud Cap Inn. Nothing.

The local media stationed at Cooper Spur trailhead is asked to move to the Mount Hood Ranger Station in the community of Mount Hood, fifteen miles down the road after several national news trucks show up and cause too much congestion. The story appears in the national news. A journalist discovers the climber's posts on two northwest climbing Internet forums but that yields few clues to their whereabouts.

Cellular technicians confirm that the last ping signal from Kelly James's cell phone occured at 1:51 A.M. earlier today.

Penny sends out another text message. *More searchers needed for tomorrow 12/13 for N side climbers. Call voice mail.* On the voice mail, Penny asks for anyone who can spare a day; they are asking for as many searchers as possible.

The climbers begin their sixth night on the mountain.

On Wednesday, December 13, the temperatures climb to above freezing but the precipitation does not stop. Midday at Cloud Cap Inn it pours rain; all the way up to 8,000 feet it rains. Nonetheless, searchers are still afoot. Crag Rat Dave Maccabee skis with his team up to 7,500 feet, to the small, dilapidated stone Cooper Spur shelter. "It was the worse day's skiing I've ever had. It rained." They come home sopping wet. Teams again attempt to reach the north-side objectives. The weather is too severe for any south-side searching.

Meanwhile, Roger Nelson shows up to take over the kitchen at Cloud Cap from Bernie. He will staff the kitchen for five straight days. Massive quantities of food are shuttled up by snowcat, much of it donated by local businesses. An auto company donates deep-cycle marine batteries to help run the electronics at Cloud Cap. A local sports store donates socks and energy bars.

The story becomes a regular headline item, topping the national evening news, smattering CNN, eventually filling papers with close to a thousand stories. Crag Rat John Ingles, traveling in Australia, hears the news. The press liaison for the Oregon National Guard gives regular news briefings now and helps Joe Wampler deal with the media. The entire media entourage is moved again, now to the Hood River Airfield, where there's more room.

Bill Pattison stations himself at the airport to be the press liaison for the Crag Rats. Penny sends out another text message. Nightfall brings diminished hopes. Not only has searching been strictly curtailed by the massive storm but also every night the missing climbers spend out decreases their chances of survival.

On Thursday, December 14, there is essentially no searching up high. The storm is unabated, and, in fact, strengthened as if reinvigorated. Two north-side teams set out; one makes it to Cooper Spur shelter but no higher. After a short pause, another storm hits with full force. On the mountain, the 100 miles per hour winds, two feet of new powder, gigantic snowdrifts, and a single-digit thermometer readings continue.

Again, conditions are too stormy to search the south side.

A private company from Colorado brings in drones, small heat-seeking remote-controlled aircraft. The boxes of electronic support equipment fill an entire snowcat. But it is too windy for the small planes. Then the camera lenses fog.

Not once does Sheriff Wampler talk about suspending the search, but he acknowledges he is running out of skilled rescuers able to search on the mountain. Volunteers are tired. We have work and family duties. The text messages continue for daily calls for help. But it looks like there will be no break in the weather.

Tonight, the massive storm peaks, leaving 1.5 million without power in Portland and Seattle.

On Friday, December 15, the storm still rages: full on, cranking. We have no power in Hood River. Schools and businesses are closed. Utility crews are working overtime to clear downed trees and fix power and telephone lines. The hospital, where I report for duty, runs on backup-generator power.

Again, searchers set out from Cloud Cap at dawn but are limited to ground-searching around the tree line.

Penny sends out what will be the last text message: *Continued searches needed for Fri., Sat., Sun.* She asks that all searchers respond to the staging area at night, to get shuttled to Cloud Cap Inn. That way, searchers can head into the field at first light. This weekend is our first chance at a clearing in the weather and our last hope at finding someone alive. Crag Rats respond by the dozens; members do whatever they can to help: shuttle food, make phone calls, deal with the media. Clackamas County is mounting a similar massive force on the south side. Volunteers call in from across the state to report for the weekend search.

A C-130 Hercules from Reno, Nevada, Air National Guard arrives with heat-seeking and infrared sensing equipment, for day and night operations. The Black Hawks are still grounded. A CH-47 giant twin-rotor helicopter for the Oregon National Guard in Salem is en route.

Bill Pattison picks Don Pattison and Dick Arnold to fly in the Black Hawks this weekend. The military spotters are keen-eyed. But they need local Crag Rat climbers who know the mountain to direct the air search and help look for likely spots the climbers may be holed up.

From Cloud Cap Inn, Bernie and Roger ask for $1,000 worth of groceries. The local grocery store donates a portion; the food is shuttled up by snow cat.

The cost of the mission becomes a prominent headline. Sheriff Wampler estimates he is spending $5,000 to $6,500 daily on the search. Fortunately, we have much donated food, supplies, and equipment. The Black Hawks cost $2,800 per hour, and will eventually fly thirty-seven hours, according to the military press liaison. A Chinook helicopter costs about $7,500 per hour and eventually flies fifteen. A Nevada Air National Guard C-130 Transport Hercules is in the air for almost two days. Although the sheriff's department funded some of the search, the military flight hours would have been used in training, if not in an actual search, says the press liaison. So they are not, according to the military brass, an extraordinary expense.

The cost issue becomes headline news possibly since the story about the weather is getting regurgitated. The debate over who should actually foot the bill then tops the debate. The discussion is not much of an issue to the sheriff's office or the Crag Rats. We will continue to search for James, Cooke, and Hall.

Tonight is night nine for the mountaineers.

The climbers have a chance only if they are hunkered down in a snow cave. These lifesaving shelters are carved into the snowbank and can easily keep a person alive for several nights or even a week. Once protected from the wind, falling snow, and cold, the cave can heat up quickly to a survivable temperature because your body heat or a camping stove warms the air and snow is an extremely efficient insulator. However, a snow cave is not just a hole in the snow. The snow cave needs to be constructed properly. If the walls are too thin or unsupported at the base, a cave can collapse. Likewise, without proper ventilation, one can suffocate by rebreathing exhaled carbon dioxide.

But even in a snow cave, climbers need warm clothing, sleeping bags, food, and water; the water can come only from melting snow with a camp stove. Nine days is a long time to survive in a mountain snow cave in the midst of a massive blizzard. But it is not unprecedented.

On Mount Hood in January 1971, two men survived a below-zero storm and 80 miles per hour gusts at 10,000 feet for five days in a snow cave. In March 1979, two climbers survived for two days at 8,000 feet. In 1976, teenagers Randy Knapp, Matt Meacham, and Gary Schneider became lost on Mount Hood. They tried for four days to descend the mountain, then dug a snow cave and waited thirteen days for the weather to clear.

For Hall, Cooke, and James, the likelihood of survival depends on coexisting factors. We know they are skilled in mountain craft and had good-quality equipment. But they were climbing light, without sleeping bags and without a tent. They likely had a minimum of extra clothes and probably only a day or two of stove fuel to melt water.

If they started out digging a snow cave on Saturday morning, they were likely exhausted from the 5,000 foot near-vertical ascent. Plus, the storm was raging, so they were probably cold and wet. Their hands and feet were probably frozen and their faces caked with frost. They were, no doubt, hungry and thirsty. They possibly might be injured. The visibility was close to zero. If they tried to climb down, the whiteout likely caused vertigo. Once in the snow cave, they may have become claustrophobic. Staying for prolonged duration at high altitude probably caused at least some degree of acute mountain sickness, which is less common on Mount Hood because people climb to the summit and return home usually within a day. And that all that probably occurred nine nights ago, now is compounded.

While the media is focusing on the storm and the cost, the mountain rescue volunteers are discussing other items. First, how much risk should rescuers take, knowing the chance of survival of the lost climbers is dramatically decreasing by the day? And, second, how much longer should we search? In past searches, like for the missing snowboarder who died in a tree well on Oregon's Mount Bachelor, it has been difficult to know when to scale back the search. The Mount Bachelor search went full force for ten days, then was scaled back to a minimum for another ten days before the body was recovered.

We had two other high-profile searches in Oregon in 2006. One was successful because of prolonged efforts, one was not despite the lengthy search.

In November, barely a month prior, the Kim family was driving to the beach across the Southern Oregon Coast Range when their car got stuck in the snow. James Kim died of hypothermia after he left the car to summon help. His wife, Kati Kim, and their two young daughters, ages four and seven months, survived for ten days by staying at the car. Kati Kim burned car tires for heat. For the first time in Oregon, searchers used cell phone pings to narrow the location of the missing family. Then a chopper hired by the Kim's family finally located the stranded car on a remote mountain road.

Similarly, in October, at Crater Lake National Park, eight-year-old Samuel Boehlke became separated from his father on a hike and disappeared. Intensive searching with more than 200 volunteers lasted a week; the scaled back search continued intermittently well into November. This boy has not been found.

The chief problem with the December Mount Hood search was not lack of resources or personnel. It was not search tactics or equipment. The volume of equipment was impressive: three helicopters, two airplanes, four snowcats, a multitude of snowmobiles, the unmanned drones, and tracked all-terrain vehicles—ATVs with snow cogs—aided in the search. The only one who didn't cooperate was Mother Nature. The extreme weather created a situation in which searching was difficult and dangerous.

In addition to focusing on the weather and the cost, much media attention was devoted to the fact that the climbers had no locators. They did not have avalanche beacons, small devices worn by climbers and backcountry skiers that broadcast a signal. If a climber or skier is buried, his or her partner can switch to Receive and home in on the signal. These devices broadcast at a range of 50 meters and are most useful for climbers locating their buried partner. They do little good for massive searches. Another option is renting a Mount Hood Locator, radio beacons similar to an avalanche beacon, but with a much greater ranger, more like an animal tracker. These locators allow rescuers to find a lost person and were developed after the disastrous Oregon Episcopal School accident. A third system, called RECCO, is available at many ski resorts. These use a harmonic radar detector to find a small batteryless reflector sewn into a ski jacket or other type of clothing. A fourth option is a personal locator beacon, a new technology that uses the Global Position System, similar to those found on airplanes and ships, which are called emergency position indication radio beacons.

Nonetheless, had we been able to locate a signal from Kelly James, we would not have been able to reach him all week. We knew his approximate location from the cell phone pings and his actual phone call on Saturday. Plus, even if we had located an exact a signal from Kelly James's location, we still would have been searching elsewhere on the mountain, knowing Hill and Cooke had left James and gone for help. So, locators, while they would have been helpful, may not have significantly altered our search tactics.

Nine days, nine nights, and one big storm.

O n Saturday, December 16, I am packed and ready to go. I had to go to the hospital for a few hours first; I couldn't switch my shift with Christmas coming. I am anxious to get on the mountain after having not been able to help all week.

At Cloud Cap, the day dawns brutally cold and still windy. The chill is minus five degrees at 7,000 feet and winds are cranking at 15 to 25 miles per hour. But it is clear enough to get field teams out and to get choppers airborne. The two Black Hawks set off at first light, scouring the upper mountains, with one Crag Rat in each helicopter. The C-130 begins circling the peak using heat-seeking radar on the upper and lower snowfields. The giant twin-rotor CH-47 Chinook helicopter from the Oregon National Guard is on standby. The goals: scour the upper mountain by air, put a team on the summit from the south, search the entire north side: Cooper Spur, Eliot Glacier, Elk Cove, Polallie Creek Canyon, and Newton Clark Glacier.

The Forest Service orders Mount Hood closed for climbing to make way for the nearly 100 searchers and to eliminate false clues, such as footprints, ski tracks, or cell phone signals. The Federal Aviation Administration closes airspace within three nautical miles of the Mount Hood summit, restricts aircraft to only those involved with the search.

I get off work midafternoon on Saturday. I am instructed to meet Jay Sherrerd and Penny Hunting, who left her post as call out person to help join the teams on the mountain, at Tilly Jane to take the snowcat to Cloud Cap Inn. Jay just arrived on the red-eye flight from the East Coast and, like me, is itching to help.

Just as I leave Hood River, Penny calls and tells me to come by dispatch, the sheriff's office command post, for the search. Jay and Penny, in addition to their regular gear, have a car full of lasagna a local Hood River woman had prepared for the crew at Cloud Cap Inn. They stop by dispatch to pick up the "special pancake mix," code name for several cases of beer requested by searchers; the cases are double wrapped in brown bags for fear the media might catch a glimpse.

At the sheriff's office, we step into a rather intense discussion. A Black Hawk earlier today had spotted a V-shaped climbing sling. The media would later call it a "trench," "signal," and "arrow." But when Penny, Jay, and I look at the pictures, it appears to be a two-point anchor system commonly used by climbers, a V-thread. It was in the approximate position of the cell phone call location.

"I want someone to check this out," says Joe Wampler. The pararescue jumpers, or PJs, from the 304th have a plan. They will get airlifted to the summit in the giant Chinook, establish some anchors, and rappel to the anchor system. The PJs, however, feel they don't have enough local knowledge or enough skilled climbers to pull this off. They need Crag Rats. Either Jay or I could volunteer to go, as we're standing there at dispatch discussing the plan and looking at the photograph and map. But this is clearly a job for our best climbers and rope rescuers. The two obvious names are Brian Hukari and Todd Wells. The problem is that they are currently at Cloud Cap, readying for the next morning's ground search.

Two hours later, Penny, Jay, and I are stuffed in the back of a snowcat from Silver Star Search and Rescue, a team in Washington who came over to do nothing but shuttle rescuers up and down the mountain by snowcat. Along with us is a member of the Snowshoe Club, a private group based in Portland, which volunteered their backcountry cabin next door to Cloud Cap Inn. The Snowshoe Club is currently housing and feeding a dozen rescuers from Eugene Mountain Rescue because Cloud Cap Inn is so crowded.

The night is dark, cold, and clear. I take only my rescue pack, so I can ski home tomorrow without a snowcat ride. I inquire about Jay's dad, and we laugh about the three boxes of "special pancake mix" that got stacked on top of the lasagna. About halfway to Cloud Cap Inn, we stop in the middle of the Old Wagon Road cross-country ski trail. At a wide spot, we pull alongside the Hood River sheriff's snowcat coming down, driven by Crag Rat Rick Ragen; he shuttles Brian and Todd off the mountain. Our snowcat stops. We tumble out to stretch. Jay briefs Brian so he and Todd can get an idea what their mission the next morning entails.

At Cloud Cap Inn that night, the cabin is roasting hot from the two woodstoves and a big fireplace. The propane lanterns are glowing brightly. Rescuers are readying their gear. We announce the arrival of the "pancake mix," and there are hails all around. Jay and I find Jim Wells and Bernie poring over the search map. Jim has the morning briefing board about halfway completed, listing team members who will head out the next morning from the Crag Rats and the mountain rescue teams from Corvallis, Eugene, and Portland. I quickly prepare a bunk and drag my sleeping bag out of the box I keep stashed in the cabin.

After a quick briefing from Jim and a handful of cookies, I bed down. But I soon awaken to the tune of three zonked searchers snoring in the main room. I drag my mattress into the kitchen in front of the woodstove and quickly fall asleep.

Sunday, December 17, as the leader of team one, I prepare to leave with Mike and Rubin from Portland Mountain Rescue. Mike, Rubin, and I test our avalanche beacons to make sure they are working properly and our SAR radios to make sure we're on the right frequency. We quickly run through a checklist: extra clothing, crampons, skis, and climbing skins (there's nothing

worse than a search party with both skiers and snowshoers, because they travel at different speeds and can't take turns breaking
trail). I've got a rope and a picket for an anchor. Rubin has a GPS
receiver. We all have bivy sacs. If we find anything, we'll instantly
call for reinforcements.

Although we are well aware of the hazards, it's Jim's job as
operations chief to caution us again: avalanches, crevasses, deep
snow, ice, cold temperatures, and wind. Beware of dangerous terrain, frostbite, hypothermia.

We ski away with our climbing skins gliding over the loose
powdery snow with a yellow glow in the sky to the East. The
temperature is single digit, but the wind is nonexistent. It's a perfect winter day to ski high on the mountain. Despite the unfortu-
nate circumstances we ski with pure delight; up the Tilly Jane
creek drainage, up to the tree line, onto the wind-scoured rocky
east moraine of the Eliot Glacier.

At sunup, aircraft seem to appear out of nowhere. The two
Black Hawks begin sweeping the upper Eliot Glacier, and the big
C-130 starts clockwise circles around the mountain. The north side
has eight teams, which varied from our three-person crew, headed
to the top of the Eliot Glacier, to a six-person team coming up two
hours later to provide support to us. On the south side, two dozen
members of Portland Mountain Rescue are searching Palmer,
Zigzag, and White River Glaciers, the summit, and establishing an
emergency route for a summit team to descend the south climb if
necessary. The third component of this massive search, the summit
team, includes eight Air Force Reserve pararescue jumpers from the
304th; two Crag Rats, Brian Hukari and Todd Wells; and two Portland Mountain Rescue members. They wait at the airport while
the Chinook makes a reconnaissance tour of the anchor system
spotted yesterday and the summit. They also wait until a south side

team on Mount Hood establishes a safe descent route. The air mission to the summit will not go until the south side evacuation route is deemed safe by a team from Portland Mountain Rescue.

Skiing up amid the aircraft and the radio chatter and hauling up the cumbersome SAR backpack feels a long way from the solace I usually experience on a winter backcountry ski. Up high, the powder snow is light and dry. The weather is spectacular: clear blue sunny sky and very cold. But the circumstances are dire.

"We have a no-sweating rule," says Rubin, meaning he doesn't want to ski too fast and thus sweat too much. Every half hour, we stop and Rubin scours the headwall with binoculars he's thoughtfully brought. I try to look around constantly.

We keep radio chatter to a minimum, but when Jim doesn't hear from a team every twenty minutes or so, he checks in.

As we reach the top of the Tilly Jane drainage, we see Black Hawks dip so low on the Eliot that they seem to be ten feet off the tops of the seracs. I radio Cloud Cap search base on Rubin's recommendation to confirm that the Black Hawks know we are on the moraine and about to descend to the glacier. Now that we are well above the tree line, we feel a brisk wind that, when we stop for a drink of water and look at the north face, cools us to the bone. Despite our high-tech clothing, we become chilled in an instant. I put on warmer gloves and a second jacket.

At 7,500 feet, we find the Pooley Trail, named after octogenarian Crag Rat Dick Pooley, a founding father of the MRA. This well-trod trail leads from the rocky moraine to the bottom of the Eliot. It's marked by a giant rock cairn, a stack of rocks the size of a car. At the Pooley Trail, ice sheets leading into the Eliot are clear, hard, and interspersed among pockets of snow that are thick and firm, compacted from the last week of wind. We unclip our skis and strap on crampons for the five-minute, 300-foot climb to the floor of the vast Eliot Glacier. As soon as we get to the bottom of the slope, we sink in new snow up to our knees. Time to put the skis back on.

We attempt to ski up the left-hand side of the Eliot Glacier, a track in which there are no crevasses. This route leads to our search objective, the uppermost section off the Eliot and the Chisholm Trail. But when we come into view of the route, we see widespread avalanche activity. We now plow through a foot of new snow, but our skis provide floatation and our skins allow us to continue uphill. Every side slope, we knock off a six-inch slab of the wind-compacted snow to find firmer snow underneath. We find all the right ingredients for an avalanche: a thick heavy layer sitting on top of a crust. We see several new cracks and loaded cornices on the cliffs above our planned route. And we see a large, one- or two-day-old avalanche on a slope above us.

"I don't like the looks of those cornices or that recent avalanche," I say.

"I'm not going anywhere near that slope," says Rubin.

"Mike?" I ask, to get all opinions.

"Looks too dangerous for me."

"I think we should stick to the middle of the glacier—much safer," says Rubin.

"Yeah, we can get to the bench and re-eval," I say.

"Cloud Cap, from team one," I say.

"Go, team one," says Crag Rat Rick Regan. He's probably giving Jim Wells a break from the radio.

"We're on the Eliot at about eight thousand feet. We see a large avalanche on skiers' left above us. We see a crown from a slide on the Cooper Spur climbing route. We've got several hanging cornices on the cliffs above us and several six-inch wind slaps we're kicking off."

"Copy," says Rick. "Do you think you can get a look at the upper Eliot?"

"Stand by," I say.

Mike, Rubin, and I have a discussion. The skiers' left is clearly too dangerous. There's an ice-climbing route up the middle of the Eliot, but we'd have to ski through the giant crevasses and seracs. Skiers' right also looks dangerous, because the slope above it is steep and loaded with new snow.

"The only thing that looks reasonable is to ski across the Eliot, up the west moraine, and up the Snowdome. There's no crevasses, and it's low angle so we'll be okay from avalanches until we get to the top."

"Once up top," says Rubin, "we might be able to belay someone on a rope over to the Eliot. But it's hard to see how we'll get a better look than the Black Hawk that was hovering ten feet from the tops of those seracs."

"We can safely ski up the bench on the Eliot, but not much farther," I say to Jim at Cloud Cap. "On the bench, we'd be okay skiing up Snowdome to have a look into the Eliot, but nothing else looks safe."

"Okay," says Jim, "Team one ski to the Snowdome."

Rubin thinks to ask about team six, our backup. "No sense of having them ski up here if there's nothing we can do."

"Good thought."

"Cloud Cap from team one," I say.

"Go, team one," says Jim.

"Have team six let us know before they drop into the Eliot. We're not sure there's a need for more rescuers up here."

"Roger that, team one. Team six copy?"

"Team six copies. We're almost at the top of Tilly Jane drainage." This is the way our morning goes. Short conversations with Cloud Cap base, stay in touch only with important and terse communications, and check in every half hour.

Rubin, Mike, and I ski to 8,000 feet on the crevasse-free bench on the Eliot Glacier. We finally stop for water and a snack. But we get cold quickly, despite the sun and very light wind.

When team six is in position, Dave Maccabee calls me for instructions. "There's widespread avalanche dangers. Not much higher we can go. Ask Cloud Cap for instructions," I say. I hear on the radio Jim Wells asking them to hold their ground to wait for further instructions.

We ski with a helicopter buzzing around us to about 9,000 feet on Snowdome. From there, Rubin and I take turns peering through binoculars at the entire north wall. We then watch the Chinook fly in, hover for ten minutes on the summit to drop the summit team, and fly away. It feels like I've been out here all day but it is only 12:30 P.M.

Once we achieve the 9,000-foot-level on the Snowdome, we feel exposed, and it seems too risky. New snow has been loaded on the Snowdome from the wind, and the convexity and steepness create a double avalanche hazard; if it slides, it goes right into the Eliot. All three of us quickly ski down to a saddle that separates Snowdome from the Coe Glacier to the west. We take a break, remove our climbing skins from our skis, and eat. Clearly, it is way too dangerous for us to try to look over the edge into the Eliot Glacier.

We share the cola I brought. The sugar and caffeine are an elixir to rejuvenate us. On the radio, we can now hear discussion of the the summit team setting up a belay and then Brian Hukari down climbing to the anchor webbing spotted off the summit. Because we are at the saddle near the Coe Glacier, I can now hear the dozen teams from the south side, too.

"Cloud Cap, from team one," I say when I hear a break in the radio communications from other teams. I need to keep it short.

"Go, team one."

"We've reached the top of Snowdome. It's too dangerous for us to drop into the upper Eliot. Do you have a new assignment for us?"

"No, team one. Head back to Cloud Cap. Which route will you descend?"

I check in with Rubin and Mike quickly.

"Team one is skiing back down Snowdome and will cross the Eliot the same way we came up," I say. "We'll rendezvous with team six."

We ski down the Snowdome, but it is not anything like skiing in a ski resort. The snow varies from thick, deep powder in some spots to sheer ice in others. Plus, we're each skiing with a forty-pound pack on our back. We ski slowly, cautiously, and defensively. And we go one at a time down any slope that is steep enough to slide.

We ski down the Snowdome, across the Eliot on the bench with no crevasses, and down to the Pooley Trail. At that point, we strap our crampons back on for the ten-minute hike back up to the east moraine. At the Pooley Trail cairn, we meet up with team six: four Crag Rats, including David Maccabee, one Corvallis Mountain Rescue member, and two friends of the climbers on snowshoes.

The radio crackles for the hundredth time; but this time, all nine of us at the Pooley Trail hear on the radio that Brian Hukari has found a snow cave at the site of the climbing webbing. He and Todd are on the uppermost section of the Cooper Spur route, about 300 feet below the summit. I hear on the radio: "It's a big cave. There are two Grivel ice tools, a section of rope that's been cut, a self-equalizing anchor with two pickets, and half a sleeping pad. No sign of anyone."

"Okay, gather the gear, try to have a look around, and return to the summit," says Jim from Cloud Cap.

Dave Maccabee gives me a turkey sandwich. Jeff Heater, another Crag Rat, recounts the tale of other north-side climbers who perished and were never found. Kenneth Budlong, a Nike executive, was lost in 1995. And Jeff recalls Karoly Orsi, a Budapest, Hungary, student who disappeared in 2001. This mountain, in particular the north side, has taken many lives.

Most of the radio chatter is communication with the Cloud Cap search base and the summit team, with relays to the command center at the sheriff's office, deciding on an extrication time to remove the summit team. I hear Todd and Brian talking about returning to the summit. Then, on the radio, one of the summit team members says, "I see some footprints heading east. Why don't we check those out quickly." Cloud Cap base says they have until 3:30. The chopper is returning at 4:00 for extrication. It's close to 2:30 P.M. and we get cold when the sun ducks behind the peak. We strap on our packs, and begin the twenty-minute ski back to Cloud Cap.

At Cloud Cap Inn, Roger has heaps of lasagna. It's lukewarm since the propane oven wouldn't light and it was heated on the woodstove top; it got rather mashed, too, from the snowcat ride with the "special pancake mix" resting on top. The noodles, cheese, and sauce are one solid color the consistency of stew. I have one bite, but for the moment I'm too tired to eat so I guzzle water.

Cloud Cap is a flurry of activity. A snowcat full of journalists came up that afternoon; a sheriff's deputy is trying to round them up to start evacuation of Cloud Cap. The fifty searchers now filtering into the inn all need rides down. Each snowcat can hold a half dozen people and takes almost two hours round trip. Several Crag Rats, including Jay and Dave, need to get home, so they ski down the Tilly Jane Trail. The trail is an easy half-hour glide through the woods to the parking lot. Penny is staying the night to help with Cloud Cap Inn cleanup. I want to stay, but I have to work tomorrow. I feel like I should at least wait until all teams are off the mountain.

The search is winding down.

Then the cabin's radio crackles. A second snow cave has been found. The rescuer saw the footprints that headed down the east side of the mountain toward the Wy'East Face and a rock formation known as the Black Spider. The searcher looked at the rock outcropping and said to himself, if I was building a snow cave, I'd build it right here. He hit pay dirt.

"Cloud Cap base, this is summit team."

"Go ahead, summit team"

"One climber in snow cave. Stand by for medical eval."

"Copy—you found one climber in a snow cave," says Jim as he motions for a propane lantern. Rick brings one over so Jim can see in order to be able to write. As the sun starts to drift to the horizon, it gets dark in the old building. It is 3:20 P.M. Every occupant in Cloud Cap Inn falls into a momentary pause, then starts bustling again. The media, previously just preparing to leave, turns on cell phones to make hurried calls, if they can get reception. The rescuers are packing, but reluctant to commit to a snowcat ride if something is happening on the mountain. Everyone mills around, sort of bumping into one another in the small cabin.

In three minutes another call comes in. At the moment we hear the transmission, there is another massive pause.

"Cloud Cap, from summit team."

"Go, summit team."

"We have a twelve fifty-nine," a code that stymies Jim and Rick Ragan. They pause for a minute, trying to figure out military code used by this PJ, a member of an elite combat search and rescue team.

"Tell them we're trying to determine the relevance of that code," says Rick, thinking quickly. And then, "Anyone know what a twelve fifty-nine is?"

"Trying to determine relevance of that code," says Jim into the radio.

"We have a delta one," replies the PJ.

"Okay," says Crag Rat Dwayne Troxell, "I know what a delta one is." He is about to explain when the radio crackled again.

"We have a deceased person in the snow cave."

A radio call comes in from Command Center for the summit team to prepare for extrication no later than 4:45 P.M. That will be right at dusk. The body will be recovered tomorrow. South side teams are instructed to remove their fixed ropes, the emergency descent route for the summit team. Jim, thinking like a skilled operations chief, checks in on team four. They are not yet back, but they are about fifteen minutes away.

At 4:45 P.M. the heavy Chinook returns to the summit and plucks the team off the top of the volcano. Instead of riding the snowcat home, I stash my pack in the cat and ski down the Tilly Jane Trail with Rubin and Mike. We glide through six inches of light, fluffy powder; skiing without a pack in the smooth, dry powder is luxurious. We glide to the Cooper Spur Resort, then make a track right down the middle of the ski run. We arrive at the Tilly Jane parking lot five minutes ahead of the snowcat, just as orange-purple alpenglow is kissing the snowfields of Mount Hood.

I am not even close to being finished with my day. I called Bill Pattison while driving down the mountain. I want to find out when debriefing is scheduled so I can give an avalanche assessment. Bill has been at the airport all week. I find Bill and Joe Wampler, chat for a while, then drive to dispatch for debriefing.

At command center, Rick Regan and I sit with Sheriff Wampler and his deputies. We look over Todd Wells's photos of the two snow caves and spread out the equipment found in the first snow cave. The body, says Joe, was probably Kelly James, based on description of the body and a wedding ring, which was too frozen to the hand to remove. In the snow cave, Rick and I figure the climbing rope had been cut with a knife; it didn't look like it was frayed by a rock. It was a clean, smooth cut. The two ice tools were expensive. Unlikely that a climber intentionally left these tools in the cave, as they would be needed for descent. The two pickets were threaded with climbing webbing, then two second pieces of webbing were attached. It appears as if two climbers were anchored at this snow cave. There was a fragment of a foam sleeping pad.

We conclude two things: first, this cave was likely the missing climbers' last known point on the mountain. And, second, something bad probably happened here. The climbers most likely were not at the spot of Kelly James's body. If they were, a fall or descent would put them down the northeast side of Mount Hood, into the Newton Clark Glacier, above Mount Hood Meadows Ski Resort. Instead, they were at this larger cave, on the Cooper Spur climbing route. The fall line from this spot would take the climbers down the Chisholm Trail into the crevasses of the Eliot Glacier. Even if they were not fifty feet into a crevasse, they were likely buried by ten feet of new snow and avalanche debris. Not only were chances slim that they survived a fall, it was simply too dangerous to get there on foot. Although Rubin, Mike, and I did not reach that search point as we would have liked, it was scoured by the Black Hawks.

We figure the three climbers probably reached the summit at dark on Friday night or Saturday morning. They tried to find the Pearly Gates chute but got disoriented in the storm. So they backtracked 300 feet down the east side of the mountain, built a snow cave, and hunkered in. On Sunday, Hall and Cooke probably traversed back to the Cooper Spur route, set up the belay point in the snow cave where the equipment was found, attempted to descend, and fell.

It is time to scale back the search

It is time for me to go home.

On Monday, December 18, the summit team returns via Chinook to extricate the body of Kelly James. At Cloud Cap Inn, the crew of Bernie Wells, Jim Wells, Roger Nelson, and Penny Hunting are on standby. No ground crew is sent out from the north or south search bases.

That night, the sheriff and his team look over the digital images recovered from Kelly James's camera. Brian Hukari confirms that the climbers were lightly equipped and did get a late start. They were low on the Eliot at daylight. Sheriff Wampler sends someone down to the Tilly Jane ski hut, where the missing climbers spent their first night, to search with a metal detector to look for cached equipment.

On Tuesday, December 19, the military crew, the three helicopters, and one airplane head back to their respective bases. Joe Wampler heads up with another deputy in his Piper Cub to search by air. Joe takes select family members of the two missing men for an air tour of the entire mountain. At a 2 P.M.

press conference, Joe announces the search will be scaled back. He will continue to search by air in good weather. He will continue the search by ground so long as he has climbers willing to go and the conditions are safe. Right now, the mountain is too dangerous. We will head up in the spring when avalanche and weather conditions improve.

On Wednesday, December 20, Joe again takes a look with the Piper Cub, notices a rock at 7,500-foot level on upper White River. I'm working as the ski doctor at Mount Hood Meadows Ski Resort, adjacent to White River. I watch the small plane make several passes that afternoon. I'm seeing a patient in the mountain clinic when the two family friends, the snowshoers who searched with team six on Sunday, ask ski patrol for a ride up the chairlift with their snowshoes so they can look into White River from the top of the ski resort.

"The ski patrol had already checked that rock," says Crag Rat Tom Scully, maintenance manager at the resort. He calls the sheriff from the clinic. Nonetheless, the two snowshoers leave late in the day to check out the rock. A few hours later, at dark, they are brought down with a ski patrol snowmobile.

The state medical examiner deems cause of death of Kelly James to be hypothermia and dehydration. Because of the holidays, our official debriefing won't occur until January 25.

On Monday, December 25, it is my turn to work Christmas Eve and Christmas Day, so I work my shifts, pick up the kids at 4:00 P.M., celebrate Christmas quickly at my house, then we catch the night train to my family's ski house in Montana. In Montana, with my sisters, my parents, and all the grandkids, the girls and I ski six straight days, at their request. I spend three predawn mornings skiing on my mountaineering skis to the top of the resort before it opens to make an attempt to decompress from a rather fraught December.

I think a lot about the climbers, the massive search, and the risk of adventuring in the outdoors. When I learned Kelly James had four kids back home, it was perhaps the saddest and most personal moment for me. James, Hall, and Cooke chose the toughest route in the toughest month up a mountain they'd never climbed. They traveled fast and light. The media would renew discussions about the high risk of climbing mountains. But most accounts lumped all mountaineering into a general class of high-risk sport.

Not all climbing is risky. But whatever the risk, the mountain and the storms do not care.

Skylar and Avrie have lots of questions about the search, the missing men, their families, the four kids Kelly James left behind, and the snow caves. I try to answer questions truthfully, in terms a six- and an eight-year-old can comprehend.

"The mountains are not necessarily dangerous," I say to them. "You just have to learn to be careful. You have to respect nature and the mountain."

On Friday, January 12, we are back from Montana and, for the first time in two years, my daughters have the ski bug, an eagerness to play in the mountains that touches me deeply. We head up to Mount Hood Meadows directly after school to make a few runs with friends. From the chairlift, we can see Mount Hood's Wy'East face and the summit. Just as the sun drifts to the horizon and alpenglow lights the summit, I point out the Black Spider and Chimney rock formations and the hanging snowfield where Kelly James was found dead.

"Where's the snow cave, Dad?" they ask, and then "I think I

see it!" Six feet of snow have fallen since that first one a month ago, but although they surely can't see the cave, my kids have genuine wonder and sorrow regarding the snow cave, the deaths, and the family James left behind, particularly his children.

Life has not gotten back to normal: I've got a book deadline, the debriefing for the Mount Hood search will run for five hours later this month, and I have a new job. But we are healthy, safe, and smiling: that is the only aspect of normalcy that really matters. My schedule, job, or rescue missions will probably never be construed as normal. I explain to the kids what the rest of the world perceives as normal: that some families live in poverty or in war, some live without clean water or adequate food, some live with very few worldly possessions, and some live with no home. I remind my daughters that this life we've build, somewhere between the summit of Wy'East and the flowing waters of the Columbia River, is precious. But they ask again about the snow cave, so I put aside my life lesson for now.

"Okay," I ask, "do you want to hike to the Cooper Spur shelter this summer and help look for the missing mountaineers?"

"Yeah! Let's go search!" Skylar and Avrie say in unison as their eyes light up and their smiles go wide. "Can we bring some friends?"

Coda

Two months after the massive December search, I am working my shift at the mountain clinic at the ski resort. It's a
powder day, lots of new snow, and white flakes are still falling
from thick clouds engulfing the mountain. Up high, the wind is
40 miles per hour. Down in the clinic, we are busy on this Sunday.
I see twenty-two patients between 9 A.M. and 6 P.M.: three patients with dislocated shoulders, four with fractured wrists, and
lots of kids with bumps and bruises. When I finally have a break,
I try to escape for an hour of snowboarding, only to be called back
to the clinic to see a few more patients.

At 3:30 P.M., as I am reading X-rays on the computer screen, I
receive a page on my cell phone. It's a call out by the Clackamas
County sheriff, the neighboring county. I call the voice mail and
hear Bill Pattison describe the mission: a search for climbers on the
south side of Hood. *Not again*, I think. This is the sixth rescue on
Hood in three months. Eight climbers reported themselves missing
via their own cell phone. Five are somewhere in a snow cave on Illumination Saddle; three others have fallen and are stuck somewhere in a canyon. Portland Mountain Rescue initially responded,

but they are now in need of much more help. The five in the snow cave are accessible by snowcat and rescued.

"I can help," I tell Bill, "but not until my shift at the mountain clinic ends at nine P.M. The good news is that I'm here, got my gear, and I'm fifteen minutes from Timberline."

"Right," he tells me. "I'll call you back. I'll let you know."

At 6 P.M. the clinic quiets down, so I head out to the ski slopes to float in the fresh powder I'm on duty as mountain doctor, so I can't leave the ski resort—I have to be within fifteen minutes of the clinic. We're in the middle of a storm cycle and it's dark now. It's cold, windy, and snowing. The snow is coming down so fast that it covers my tracks every other run. The place is magical: good snow comes only a few times a month in winter. I'm right in the best part of the storm. I feel a bit anxious that I can't help with the rescue. I cruise back to the clinic just before the resort closes at 9 P.M. fully expecting to be told by Bill to head home. I'm almost certain the climbers have been found, at least the five in the snow cave.

I call Todd Wells, who's in the field.

"I'm skiing to White River with an MLU," he shouts over the wind into his cell phone. "Can't see anything." The mountain locator unit (MLU) is like an animal-tracking device. It was developed specifically for use on Mount Hood after the Oregon Episcopal School tragedy in 1986. They can be rented by climbers and activated in an emergency. The battery-powered transmitters send out a signal, and rescuers then can locate the missing people using a bulky antenna and receiver. Rentals fell off to a minimal level until the December 2006 search that garnered massive media attention.

I call Bill Pattison again. He says the five climbers in a snow cave have been rescued by snowcat, but the three climbers are thought to be huddled in White River Canyon, the massive glacial remnant that separates Timberline Lodge ski resort from Mount Hood Meadows Ski Resort. The walls of the canyon are 2,000 feet high in some places. Todd Wells's team at Timberline had located the missing climbers' signal using the MLU, which doesn't give distance but only approximate direction. The missing climbers could be anywhere along a two-mile-long vector. They are not, as first thought, at Illumination Saddle. But they are in White River Canyon, which puts them in Hood River County, our responsibility. If the climbers had an altimeter or a GPS, it would be easier to pinpoint their location.

I call Crag Rat Jeff Prichar, who is standing by at Timberline Lodge with new Crag Rat Richard Hallman, a nurse. They have been dubbed team six and told to meet me at Mount Hood Meadows. Our assignment is to ski or, if possible, catch a ride from the ski patrol, to the top of White River Canyon to attempt to get an MLU vector. When plotted on a map, our vector and the vector from Timberline should bisect at the exact location of the missing climbers. Without this second vector, the MLU isn't nearly as useful.

Sheriff Joe Wampler is en route to the mountain clinic with the MLU receiver, says Bill Pattison when I call him back to confirm. Prichar and Hallman are coming over from Timberline. My job, while I wait, is to ready my backcountry ski gear, change out of snowboard clothes into my ski mountain ones, gather my equipment, and try to find a ride up the hill for team six. I call ski patrol and reach night manager Paul Klein, son of Crag Rat Dennis Klein. I really have to talk him into taking us, as he's closing down the mountain and leaving for the night. Paul says something about a "girlfriend." But riding up to the top of the ski resort at night in a storm is too tempting. Not to mention, Paul knows this section of the mountain probably better than anyone else in the world. Paul clocks out and commandeers a snowmobile to shuttle us up the hill.

The mountain closes at 9 P.M. but it's 11 P.M. before the team six crew and sheriff have arrived, the MLU is assembled and tested, and we are ready for the mission. The winds have increased to 60 miles per hour and the temps have dropped below 20 degrees.

I'm bundled in four layers, with no exposed flesh. I stash my skis and poles on the back of the snowmobile and jump on behind Paul. Paul flicks on the light and guns the motor. We race full-throttle to the top of the hill, over huge drifts, through blinding sheets of horizontally blowing snow, and through dark woods. When we pop out of the woods above the tree line, it's as if Paul's navigating by feel: everything looks the same, the snow-covered slope, the black sky, and the blinding snow that are lit up by the snowmobile's headlamp. Paul guns the heavy snowmobile to get over the huge drifts and almost rolls the machine over. Finally we reach the exposed, windswept Vista Ridge, the edge of the massive White River Canyon. Paul stops and lets me off at a lone tree. I can see the shadow of the uppermost chairlift on Vista Ridge and the faint glow of distant lights from the night ski area in the next canyon below.

"The resort lights are about to go out," yells Paul over the howling wind. "If you need to get down, walk over there." He points to the west. "There's a rope line that you can follow all the way down," he says, pointing out a ski resort boundary line. He jumps on the snowmobile, guns the motor, heads down into the night, and disappears.

Surprisingly, I'm not cold, a testament to the high-tech clothing I'm wearing. Thick gauntlet gloves, four layers on my torso and legs, and a neck gaiter that covers my mouth and nose and which tucks into my goggles and ski helmet. Luckily, I had dry socks and gloves in my ski bag.

The wind is now pushing 80 miles per hour, and when my neck gaiter slips below my goggles, the wind feels like pins and needles on my face. When I slip my hand out of my glove for ten seconds to work my radio, which is tucked beneath my parka and a thick sweater, my hand instantly goes numb and cold.

"SAR base, team six," I say.

"Go, team six,"

"We're establishing an MLU vector position at sixty-five hundred feet, top of Vista Ridge chairlift at Meadows. We'll have a bearing for you in twenty minutes."

"Roger, team six. We need that as soon as possible."

It takes me two or three minutes to warm my hand back up. As I wait by the tree, the ski resort lights go out, and it becomes instantly dark. I strap my headlamp on my ski helmet—an awkward task since I'm wearing thick gloves and ski goggles—and shine the light, then blow my whistle. The missing climbers won't hear this unless they are right in front of me; in this weather, the whistle has a range of fifty feet.

In fifteen minutes, Paul arrives with Jeff and the large MLU receiver. We huddle behind the tree to assemble the antenna—similar to the rabbit ears that sit on top of a TV—with a handheld unit and headphones that look like something used in a movie about the Vietnam war. What's more, this MLU hasn't been used in years and the battery failed in the parking lot. Sheriff Joe and Jeff had stripped the wires and connected them to a battery meant for jump-starting cars. The work is difficult, with the dark, wild weather and bulky equipment, not to mention our thick gloves, ski goggles, and helmets.

Finally, with the MLU assembled, we walk over to the edge of White River Canyon; turn on the unit; adjust the dials for the gain, squelch, and volume; and wave the antenna in the wind. It's a two-person job: I point the antenna and Jeff holds the earphones to his ears. We instantly pick up the signal, a strong beep. But the challenging part of the task is to locate the point of its maximum strength. We are quick to pin down the loudest signal to an approximate quadrant to northwest. The howling wind is making so much racket we can barely hear each other. Richard and Paul show up on the snowmobile, and we walk farther to the edge of the giant White River Canyon to attempt to get a better signal.

It takes twenty minutes with Jeff and I swapping headphones and antenna a few times. Finally we agree on the point of maximum intensity. I line up my ski pole with the antenna, and lay it across a snowbank.

"That's it!" I exclaim. Then, "Whoa," I say, "they are really high on the White River." Although it's pitch-black, superwindy, and snowing, I realize our vector is pointing into the headwall of the White River Glacier.

Now that we have the vector, we need to take a compass bearing. Jeff pulls out his GPS, which has an electronic compass, and we confirm the bearing with my watch compass and Richard's liquid-filled compass. All three line up, and after another ten minutes of checking and rechecking, we determine the vector is 330 degrees north northwest.

I dread the moment but pull off my warm glove, unzip both jackets, dig out my radio, and make the call.

"SAR base, team six."

"Go, team six,"

"We've got a bearing for you: three thirty, that's three, three, zero."

"Confirm, team six. Three, three, zero. Operations, do you copy." Apparently SAR base and search operations are at two different locations.

"Operations copies. Team six, do you have your location?"

"We're at sixty-five hundred feet on Vista Ridge, at the top terminus of Vista Ridge chairlift at Meadows." I bury my head in my jacket to speak into the radio that is strapped to my chest.

"We don't have that ski lift on our map. Can you give us co-ordinates?"

"Stand by," I say. Jeff takes a reading with his GPS, then I relay our coordinates to operations command.

"Do you have another assignment for us?" I ask on Richard's request. On the one hand, we're ready to get back down the mountain, but on the other hand, we've only been out here an hour—not very long for a night SAR mission. We are able to continue the search if needed. "Conditions are very windy and cold with no visibility," I report.

"Okay. Look around if you can, see if you can find an entrance to White River for tomorrow's team. Then head home."

"Okay," I say.

"Forget that," says Paul. "There's no looking around here at all." He's right. Even with our high-powered headlamps, we can see only fifty feet in any direction. It's too dangerous to wander around this ridge tonight.

We pack away the MLU. Jeff straddles the snowmobile behind Paul, and Richard and I click into our skis. When Paul peels away on the snowmobile, Richard and I are left in the black night, with only the distant light of the snowmobile. It's spooky. I can't imagine how the three climbers can spend the night without a snow cave. Richard and I start down cautiously over the hard ice and exposed rocks. It's like being on the moon: barren, forlorn, ghostly. We quickly catch up to the snowmobile—its light is like an oasis in the desert. The machine is bogged down in a deep drift. After Paul gets the machine going again, Richard and I ski behind the snowmobile, using its light to see the changing terrain: rocks and logs jut haphazardly from the snowpack, which is rock-hard ice in wind-scoured spots and soft and powdery in others. The sound of our skis changes from hard and loud over the ice, to soft and quiet over the velvety powder in seconds.

When we get down to the mountain clinic, we give report to Sheriff Wampler. Jeff relays conditions of the wind and snow, and Richard shows images from his digital camera. I'm responsible for closing up the clinic, and afterward I ski to my car, which is piled high with snow after the day-long storm.

B ack home, at 2 A.M., I finally make it to sleep, but have a fitful night. At 3:02 A.M. I get a page from Bill Pattison, stating that the search will start at 5:30 A.M. at Mount Hood Meadows. As much as I try, I just can't leave my phone off. I have to work today, or I would have stayed on the mountain at the clinic to help search. I doze off and get another page at 4:30 A.M., a second call for searchers.

The Crag Rats send a team to search the Vista Ridge side of White River that day. Later that morning, a team from Portland Mountain Rescue locates the climbers and walks them out. I later hear our vector was spot-on and contributed to the rapid location of the climbers.

Six missions in three months on Mount Hood are too many to ignore. In the days following this most recent rescue, the Oregon lawmakers are determined to pass a law to discourage climbers from getting lost and to lessen the burden on volunteer rescuers. House Bill 2059 would require climbers in Oregon to wear a signaling device in the winter. Rescuers are universally opposed to any legislation, and several colleagues from Portland Mountain Rescue and the 304th Air Rescue Squadron take a day off work to testify at the state capital in Salem. Paul Crowley, Crag Rat president, and Fran Sharp, president of Mountain Rescue Association, write letters in opposition. It's not that rescuers are opposed to any law, but requiring locators can do more harm than good and will not realistically solve the problem of climbers needing rescue.

Of the 730 SAR missions in Oregon the year prior, only 30 were for climbers. To require that climbers carry, signaling devices would single out that group unfairly. The law should include hunters, hikers, and boaters as well. And the mountain-locator unit is an outmoded technology, based on animal tracking devices developed decades ago. The only reasonable signaling device nowadays is a personal locator beacon, which uses a satellite signal to pinpoint a location. However, these units cost around $700, so they are not easily affordable. They aren't 100 percent reliable: batteries can fail, and weather and terrain can obstruct the signal. If a climber carries a GPS along with a cell phone, those two devices can actually speed rescue and are ubiquitous now in the backcountry, but they are not active signaling devices.

Some lawmakers want to know why the Forest Service doesn't close Mount Hood during the winter to prevent accidents. But as Jon Jarvis, superintendent of Mount Rainier National Park said, to reopen the mountain after the winter would imply that conditions are safe. The mountains are never, ever safe. That's like saying driving a car is safe. During the ten-day December 2006 storm that killed the three climbers on Mount Hood, thirteen people died on Oregon roads in car accidents. Cars take 50,000 lives annually. Mount Hood has claimed thirty-five lives in twenty-five years.

People ask again why taxpayers should foot the bill for SAR. In Oregon, we already have a law that allows a sheriff's department to send the bill to a negligent person who needed rescue. But asking why taxpayers should foot the bill for SAR is somewhat like asking why taxpayers should pay for law enforcement or fire departments.

The biggest problem from a rescuer's point of view is that mandating the use of an emergency-signaling device may give people a false sense of security—that they can climb higher and farther in bad conditions, knowing they have a fail-safe. But as the December 2006 rescue showed, even if we had known the exact location of the three climbers, we still would not have been able to reach them for a week.

What it really comes down to is prevention and education. If people learn to climb safety and, perhaps most important, to turn back when conditions are bad, they can prevent many, but not all, accidents. I see that as part of my job as a mountain rescuer, a doctor, and a parent: to teach my kids to play safely in the mountains. But when bad things happen to good people, when you do everything correctly and you have an accident, you should know someone will come help you.

Although location devises will help rescuers, they won't eliminate our job. People will still get lost and injured. And we'll still head up to the mountains to get them. Day or night.